Statistical Methods in Language and Linguistic Research

Statistical Methods in Language and Linguistic Research

Pascual Cantos Gómez

Published by Equinox Publishing Ltd.

UK: Unit S3, Kelham House, 3 Lancaster Street, Sheffield S3 8AF
USA: ISD, 70 Enterprise Drive, Bristol, CT 06010

www.equinoxpub.com

First published in 2013

ISBN: 978-1-84553-431-8 (hardback)
          978-1-84553-432-5 (paperback)

British Library Cataloguing-in-Publication Data
A catalogue record for this book is available from the British Library.

Library of Congress Cataloging-in-Publication Data
Cantos Gómez, Pascual.
    Statistical methods in language and linguistic research / Pascual Cantos Gómez.
      p. cm.
    Includes bibliographical references and index.
    ISBN 978-1-84553-431-8 (hb) – ISBN 978-1-84553-432-5 (pb) 1. Language and languages—Statistical methods. 2. Language and languages—Study and teaching—Statistical methods. I. Title.
    P123.C28 2009
    407'.27—dc22
                                                              2009005206

Typeset by JS Typesetting Ltd, Porthcawl, Mid Glamorgan
Printed and bound in Great Britain by Lightning Source UK, Milton Keynes

To the memory of my father

Contents

Acknowledgements

When I first started writing some of the parts now present in this book, I never thought and planned writing a book like this. They were mere drafts, a simple informal collection of lecture notes for my PhD module on *Quantitative Data Analysis* at the University of Murcia. I am particularly grateful to those friends, colleagues and students who encouraged and persuaded me to get into this project.

Thanks are also due to Professor Aquilino Sánchez who was responsible for first encouraging my interest in statistics. I am particularly indebted to Liz Murphy, who has helped me refine this book; each page of this work has benefited from her careful revision and analysis. Thanks, Liz, for having taken much of your time to read and comment on drafts.

I would also like to thank the people from Equinox Publishing (Janet Joyce, Valerie Hall and Kate Williams, among others) for believing in this project and for their assistance and support throughout the production of this book. Thanks also to copy-editor Judy Napper, Hamish Ironside, Gina Mance and Christine James.

Thanks go also to my wife Andrea and daughters, Andrea and Belén, for the many sacrifices they made to allow me to work on this book; I would still be working on the index if it had not been for Belén.

This book is dedicated to the memory of my father. He has always shown a genuine interest in and concern for my life, my work and my well-being.

Preface

Statistics is known to be a quantitative approach to research. However, most of the research done in the fields of language and linguistics is of a different kind, namely qualitative. Succinctly, qualitative analysis differs from quantitative analysis in that in the former no attempt is made to assign frequencies, percentages and the like to the linguistic features found or identified in the data. In quantitative research, linguistic features are classified and counted, and even more complex statistical models are constructed in order to explain these observed facts. In qualitative research, however, we use the data only for identifying and describing features of language usage and for providing real occurrences/examples of particular phenomena.

This book is an attempt to show how quantitative methods and statistical techniques can supplement qualitative analyses of language. We shall attempt to present some mathematical and statistical properties of natural languages, and introduce some of the quantitative methods which are of the most value in working empirically with texts and corpora, illustrating the various issues with examples and moving from the most basic descriptive techniques to decision-taking techniques and to more sophisticated multivariate statistical language models.

Among the linguistic community, statistical methods or more generally quantitative techniques are mostly ignored or avoided because of lack of training, and also fear and dislike. The reasons: (1) these techniques are just not related to linguistics, philology or humanities; statistics falls into the province of sciences, mathematics and the like; and/or (2) there is a feeling that these methods may destroy the "magic" in literary text.

There currently exist quite a few introductory statistics texts for linguists. Some of these books are either (1) statistically and mathematically too demanding, not really intended for linguists, (2) restricted to applied linguistics and with little statistical coverage, or (3) not directly related to linguistics but more social science oriented. The aim of this book is to try to illustrate with numerous examples how quantitative methods can most fruitfully contribute to linguistic analysis and research. In addition, we do not intend here to offer an exhaustive presentation of all statistical techniques available to linguistics, but to demonstrate the contribution that statistics can and should make to linguistic studies.

We have tried to keep the writing simple and have sought to avoid too much statistical jargon whenever possible in an attempt to be user-friendly. This explains also why we have deliberately avoided using references within the text; these are normally given in footnotes, although an extensive reference section is given at the end of the book for the interested reader.

This book presents an accessible introduction to using statistics in language and linguistic research. It describes the most popular statistical techniques, explaining the basic principles and demonstrating their use in a wide range of linguistic research: (1) observations and descriptions of some aspects of language phenomena including the areas of applied linguistics, sociolinguistics, dialectology and so on, as far as they can be modelled by means of quantitative mathematical methods, (2) applications of methods, models or techniques from quantitative linguistics to problems of natural language description and language teaching, and (3) methodological problems of linguistic measurement, model construction, sampling and test theory.

The range of techniques introduced by the book will help the reader both to evaluate and make use of literature which employs statistical analysis and apply statistics in their own research. Each chapter gives step-by-step explanations of particular techniques using examples from a number of linguistic fields. None of the techniques requires the reader to have a grasp of mathematics more complex than simple algebra.

We have deliberately sought to write and design this book not for mathematicians but for linguists, in an attempt to demonstrate the use of statistical techniques in a wide range of linguistic research.

1 Some basic issues

1.1 Introduction

There are various means that can help us to represent summarized data: frequency and contingency tables, charts or graphs (histograms or frequency polygons). However, we may sometimes wish to compare data or sets of data, in order to look for similarities or differences. Tables, graphs and charts may not always be useful in this respect as it is not easy, on some occasions, to talk succinctly about a set of numbers. Consider the two histograms in Figures 1.1 and 1.2, which show the sentence length in words of two linguistic samples; one contains written texts and the other is made up from written-to-be-spoken text samples, such as speeches, conferences, and so on. In this case, a mere glance at them allows us to realize immediately that the sentence length in written texts tends to be longer than that in written-to-be-spoken texts.

However, the normal shape of things is that situations are rarely that neat and clear. For example, Table 1.1 compares the data on sentence length (in words) of written texts and written-to-be-spoken texts.

The figures relative to each variety are very similar but there are some slight differences. With this simple data display, it is very hard, if not impossible, to make any precise statement about these dissimilarities in the overall sentence length of written texts and written-to-be-spoken texts.

Studies in our field often omit the use of graphs. However, graphs usually just provide some form of description (descriptive statistics), that is, a numerical

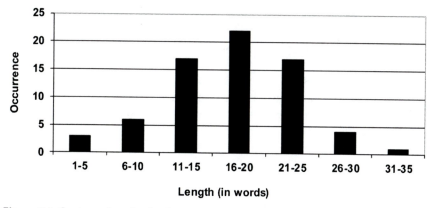

Figure 1.1 Sentence length of written texts.

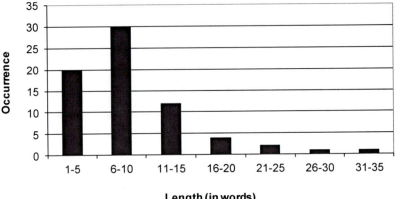

Figure 1.2 Sentence length of written-to-be-spoken texts.

representation of the data that might help us in creating a mental picture of how a linguistic phenomenon performs. It is our responsibility not just to get a "picture" of the situation but also to look at the information or data provided. Both aspects are important.

Table 1.1 Written versus written-to-be-spoken-texts.

	1–5	6–10	11–15	16–20	21–25	26–30	31–35
Written texts	3	6	17	22	17	4	1
Written-to-be-spoken texts	20	30	12	4	2	1	1

One way to look at the information is to represent the data for a group of items by means of scores. That is, single measures that are the most typical scores for a data set.

1.2 Measures of central tendency

The central tendency indicates the typical behaviour of a data set. There are different ways or measures to estimate it. The measures of central tendency can provide us with information on how a group or collection of data performed overall. Therefore, central tendency is a representative or typical score. For example, if a foreign language teacher is asked to provide a single value which best describes the performance level of her group of students, she would answer with a measure of central tendency. The three measures of central tendency that will be discussed are the mode, the median and the mean.

1.2.1 Mode

The mode is the value or score that occurs most frequently in a given set of scores. If we take the above data on sentence length of written and written-to-be-spoken texts (Table 1.1) then the mode for written texts would be sixteen to twenty words, because this sentence length occurs most: twenty and twenty-two words. It would be six to ten words for written-to-be-spoken texts. To keep the mode clear in your mind, associate the term with its near-synonym: fashionable. Thus, the mode is the score or value that is most fashionable. This score has no statistical formula and is straightforward. The mode is easily identifiable in frequency polygons, that is, graphic displays of frequency tables, as it corresponds to the score with the highest point. A distribution may have more than one mode if two or more scores occur the same number of times. Such distributions are called bimodals (two modes), trimodals (three modes), and so on.

This central tendency score is easy to use and quick to compute. However, it is not very useful as it does not give much information about the distribution and it is easily affected by chance scores, although for large data sets this is less likely to happen.

1.2.2 Median

In any group of scores the median is the middle point or central score of the distribution, with half of the scores lying above and half falling below. It is that point below which 50 per cent of the scores fall and above which 50 per cent fall, dividing any set of scores into two equal subgroups; one of these contains all the scores lower than the median and the other all those greater than the median. For example, in a corpus consisting of sentences with the following number of words: 15, 16, 20, 22, 12, 12, 13, 15 and 14; the median is 15 (12, 12, 13, 14, **15**, 15, 16, 20 and 22), as four of the sentences are shorter (12, 12, 13 and 14) and four are longer or equal (15, 16, 20 and 22). If there is an even number of scores as, for example, in this distribution: 12, 12, 13, 14, 15, 16, 16, 17, 20, 22, then the median is the midpoint between the two middle scores: 15.5, which is calculated by adding the two middle scores and dividing by 2:

$$\frac{15 + 16}{2} = 15.5$$

1.2.3 Mean

The mean, also known as the average, is the sum of all scores divided by the total number of scores. Application of it to our sentence length example yields the result in Table 1.2.

That is, the mean sentence length for the data set in Table 1.2 is 15.7 words per sentence. The mean is defined by the formula:

Table 1.2 Calculation of the mean.

Sentence	Sentence length (in words)	Calculations
1	12	1. Sum of scores: $\sum x$
2	12	$= 12 + 12 + 13 + 14 + 15 + 16 + 16 + 17 + 20 + 22$
3	13	$= 157$
4	14	
5	15	2. Number of scores: N
6	16	$= 10$
7	16	3. Mean: $\bar{X}$
8	17	
9	20	$= \dfrac{157}{10} = 15.7$
10	22	

$$\bar{X} = \frac{\sum x}{N}$$

Where $\bar{X}$ = mean, N = number of scores and $\sum x$ = sum of all scores.

The mean is the preferred measure of central tendency, both as a description of the data and as an estimate of the parameter. Its major drawback is that it is sensitive to extreme scores. If the data are not normally distributed (see section 1.6.1 below), for example if most of the items are grouped towards the higher end of the scale, then the median may be a more reliable measure.

1.3 Proportions and percentages

On many occasions data are presented as proportions or percentages. Suppose we are interested in the distribution of a linguistic variable in relation to some other variable: for example, the use of modal verbs (linguistic variable) in relation to arts texts versus science texts. To simplify matters we shall concentrate on the distribution of just ten modal verbs (*can, could, may, might, must, ought to, shall, should, will* and *would*). Table 1.3 shows the number of times each modal verb occurs in each linguistic domain (arts and science).

However, we could also represent the data as fractions of the total number of modal verbs, in percentages (see Table 1.4). This table displays the partial percentages and total percentages. If we take the second arts column, we see that *can* makes up 15.07 per cent of all modal verbs used in arts texts. Similarly, in the second totals column we find that, for example, *should* makes up 5.11 per cent of all modal verbs used in arts and science. Comparing arts and science, scientific communication uses many more modals than arts does: 65.03 per cent versus 34.97 per cent.

Percentages and proportions are particularly useful to summarize data. However, we should also note that simple averages of percentages and proportions are not

Table 1.3 Modal verbs in arts and science texts.

Modal verb	Arts	Science
Can	265	778
Could	296	307
May	187	547
Might	157	113
Must	130	236
Ought to	12	6
Shall	18	44
Should	98	159
Will	174	593
Would	421	485

Table 1.4 Modal verbs in arts and science texts in percentages.

Modal verb	Arts		Science		Total	
Can	265	15.07%	778	23.80%	1043	20.75%
Could	296	16.83%	307	9.39%	603	11.99%
May	187	10.63%	547	16.73%	734	14.60%
Might	157	8.93%	113	3.45%	270	5.37%
Must	130	7.39%	236	7.22%	366	7.28%
Ought to	12	0.68%	6	0.18%	18	0.35%
Shall	18	1.02%	44	1.34%	62	1.23%
Should	98	5.57%	159	4.86%	257	5.11%
Will	174	9.89%	593	18.14%	767	15.26%
Would	421	23.94%	485	14.84%	906	18.02%
Total	1758	34.97%	3268	65.03%	5026	100.00%

always appropriate, particularly whenever the data are presented only as percentages and proportions without the original values being given. This is a serious error that often prevents analysis of the data by another researcher. In addition, it may be difficult to interpret a mean proportion or percentage when it is not clear what the total number of observations was over which the original proportion was measured, especially when the original values which the percentages were based on are omitted.

1.4 Dispersion

The mean and the median can be very useful for the comparison of data sets as they help us to interpret the typical behaviour of the data in the form of central tendency. If these data sets are very different, then we are likely to have made a significant discovery. However, if the two means or medians are very similar, then it is difficult to make any statement on the complete set of scores. Let us consider the artificial example in Table 1.5, showing the distributions of nouns in arts and science texts over five samples of equal length:

Table 1.5 Nouns and verbs in arts and science texts.

	Sample 1	Sample 2	Sample 3	Sample 4	Sample 5
Nouns	20	29	24	15	22
Verbs	25	23	18	25	19

Comparing the mean of nouns and verbs, we get 22 for both cases, and two very similar medians: 22 (nouns) and 23 (verbs). Both the mean and the median reveal that both linguistic items are very similar in shape or structure. A closer look at the data, however, reveals that both samples have a dissimilar variability, that is, a different spread or dispersion of scores. Thus, for nouns, the highest score is 29 and the lowest 15, and data dispersion range is 15 (29 − 15 + 1), whereas for verbs, we get a dispersion of 8 (25 − 18 + 1). These two measures, 15 and 8, provide the range of nouns and verbs respectively, giving us an idea of how the various samples vary from the central tendency.

1.4.1 Range

The range is defined as the number of points between the highest score and the lowest one plus one (plus one in order to include the scores of both ends). The range is a quick measure of variability, as it provides information on how data scores vary from the central tendency.

Occasionally, it may give a distorted picture of the data as it just represents the extreme scores of the variation and, as a result, it is strongly affected by behaviour that may not necessarily be representative of the data set as a whole. For instance in Table 1.5, if there were a text sample with just 5 nouns, then the noun range would change dramatically from 15 to 25 (29 − 5 + 1). This range would not really represent the behaviour of noun occurrence, as it was strongly affected by a single score (5). The range should be taken cautiously just as a dispersion indicator and should be interpreted simply as the number of points between the highest and the lowest scores, including both.

1.4.2 Variance and standard deviation

Recall our sentence length data above (section 1.2.3). As we know its mean length (15.7), we can calculate the difference between each sentence length value and the mean length:

$$difference_i = X_i - \overline{X}$$

Intuitively, this difference measure might give us some kind of information on how far apart the individual sentence length values cluster around the mean length. Table 1.6 shows all the calculations. A close look at the figures reveals that not all differences are positive, some are negative, indicating that the sentence length of these samples are less then the mean. Furthermore, if we add all the difference values, we come up with zero. This happens not just here but will occur with any data set, if the calculations are performed correctly.

Table 1.6 Differences with the mean.

Sentence length (in words)	Differences (*diff*) with mean
12	−3.7
12	−3.7
13	−2.7
14	−1.7
15	−0.7
16	0.3
16	0.3
17	1.3
20	4.3
22	6.3
$N = 10$	$\Sigma diff = 0$

One way to avoid getting always the same calculation (zero) is squaring the differences, as we shall, then, get only positive figures (see Table 1.7).

Once we have the squared sum differences ($\Sigma diff^2 = 98.1$), we can calculate the variance straightforwardly:

$$V = \frac{\Sigma diff^2}{N}$$

$$V = \frac{98.1}{10} = 9.81$$

The variance is thus the arithmetic mean of the squared sum differences or square deviations. However, dividing by N (number of cases) is only correct whenever N is very large. In our case, with only ten scores, it would be wise to divide the square deviations by $N - 1$, instead.[1] This would result in:

$$V = \frac{\Sigma diff^2}{N - 1}$$

$$V = \frac{98.1}{9} = 10.9$$

---

1. Generally, the denominator of N is used for a population and $N - 1$ for a sample.

Table 1.7 Squared differences with the mean.

Sentence length (in words)	Differences (*diff*) with mean (15.7)	*diff*^{2}
12	−3.7	13.69
12	−3.7	13.69
13	−2.7	7.29
14	−1.7	2.89
15	−0.7	0.49
16	0.3	0.09
16	0.3	0.09
17	1.3	1.69
20	4.3	18.49
22	6.3	39.69
$N = 10$	$\Sigma diff = 0$	$\Sigma diff^2 = 98.1$

To summarize, the calculation of the variance is performed in the following steps:

1. Find the mean of the scores.
2. Subtract the mean from each score.
3. Square the results of step two.
4. Add up all the results of step three.
5. Divide the sum of step four by the number of scores minus one.

The main problem with the variance is the units of measurement it uses. The variance measures variability in squared units. For instance, take the above example where we measure sentence length in words: the units we get with the variance (10.9) will be in words squared. But what are these units? What do they mean? This concept is not very helpful for empirical interpretation. In contrast, if we take the square root of the variance (10.9), then we are given word units; and this is precisely what the *standard deviation* (SD) does. The standard deviation measures variability in units of measurement. For this reason, the standard deviation is the preferred measure of variability and is one of the most important statistical measures. To calculate the standard deviation, we just need to add a further step to the variance calculation presented above:

6. Take the square root of step five.

Recall our sentence length measure above; its standard deviation is:

$$SD = \sqrt{10.9} = 3.3015$$

And its empirical interpretation is straightforward: the variability of distribution of sentence length is 3.3015 words.

In more complex analyses with various variables, the means and the standard deviations can be compared in order to find differences in distribution. Suppose we get the following data referred to sentence length, domain and written versus oral medium (see Table 1.8).

Table 1.8 Sentence length in words referred to different domains and media.

Sentence length (in words)	Domain	Medium
12	Mathematics	oral
12	Literature	written
13	History	oral
14	Mathematics	oral
15	Mathematics	written
16	History	written
16	Literature	written
17	Literature	oral
20	History	written
22	Literature	written

It is now possible to compare sentence length of oral and written sentences by first calculating the mean and the standard deviation of oral medium only and then for written medium alone. So the data set is split into two sets: one for oral and one for written (Table 1.9).

Table 1.9 Sentence length regarding oral and written language samples.

Oral	Written
12	12
13	15
14	16
17	16
	20
	22

The means and standard deviations of oral and written sentences can be seen in Table 1.10.

Table 1.10 Mean and SD regarding oral and written language samples.

Medium	N	Mean	Standard deviation
Oral	4	14	2.16
Written	6	16.83	3.6
Total	10	15.7	3.3

From this data, we can seen that written sentences are longer as evidenced by the larger mean and have greater variability. In addition, the total variability is less than the variability of written sentences.

A similar analysis can be performed for sentence length by domain, producing the data displayed in Table 1.11.

Table 1.11 Mean and SD regarding different domains.

Medium	N	Mean	Standard deviation
Mathematics	3	13.67	1.53
Literature	4	16.75	4.11
History	3	16.33	3.51
Total	10	15.7	3.3

The means and standard deviations above reveal that sentence length in mathematics is shorter than in literature and history, and that the distribution of variability in mathematics is also least: mathematics is in this respect more homogeneous.

This preliminary analysis can become a powerful tool for examining relationships between variables. In addition, it is central to the understanding of other more sophisticated statistical tools such as the *analysis of variance (ANOVA)*.

1.5 Standard scores

Before we continue, imagine the following case: a researcher is faced with two sets of data (raw data) corresponding to scores students achieved in two different language tests. Naively, one might think that it would be enough to just compare the two data sets and compare how students performed in test A versus test B. This would be fine if students had been examined by the same methods and questions in both tests. However, if the testing methods and questions were different, then we cannot compare the two data sets directly; we need to standardize the scores. And here is where the standard deviation has a prime application. Transforming scores from raw scores into standard scores has two main purposes:

- it gives sense and meaning to the scores and allows their interpretation, and
- it allows direct comparison between two or more scores.

Let us assume the hypothetical scores of five students in two different language tests (A and B; see Table 1.12).

Table 1.12 Scores in two different language tests.

	Student 1	Student 2	Student 3	Student 4	Student 5
Test A	120	90	130	125	110
Test B	4	3	5	4	3

Suppose we want to compare two scores: student one's score in test A (120) and student five's score in test B (3). In principle, it does not look that neat, as they have clearly been examined by two different methods. Let us move one step further, and calculate the mean of both tests; the two mean scores are: 115 (test A) and 3.8 (test B). We can now say that student one scored above the average in test A and that student five scored below the mean in test B. There is some sense in thinking that student one performed in test A better than student five in test B, although the comparison is not that obvious.

A more precise method is to standardize the scores into a single scale: *z-scores*. This will tell us how far a given raw score is from the mean in standard deviation units and, additionally, will allow us to compare both tests directly. This is done by means of the following formula:

$$z = \frac{score - mean}{SD}$$

To find a student's z-score we subtract the mean from the student's score and divide the result by the standard deviation. If we apply this formula to our hypothetical data above we get the data given in Table 1.13 for test A (SD = 15.81).

Table 1.13 *Z-scores for test A.*

Student	Score	Score – mean	Z-score
1	120	5	0.31
2	90	−25	−1.58
3	130	15	0.94
4	125	10	0.63
5	110	−5	−0.31

So student one's score in test A is 0.31. In other words, his score is roughly one third of a standard deviation unit above the mean, whereas student two's score is about one and a half standard deviation units below the mean on the same test. Let us compare the z-scores of test A with those of test B (SD = 0.83; see Table 1.14).

Table 1.14 Z-scores for test B.

Student	Score	Score – mean	Z-score
1	4	0.2	0.24
2	3	−0.8	−0.96
3	5	1.2	1.44
4	4	0.2	0.24
5	3	−0.8	−0.96

We are now able to make full comparisons of both test scores (Table 1.15).

Table 1.15 Comparing z-scores for test A and B.

	Student 1	Student 2	Student 3	Student 4	Student 5
Test A	0.31	−1.58	0.94	0.63	−0.31
Test B	0.24	−0.96	1.44	0.24	−0.96

For example, student one obtained nearly the same score in both tests. In contrast student three scored significantly better in test B than in A.

Summing up, the z-score expresses in standard deviation units how far a score is from the mean. Note that once the scores are standardized, the mean is always 0. If the units are positive then the score is above the mean, whereas if the units are a negative figure then it is below average.

Alternatively, we could have used other standard score methods such as *t-score* and/or transformed scores into percentile ranks. To convert z-scores into t-scores is pretty straightforward; we just need to apply this formula:.

$$T = 10z + 50$$

The most positive advantage of t-scores is that all scores become positively marked. The equivalent t-scores for tests A and B are given in Table 1.16.

Table 1.16 Comparing t-scores for test A and B.

	Test A	Test B
Student 1	53.1	52.4
Student 2	34.2	40.4
Student 3	59.4	64.4
Student 4	56.3	52.4
Student 5	46.9	40.4

Such scores are probably easier to explain to laymen. Note that the mean for t-scores is always 50 and that standard deviation units are represented in units of 10.

Regarding percentile ranks, succinctly, these are the percentages that fall below a given score. For example, take the raw score of student four in test A: 125. If we transformed the data into a percentile rank of 60, we could interpret that: student four did better than 60 per cent of all the students who took the test. The calculation procedure is as follows:

1. Order the scores from lowest to highest.
2. For each score, add the percentage of scores that fall below the score to one-half the percentage of scores that fall at the score.

The result is the percentile rank for that score. To demonstrate this, take the scores of test A:

120   90   130   125   110

Order the score from lowest to highest:

90   110   120   125   130

Now calculate, for example, the percentage falling below 125:

$$\frac{3}{5} = 0.6 \text{ or } 60\%$$

where 3 stands for the number of scores below 125, namely 90, 110 and 120; and 5 for the total amount of scores. The percentage falling at score 125 would be:

$$\frac{1}{5} = 0.2 \text{ or } 20\%$$

Again, the numerator is the number of scores with the value 125 and the denominator the number of total scores. One half of 20 is 10, which added to the percentage falling below 125 gives:

$$10 + 60 = 70\%$$

In other words, the student score of 125 on test A has been transformed into a percentile rank of 70 and is interpreted as that this student in particular did better than 70 per cent of the students who took the test. The percentile ranks for all the scores are as follows:

90	110	120	125	130
10%	30%	50%	70%	90%

1.6 Distributions

Before we explore the concepts of distribution, and normal distribution in particular, consider this simple example: toss an unbiased coin and examine the possible outcomes. No doubt, the probability of this coin coming up tails would be 50 per cent. More formally, the probability of getting tails is 1 in 2; this is determined by the formula:

$$p = \frac{e}{n}$$

where p = probability, e = expected outcome (1: tails) and n = possible outcomes (2: heads and tails). Similarly, the probability of getting heads is also 50 per cent, and this is important, since heads and tails account for all possibilities:

$$p(tails) \quad = \frac{1}{2} = 0.5 = 50\%$$

$$p(heads) = \frac{1}{2} = 0.5 = 50\%$$

$$p(tails) + p(heads) = 0.5 + 0.5 = 1 = 100\%$$

What is the probability of flipping two coins and getting a head followed by a tail? As already seen *p(tails)* is 50 per cent and *p(heads)* is 50 per cent and as the outcome of one spin of the coin does not affect the outcome of the next one, the outcomes are said to be independent. In this case, the conjunction of independent outcomes is the result of multiplying the individual probabilities, that is:

$$p(heads \, \& \, tails) \quad = \quad p(heads) \times p(tails)$$

$$p(heads \, \& \, tails) \quad = \quad 0.5 \times 0.5 \quad = \quad 0.25 \quad = \quad 25\%$$

The probability ratio ranges from 0 to 1 and can also be stated in percentages; both can help us to look at how probability is related to distribution and to the description of patterns in events.

An alternative way to represent probability and pattern of events is using histograms such as Figures 1.1 and 1.2 above. The two histograms shown in Figures 1.3

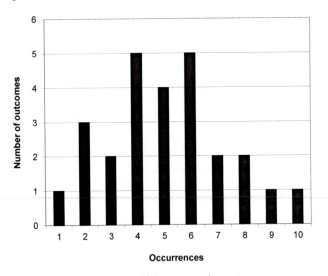

Figure 1.3 Occurrences within twenty-six sentences.

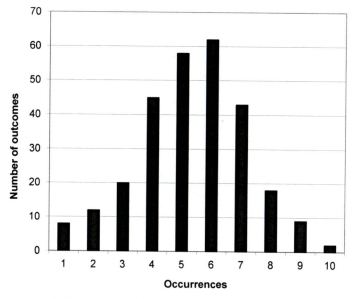

Figure 1.4 Occurrences within 277 sentences.

and 1.4 present the hypothetical number of occurrences when determiners of some sort (articles, quantifiers, etc.) occur in a sentence.

Roughly, among the twenty-six test sentences, the most common outcomes are 4 and 6: that is, the most likely occurrences of determiners within a sentence is four or six times. However, if we increase the test sample, it becomes more evident that the most probable frequency of determiners within a sentence is 6 (mode). Similarly, as we increase the sample, the histogram gets more peaked and more bell-shaped. In mathematical terms, distributions like this are known as binomial distributions and the resulting histograms would take the shape shown in Figure 1.5.

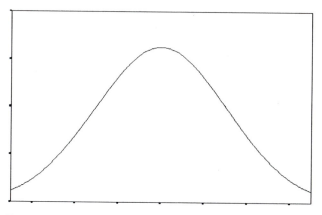

Figure 1.5 A binomial distribution.

1.6.1 Normal distributions

A normal distribution is symmetrical and exhibits no skewness (asymmetrical distribution). In a theoretical normal distribution, the mean, median and mode all fall at the same point: the centre or middle (mean = median = mode; see Figure 1.6).

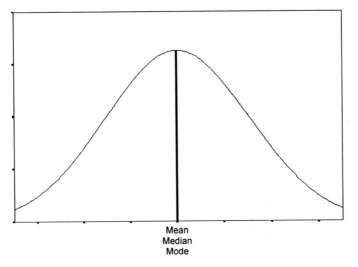

Mean
Median
Mode

Figure 1.6 Mean = median = mode.

The normal distribution is a very stable and very important statistical phenomenon. If the sample size is very large three features always occur:

- The plotted graph is symmetrical.
- The sample mean is very close to the population mean, that is, of every instance in the whole population.
- The standard deviation of the sample mean is very close to the population standard deviation divided by the square root of the sample size.

Normal distribution, normal curve or Gaussian curve is also called a family of distributions. Each member of this family differs from the rest in two parameters or values: the mean and the standard deviation. The mean determines the centre of the curve and the standard deviation determines the peak (high or flat). A large standard deviation results in a more spread curve, whereas the opposite shows a higher peaked one (see Figures 1.7, 1.8, 1.9 and 1.10).

However, as already mentioned, all members of the normal distribution family, although different, exhibit the same visual features: symmetrical shape, tails nearing (but never touching) the x-axis, and an area under the curve.

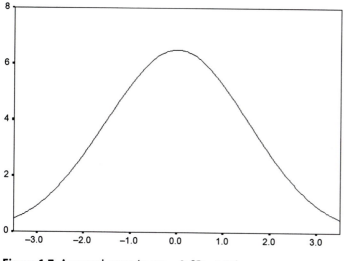

Figure 1.7 A normal curve (mean = 0, SD = 1.53).

Normal distribution is common in many phenomena in nature and as it provides the behaviour for the sample mean it can help us to construct models of the whole population from any experiment. It turns out that most variables can be modelled successfully as a normal distribution. Let us illustrate this, by taking our hypothetical data above (occurrences of determiners within sentences). Suppose we want to determine the probability of a sentence with less than three determiners. To do this, what we know is that the mean occurrence of determiners in the 277 test sentences is 5.34 and the standard deviation 1.82. If we take a random sentence and obtain its determiner occurrence x, what would be the likelihood that the inequality $x < 3$ will

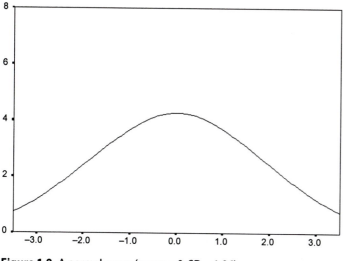

Figure 1.8 A normal curve (mean = 0, SD = 1.86).

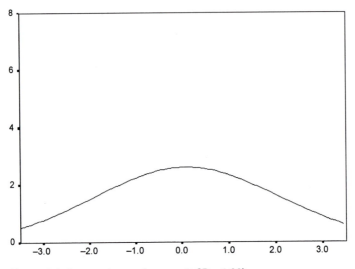

Figure 1.9 A normal curve (mean = 0, SD = 1.98).

be true? Now, one way to proceed is to transform the inequality until it becomes a standardized score (*z*-score); we have:

$x < 3$

which is the same if we subtract the mean from each side:

$x - 5.34 < 3 - 5.34$

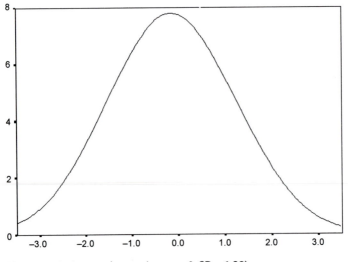

Figure 1.10 A normal curve (mean = 0, SD = 1.38).

and still the same if we divide both sides by the standard deviation:

$$\frac{x - 5.34}{1.82} < \frac{3 - 5.34}{1.82}$$

What we have done here is to transform the x into its standardized z-score, with mean 0 and standard deviation 1 (see above section 1.6). The result is thus:

$$z = \frac{x - 5.34}{1.82}$$

$$z < \frac{3 - 5.34}{1.82}$$

$$z < -1.28$$

This is the same as saying that in our data a sentence with less than three determiners has a standardized z-score of -1.28. The minus sign indicates that the score is below the mean (mean = 0). If we check the probability for -1.28 on the appropriate table (see Appendix 1), we have two columns: the z-scores and the probability associated with it. In our case, the z-score we get is -1.28, which is roughly between -1.2 and -1.3 with a probability of 0.10. Hence we can say that about 10 per cent of the sentences will have less than three determiners. In other words, if I took a random sentence, the probability of this sentence having less than three determiners will be roughly 10 per cent. We would like to warn the reader that the precision of this approach will depend on how close the distribution of our sample is to the whole population of English sentences, regarding the use of determiners. In addition, a further issue is whether or not the distribution of determiners is a normal distribution. If the population does not have a normal distribution then it would be inappropriate to use standard scores.

As we mentioned earlier, normal curves have the same mean, median and mode, and area under the curve. So, in a normal curve, we can accurately predict that 50 per cent of all scores will fall above the mean, median and mode, and the remaining 50 per cent below. Similarly, approximately 34 per cent of the scores will fall within one standard deviation above or below the mean (see Figure 1.11). Let us look again at our determiner data: using the approximate percentages falling throughout the normal distribution, we can say that the percentage of sentences with more than five determiners per sentence would roughly be 50 per cent (note that the mean is 5.34), since the bell-shaped curve is very symmetrical. The percentage distribution of this data would be as shown in Figure 1.11.

Figure 1.11 compares the raw data of our experiment and the equivalent standardized scores. The shaded area represents the probability of a random sentence having fewer than three determiners (raw score: 3; z-score: -1.28), approximately 10 per cent of our normal curve model. You can also observe that nearly 68 per cent of all sentences account for roughly three to seven determiners (34% + 34% = 68%)

No. of outcomes

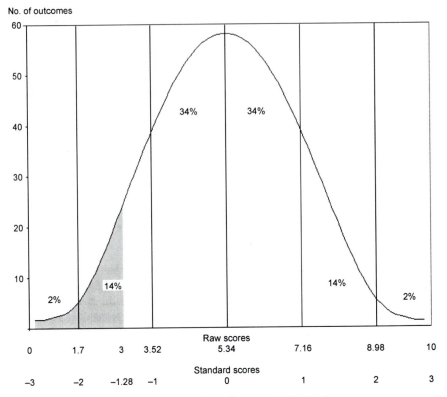

Figure 1.11 Percentages falling throughout the normal distribution.

and that 32 per cent (100% − 68%) account for less than three and more than seven determiners overall. Likewise, 34 per cent will score between the mean and one standard deviation above the mean (1 SD; five to seven determiners). We can account for nearly 96 per cent of all cases in the distribution (sentences with two to nine determiners: 14% + 34% + 34% + 14% = 96%). Of course, if the sample is large enough, then the percentage patterns within the various areas of the normal distribution will be very regular and predictable.

1.6.2 Skewed distributions

Normal distributions are by no means just theoretical distributions. There is countless research and evidence in many disciplines where normal data distributions occur. The importance of this distribution for language and linguistics research is that many statistical tests assume that the data are normally distributed. Consequently, these tests can only be applied on language data where this holds true.

Suppose we are interested in accounting for lexical items (types) that occur for the first time in a text. That is, we count newly encountered items in a text. One way to do this is to divide the text into equal chunks, say of 10,000 words (tokens). So, a text of 200,000 word length is split into twenty fractions of 10,000 words each. We now go through the first chunk and count the different lexical items it contains, take the next fraction and count the newly occurring different lexical items (those that did not occur in chunk 1), and so on and so forth until we have extracted the newly encountered lexical items in chunk 20 (that did not occur previously in chunks 1, 2, 3 ... 19). The resulting hypothetical data are given in Table 1.17.

Table 1.17 Token and type distribution.

Text fraction	Tokens	Cumulative tokens	Types	Cumulative types
1	10,000	10,000	2,600	2,600
2	10,000	20,000	1,076	3,676
3	10,000	30,000	827	4,503
4	10,000	40,000	697	5,200
5	10,000	50,000	613	5,813
6	10,000	60,000	555	6,368
7	10,000	70,000	510	6,878
8	10,000	80,000	475	7,353
9	10,000	90,000	447	7,800
10	10,000	100,000	421	8,221
11	10,000	110,000	402	8,623
12	10,000	120,000	383	9,006
13	10,000	130,000	368	9,374
14	10,000	140,000	354	9,728
15	10,000	150,000	341	10,069
16	10,000	160,000	331	10,400
17	10,000	170,000	320	10,720
18	10,000	180,000	310	11,030
19	10,000	190,000	303	11,333
20	10,000	200,000	294	11,627

And the corresponding plot is shown in Figure 1.12.

From this histogram, it becomes apparent that the data it represents are neither normally distributed nor symmetrical. This distribution is known as *skewed*. In a skewed distribution, scores are grouped asymmetrically, either towards the higher score or towards the lower score. Furthermore, the mean and median are not the same and are allocated differently along the histogram. In our data the mean is 581.25, whereas the median is 411.5. The marked difference between the mean and median evidences a substantial lack of symmetry: skewness.

The skewness is normally defined depending on the direction of the longer tail. So if the longer tail points in the positive direction (Figure 1.13), we have a skewed data set to the right: positively skewed distribution; and if the longer tails points left, in the negative direction (Figure 1.14), then we have a negatively skewed distribution. In a positively skewed distribution, most of the data are below the

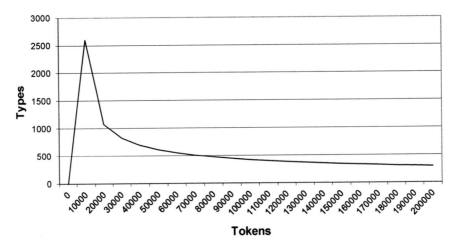

Figure 1.12 Distribution of newly found lexical items throughout a text.

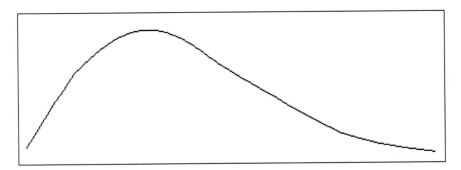

Figure 1.13 A positively skewed distribution.

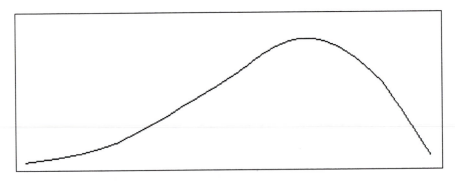

Figure 1.14 A negatively skewed distribution.

mean; and the converse is true for negatively skewed distributions: most items are above the mean.

A closer look reveals that the mean, median and mode are not located in the same place as in a normal distribution. The median cuts the distribution in the x-axis such that 50 per cent falls on each side; the mean is the balance point of the distribution and the mode the most common score. In a positively skewed distribution, the mode comes first, and the mean is pulled towards the larger scores (direction of the skewedness), thus the mean is greater than the median. So, the order in a positively skewed distribution is: mode, median and mean (Figure 1.15). A negatively skewed distribution points in the opposite direction. The order of the measures of central tendency would be the reverse: mean, median and mode (Figure 1.16).

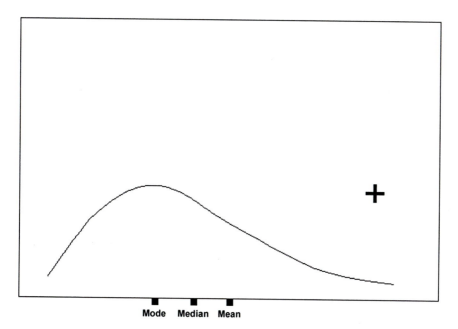

Mode   Median   Mean

Figure 1.15 Mode, median and mean (+).

The normal distribution has a single mode. However, we can also find frequency distributions with more than one modal peak. Figure 1.17 shows a bimodal distribution. Note that the distribution is symmetrical and the mean and median fall at the same point, while the modes correspond to the two highest points of the distribution.

Unless otherwise indicated, it is customary to assume that a data set is normally distributed: symmetrical and bell-shaped. A first approach to the data would be to display it graphically. Histograms clearly reveal skewed distributions, such as the ones mentioned above, or others such as U-shaped, J-shaped or totally irregular, unpredictable distributions (Figure 1.18).

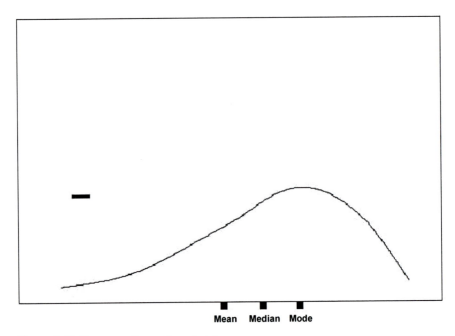

Figure 1.16 Mean, median and mode (–).

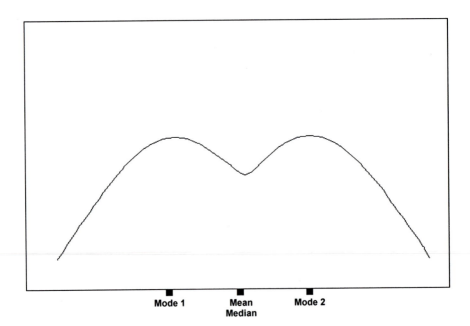

Figure 1.17 A bimodal distribution.

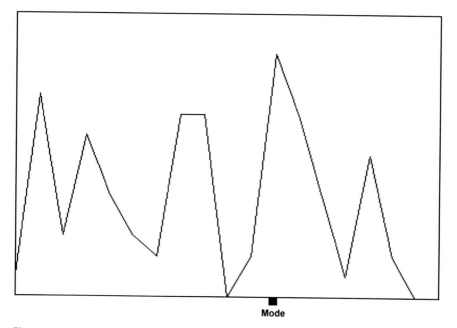

Mode

Figure 1.18 An irregular distribution.

1.7 Probability

It is not always possible or practical to study a whole data set. Thus, if anyone is interested in analysing the preposition *of*, it would not be wise to extract all instances of this preposition from the British National Corpus (BNC hereafter). A positive solution would be to select a sample of the BNC and retrieve just the instances found in that sample. This sample might be enough to allow us to draw conclusions, probably as confidently as if the whole BNC had been used. That is, we take a representative portion (sample) of the whole corpus (population) for which generalization is intended, and where the sample is representative only if it is a random sample. The point of a random sample is to ensure that each item or occurrence of the population has an equal chance of being selected for a sample. This eliminates biases as each item or occurrence is assumed to represent the population from which it has been retrieved.

Now intuitively, probability provides the bridge between the properties of a sample and the population it has been selected from (we already introduced in section 1.6 a brief note on probability). Suppose that we have the following sentence: *John has a box with a book, a map and a ruler in it*. If we tag the sentence for part-of-speech, we get:

John	has	a	box	with	a	book	a	map	and	a	ruler	in	it
Noun	Verb	Art	Noun	Prep	Art	Noun	Art	Noun	Conj	Art	Noun	Prep	Pron

In this fourteen-word long sentence we find: five nouns, four articles, two prepositions, one verb, one conjunction and one pronoun. Now, if we randomly draw a word from this sentence, what proportion of draws will turn out to be nouns? You would probably agree if we said five draws out of fourteen. Since there are five nouns in the fourteen-word sentence, we would expect that a noun would be drawn about five-fourteenths of the time in a large number of trials. This means that the probability of drawing a noun from the sentence above on any one occasion is:

$$p(noun) = \frac{5}{14} = 0.357$$

Similarly, we can also determine the probability of drawing a word from the sentence that is not a noun ($\neg noun$):

$$p(\neg noun) = \frac{9}{14} = 0.6429$$

The logic for 9 is that the number of words within the sentence that are not nouns is: 14 (words) − 5 (nouns) = 9 ($\neg noun$).

The probabilities for all parts-of-speech within the sample sentence are given in Table 1.18.

Table 1.18 Part-of-speech probabilities.

Parts-of-speech	Occurrence in sentence	Probability
Noun	5	0.3571
Article	4	0.2857
Preposition	2	0.1428
Verb	1	0.0714
Conjunction	1	0.0714
Pronoun	1	0.0714

As mentioned earlier, probabilities range from 0 to 1 and can also be stated in percentages. So, if we add them all up, we get 1:

$$p(noun) + p(\neg noun) = 0.3571 + 0.6429 = 1$$

A probability of 1 indicates that an event is absolutely certain to happen. Of course, the probability of a word being a noun plus the probability of that word not being a noun account for all possibilities (any word whether a noun or not). To facilitate interpretation, we can also state probabilities in percentages. This is simply done by multiplying ratios by 100:

$p(noun) = 0.3571 \times 100 = 35.71\%$

$p(\neg noun) = 0.6429 \times 100 = 64.29\%$

1.7.1 Conditional probability and statistical independence

Nouns can be modified by adjectives or by other nouns, either pre-nominally or post-nominally:

Pre-nominally (adjectives): *red cars*
Pre-nominally (nouns): *telephone directory*
Post-nominally (adjectives): *president elect*
Post-nominally (nouns): *book of literature*

Consider the following data relative to two hypothetical languages. The data refer to noun modification. The data for languages A and B are given in Tables 1.19 and 1.20 respectively.

Table 1.19 Distribution of nominal modification for language A.

	Adjectives	Nouns	Total
Pre-nominal	1,000	500	1,500
Post-nominal	100	50	150
Total	1,100	550	1,650

Table 1.20 Distribution of nominal modification for language B.

	Adjectives	Nouns	Total
Pre-nominal	1,070	430	1,500
Post-nominal	30	120	150
Total	1,100	550	1,650

Both of the languages exhibit the possibility of adjectives and nouns in pre- or post-nominal-modifying positions. Each language sample contains the same number of cases, 1,650, of which 1,500 are pre-nominal modifiers and 150 post-nominal modifiers.

Comparing both languages, language A has the same proportion of pre-nominal adjectives (1,000 / 1,100) and pre-nominal nouns (500 / 550), namely 0.91. In contrast, in language B, the proportions of pre-nominal adjectives and pre-nominal nouns are different, 0.97 (1,070 / 1,100) and 0.78 (430 / 550) respectively. These basic proportions suggest that language B is more likely to resort to adjectives for pre-modification than to nouns. In contrast, language A uses both equally: nouns and adjectives.

Let us now choose a noun modifier at random. What would be the probability of this modifier being an adjective? For language A it would be:

$$p(adjective) = \frac{1,100}{1,650} = 0.66$$

And for language B:

$$p(adjective) = \frac{1,100}{1,650} = 0.66$$

The probability of choosing a noun instead is for language A:

$$p(noun) = \frac{550}{1,650} = 0.33$$

The same as for language B:

$$p(noun) = \frac{550}{1,650} = 0.33$$

Both languages have the same proportions of adjectives and noun modifiers. However, language A and B have different structures. A more fine-grained analysis reveals the following for language A:

$$p(adjective \ \& \ pre\text{-}modifier) = \frac{1,000}{1,650} = 0.606$$

$$p(adjective \ \& \ post\text{-}modifier) = \frac{100}{1,650} = 0.06$$

$$p(noun \ \& \ pre\text{-}modifier) = \frac{500}{1,650} = 0.303$$

$$p(noun \ \& \ post\text{-}modifier) = \frac{50}{1,650} = 0.03$$

Whereas language B has the following structure:

$$p(adjective \ \& \ pre\text{-}modifier) = \frac{1,070}{1,650} = 0.648$$

$$p(adjective \ \& \ post\text{-}modifier) = \frac{30}{1,650} = 0.018$$

$$p(noun\ \&\ pre\text{-}modifier) = \frac{430}{1,650} = 0.26$$

$$p(noun\ \&\ post\text{-}modifier) = \frac{120}{1,650} = 0.072$$

In both cases, the total probability of all partitions is always 1 (note the rounding off):

Language A: $0.606 + 0.06 + 0.303 + 0.03 = 1$

Language B: $0.648 + 0.018 + 0.26 + 0.072 = 1$

   In the light of the data above, suppose we want to know the probability of an adjective being a pre-modifier. This is different from asking about the probability of a pre-modifying adjective (see *p(adjective & pre-modifier)* above). What we ask is this: if you have an adjective, what is the probability of this adjective pre-modifying a noun? That is, we impose a condition: *given X, what is the probability of getting Y?* This is known as a conditional probability and is re-written in standard notation as:

p(Y|X)

Returning to our previous sample, the probability of a given adjective pre-modifying a noun in language A is:

$$p(pre\text{-}modifier|adjective) = \frac{1,000}{1,100} = 0.91$$

This is the same as the probability of any noun or adjective functioning pre-nominally:

$$p(pre\text{-}modifier) = \frac{1,500}{1,650} = 0.91$$

This means that, in language A, the probability that a linguistic item, irrespective of whether it is a noun or an adjective, will function as a pre-modifier is exactly the same as the probability of an adjective functioning as a pre-modifier.

p(pre-modifier|adjective) = *p(pre-modifier)*

   A first practical consequence of this data is that the probability of a linguistic item (whether an adjective or a noun) functioning as a pre-modifier does not depend on its parts-of-speech. This implies that:

p(pre-modifier|noun) = *p(pre-modifier|adjective)* = *p(pre-modifier)*

This is indeed true, as:

$$p(pre\text{-}modifier|noun) = \frac{500}{550} = 0.91$$

Similarly, we could also impose a different condition on the data, such as the probability of a given pre-modifier being an adjective:

$$p(adjective|pre\text{-}modifier) = \frac{1,000}{1,500} = 0.66$$

Which is the same as:

$$p(adjective|post\text{-}modifier) = \frac{100}{150} = 0.66$$

And:

$$p(adjective) = \frac{1,100}{1,650} = 0.66$$

This implies that in language A, the probability of noun-modifying adjectives is irrespective of their positioning with respect to the noun (before or after it). So, in language A whatever restrictions are imposed, part-of-speech (adjective/noun) or positioning (pre-nominal/post-nominal), the probabilities remain unaltered. This means that the variables "part-of-speech" and "positioning" are statistically independent.

Let us now consider language B. The probability of finding noun pre-modification is the same as in language A:

$$p(pre\text{-}modifier) = \frac{1,500}{1,650} = 0.91$$

However, we see that:

$$p(pre\text{-}modifier|adjective) = \frac{1,070}{1,100} = 0.97$$

and that:

$$p(pre\text{-}modifier|noun) = \frac{430}{550} = 0.78$$

Clearly, language B exhibits a different structure where

$$p(pre\text{-}modifier|noun) \neq p(pre\text{-}modifier|adjective) \neq p(pre\text{-}modifier)$$

A practical implication of this is that the variable "positioning" is statistically dependent on "part-of-speech". That is, if we choose an adjective, then there are higher chances that this adjective will be positioned pre-nominally than if a noun had been taken.

Consider now this:

$$p(adjective|pre\text{-}modifier) = \frac{1,070}{1,500} = 0.71$$

This is different from:

$$p(adjective|post\text{-}modifier) = \frac{30}{150} = 0.2$$

And again different from:

$$p(adjective) = \frac{1,100}{1,650} = 0.66$$

That is to say, if we choose pre-modification, we are much more likely to find an adjective than a noun, so part-of-speech is dependent on positioning.

There is a general rule by means of which we can calculate the probability that X will occur, given that Y has already occurred:

$$p(X|Y) = \frac{p(X \& Y)}{p(Y)}$$

So:

$$p(adjective|post\text{-}modifier) = \frac{p(adjective \& post\text{-}modifier)}{p(post\text{-}modifier)}$$

where:

$$p(adjective \& post\text{-}modifier) = \frac{30}{1,650} = 0.018$$

and:

$$p(post\text{-}modifier) = \frac{150}{1,650} = 0.09$$

That is:

$$p(adjective \& post\text{-}modifier) = \frac{0.018}{0.09} = 0.2$$

Recall language A and its statistical independent variables, "part-of-speech" and "positioning", in contrast to language B's dependency. Consider the probability of there being a noun and post-nominal modifier, in language A. That is:

$$p(noun \ \& \ post\text{-}nominal) \ = \ \frac{50}{1,650} \ = \ 0.03$$

where:

$$p(noun) \ = \ \frac{550}{1,650} \ = \ 0.33$$

and:

$$p(post\text{-}nominal) \ = \ \frac{150}{1,650} \ = \ 0.09$$

We find here an important property of statistically independent variables (note that decimals are reduced to two places):

$$p(noun \ \& \ post\text{-}nominal) \ = \ p(noun) \times p(post\text{-}nominal)$$

$$0.03 \ = \ 0.33 \times 0.09$$

Whereas this does not hold for language B:

$$p(noun \ \& \ post\text{-}nominal) \ = \ \frac{120}{1,650} \ = \ 0.07$$

$$p(noun) \ = \ \frac{550}{1,650} \ = \ 0.33$$

$$p(post\text{-}nominal) \ = \ \frac{150}{1,650} \ = \ 0.09$$

$$p(noun \ \& \ post\text{-}nominal) \neq p(noun) \times p(post\text{-}nominal)$$

$$0.07 \neq 0.33 \times 0.09$$

It only holds for language A because the two variables, "part-of-speech" and "positioning", are independent. The lack of this property in language B indicates that the variables "part-of-speech" and "positioning" are statistically dependent here. However, what holds for language B is:

$$p(noun \ \& \ post\text{-}nominal) \ = \ p(noun|post\text{-}nominal) \times p(post\text{-}nominal)$$

This is a simple derivation of the more general rule:

$$p(noun|post\text{-}modifier) = \frac{p(noun \ \& \ post\text{-}modifier)}{p(post\text{-}modifier)}$$

Additionally, it also holds for language A as:

$$p(noun \ \& \ post\text{-}nominal) = p(noun|post\text{-}nominal) \times p(post\text{-}nominal)$$

$$\frac{50}{1,650} = \frac{50}{550} \times \frac{550}{1,650}$$

We conclude that the more general rule can be used to calculate the conditional probability of either of the two cases: statistical dependency (language B) and statistical independence (language A):

$$p(X \ \& \ Y) = p(X|Y) \times p(Y) = p(Y|X) \times p(X)$$

2 Scales and variables

2.1 Types of scales

The main goal of quantifying data is to assign numbers to objects in such a way that the relationship between objects is expressed in the number assigned to the objects. The problem is that not all data or objects can be measured in the same way or by means of the same measurement system. Variables like the nationality or sex of some authors can be typified using numbers:

English = 1
Spanish = 2

or:

Female = 1
Male = 2

Consequently, we could combine both variables (nationality and sex) into a two-place variable and typify texts. For example, 1.2 would correspond to an English male writer and 2.1 to a Spanish woman. Note that the first figure corresponds to nationality and the second to sex.

Similarly, we could also quantify the number of nouns, verbs, adjectives and adverbs that various texts contain. In this sense, the two novels of the hypothetical writers above (1.2 – English male writer – and 2.1 – Spanish female writer) might result in the content word counts shown in Table 2.1.

Table 2.1 Content word counts for two novels.

	Nouns	Verbs	Adjectives	Adverbs
Novel 1.2	120	75	34	12
Novel 2.1	100	95	44	2

If we compare the two examples (text typification and part-of-speech counts), we immediately see that they are different. Whereas in the first case we have a set of categories (for overall; 1.1, 1.2, 2.1 and 2.2), in the second example we have a set of scores or counts. A practical consequence is that, for example, in case one we cannot calculate the mean. The reason for this is that in statistics we have different types of scales.

Succinctly, different scales are associated with different ways of observing, organizing and assigning numbers to data. The choice of which statistical test to use often depends on what is called the level of measurement of the data. There are four levels of measurement or types of scales: interval, rational, nominal and ordinal. Certain statistical tests are only appropriate for certain levels of data.

2.1.1 Interval scale

An interval scale is a scale of measurement where the distance between any two adjacent units of measurement is the same. That is, if we measure in centimetres, the units on the scale are the same, and so the difference between 2 and three centimetres is the same as the difference between 20 and 21 centimetres. Similarly, if text A is made up of 1,000 words, text B of 2,000 and text C of 3,000, then we say that text B is twice as long as text A and text C three times bigger than text A. This is true because an equal difference between two numbers (i.e. 1,000 and 2,000 words) reflects an equal difference between the two objects (text A and text B) that were assigned the numbers.

Interval variables allow us not only to rank order the items that are measured, but also to quantify and compare the sizes of differences between them.

What is important in determining whether a scale is considered interval or not is the underlying intent regarding the equal intervals. For an IQ scale, it would not be valid to say that a person with a score of 110 was twice as intelligent as a person with a score of 55. The intervals in an IQ scale are not necessarily equal (e.g. the difference between 105 and 110 is not really the same as between 80 and 85). Behavioural scientists are willing to assume that most of their measures are interval scales as this allows the calculation of averages, the range and standard deviation. A good example of an interval scale is the Fahrenheit scale for temperature. Equal differences on this scale represent equal differences in temperature, but a temperature of 30 degrees is not twice as warm as one of 15 degrees.

2.1.2 Rational scale

A rational scale is just like an interval scale, but in addition to all the properties of the interval scale, it features an identifiable absolute zero point; it thus allows for statements such as A is two times more than B. This zero indicates that the data or objects lack this attribute. For example, if a text has 0 adverbs, we say that it lacks the property or attribute of having adverbs.

Typical examples of rational scales are measures of time or space. For example, as the Kelvin temperature scale is a ratio scale, not only can we say that a temperature of 150 degrees is higher than one of 75 degrees, but we can correctly state that it is twice as high. Interval scales do not have the ratio property. Most statistical data analysis procedures do not distinguish between the interval and ratio properties of the measurement scales.

2.1.3 Nominal scale

In nominal scales, we categorize items; a nominal scale is really a list of categories into which objects can be classified. Nominal measurement consists of assigning items to groups or categories. No quantitative information is conveyed and no ordering of the items is implied. The numbers we assign to these objects are arbitrary and do not reflect any kind of ordering or primacy of any category over the other (see examples above on nationality and sex). Nominal scales are therefore qualitative rather than quantitative. Variables measured on a nominal scale are often referred to as categorical or qualitative variables. Examples of nominal scales are, for instance, the renaming of texts in linguistic corpora. So, instead of typifying a text sample category as, say, *Peninsular-Spanish Oral Television Debate Economy*, we can just rename it as "0101030414", where the first two figures, 01, stand for Peninsular-Spanish, the next two figures, 01, for Oral, the next two, 03, for Television, 04 for Debate and 14 for Economy.

2.1.4 Ordinal scales

Ordinal scales are used to rank data. An ordinal scale is a measurement scale that assigns values to objects based on their ranking with respect to one another. For instance, we might use a scale of 0–10 to indicate the degree of autobiographicity (i.e. use of first person pronouns: I, me, my, mine, myself, etc.) of various novels, from 0 (non-autobiographical novel) to 10 (autobiographical novel). While you know that a 4 is more autobiographical than a 2, there is no implication that a 4 is twice as autobiographical as a 2. Nor is the autobiographicity from 2 to 4 necessarily the same "amount" of autobiographicity as the autobiographicity from 6 to 8. All we know is that there are 11 categories, with 1 being more autobiographical than 0, 2 being more autobiographical than 1, and so on.

To sum up, we can say that all four types of scale are somehow related and build on one another. Nominal scales name and categorize items. Ordinal scales name, categorize and provide ranking or ordering of items. Interval scales reveal information on ordering within categories, but provide additional information on the distances between points in that ordering or ranking. Finally, rational scales give all the information of nominal, ordinal and interval scales, but with considerably more information because there is an interpretable zero, and multiples of points along the scale make sense. However, in language studies ratio scales are seldom used. Appendix 2 gives some examples of statistics that are appropriate for each scale.

2.2 Types of variables

The understanding and knowledge scientists have about the world is often represented by means of models. So the main aim of the scientific method is to simplify and explain events in the real world. This is done by creating new models or verifying and/or modifying existing models of the world. Next, these models are used by applied sciences to predict and control real events in the world.

One possible set of models are statistical models, which have turned out to be most useful and profitable within linguistic research. Succinctly, a model can be defined as a representation containing the essential structure of some object or event in the real world. Of course, this implies that models are, by definition, necessarily incomplete.

A possible object or event subject to be modelled can be, for example, *proficiency in Russian*. Now, proficiency in Russian is an underlying human characteristic or ability that somehow goes on inside Russian learners' heads. Suppose we want to approach the construct and measure it. In that case what we need is to define the structure of this construct; that is, the observable characteristics or abilities involved in this construct, or in other words, the variables that are essential to it.

Variables, in contrast to constructs, are the observed quantifiable pieces of a more complex structure (object or event in the real world). In our example, the event or object we are interested in is a human characteristic or ability represented by the construct *proficiency in Russian*. Thus, if we were to measure or quantify the amount of the construct *proficiency in Russian*, it could be represented by the variable *test scores in Russian proficiency*. Similarly, the scores obtained by this variable would not be the construct *proficiency in Russian* but just the observed and quantified reflection of the ability.

Researchers are constantly faced with the problem of how to explain or define a construct by means of variables, and even worse, researchers need to know exactly how these variables interact. The classification and manipulation of variables is prime in statistical analysis in order to better understand what goes on.

In statistical analysis, we distinguish five types of variables: dependent, independent, moderator, control and intervening variables.

2.2.1 Dependent variables

This is the central variable on which other variables intervene where a relationship exists. In fact, a dependent variable is the variable observed in order to determine if there is any effect, caused by the action of other variables. This explains why a dependent variable can only be understood in the context of other intervening variables.

As an example, assume a researcher is interested in operationalizing (basically, measuring) the construct *proficiency in Russian* in her students. This is done by means of applying a standardized Russian proficiency test to all language learners. Our researcher's main interest is to investigate whether or not a new language learning/teaching methodology increases the learning pace in second-year Russian language students. To compare the new method with a traditionally existing one, the researcher takes two groups of students, group A and group B, where group A is taught in the traditional way and B in the new way. A standardized Russian language proficiency test is administered at the beginning of the course (pre-test) to both groups and at the end of the course, after completing a semester of study (post-test). The test scores are given in Table 2.2.

Table 2.2 Scores for Groups A and B in two tests.

	Group A	Group B
Pre-test	50	50
Post-test	70	85

With the data of Table 2.2, what would be the variable of interest or the dependent variable for the researcher? The students' grouping? The number of tests administered? The length of the course taught? The various scores in the Russian proficiency test?

One way to determine the dependent variable is to ask what has been measured to determine the effect of other variables on it. In fact, what has been measured here is proficiency in Russian by means of a standardized language proficiency test for Russian. Furthermore, the test scores on language proficiency determine how the teaching method has affected the dependent variable: *proficiency in Russian.*

2.2.2 Independent variables

An independent variable is a variable that has been selected by the researcher in order to determine the relationship with or the effect on the dependent variable. The researcher can choose or select more than one dependent variable. In our previous example, the researcher selected the teaching method as the dependent variable.

In contrast to dependent variables, independent variables are manipulated by the researcher to determine their effect on and relationship with the dependent variable. If we continue with the above example of *proficiency in Russian*, we can select various independent variables:

- one year of Russian study
- second-year Russian students
- a first test was administered at the beginning of the experiment: pre-test
- a second test was administered at the end of the experiment: post-test.

Thus, the researcher systematically manipulates, or varies the independent variables to determine whether, or the degree to which, they have any effect on the dependent variable: *proficiency in Russian.*

2.2.3 Moderator variables

This is a special kind of independent variable. The main difference between an independent variable and a moderator variable is that in the former the researcher is much more concerned with its direct relationship to the dependent variable, whereas in the latter the concern is with the effect on that relationship.

To illustrate this, recall our previous Russian proficiency example and imagine that our researcher is interested not just in investigating the relationship between proficiency in Russian (dependent variable) and teaching method (independent variable), but also how this relationship is different between female and male students. In this case, the researcher selects sex as a moderator variable. It may turn out to be the case that there are no differences between males and females in terms of the relationship between the teaching method and Russian proficiency. The fact that the researcher included sex as a possible moderator makes it a moderator variable.

2.2.4 Control variables

In any research, we must attempt to neutralize or control all variables that are likely to distort or have some effect on the dependent, independent or moderator variables. This is done by selecting those extraneous variables and neutralizing them, or just eliminating them from our study.

Take our previous example. Suppose that in one of the groups, B, 80 per cent of the students are bilingual in Russian, as their parents are Russian immigrants living in Spain. This finding would, no doubt, distort our research as the scores in proficiency in Russian (dependent variable) would not be due to the effect of the teaching method (independent variable), but mainly to the fact that most of the students are already bilingual in Russian.

One possible way to control this is to eliminate this variable (being bilingual), which can easily be done by, for instance, interviewing all students about their knowledge of Russian, and eliminating Russian bilingual students and other very competent students in Russian. This would control, neutralize and eliminate any unrelated effect on the dependent, independent or moderator variables under investigation.

2.2.5 Intervening variables

These variables are, in principle, not observable; they are abstract, theoretical labels applied to the relationship or process that links the independent and dependent variables. In our example, one possible way of labelling or stating the intervening variable could be *teaching method effectiveness* or more generally *language learning*. The problem is that language learning is a process that goes on inside the student's head and is not directly observable. However, there is no doubt that there is a conceptual link between language teaching methodology and language proficiency. Thus, an intervening variable is a theoretical or abstract label that relates the independent and dependent variables.

2.2.6 Interrelationship among variables

As already stated, the main relationship among variables in a study is the one between the independent variable(s) selected by the investigator and the dependent variable(s). The central aim is to determine the relationship and/or effect of the independent variables on the dependent one. Furthermore, if the researcher wants to consider how particular independent variables affect or alter the relationship between the independent and dependent variables, then she might choose or select one or more moderator variables. The intervening variable(s) just illustrate or label the process or relationship that link(s) the independent and dependent variables. Finally, to ensure that the research is under control and no extraneous variables affect it, we must neutralize any potential variable likely to distort our study: that is, we must control variables.

To sum up, the general relationship between variables looks graphically like Figure 2.1.[1] Note that the arrows indicate the direction of focus in the researcher's design and thinking of the study.

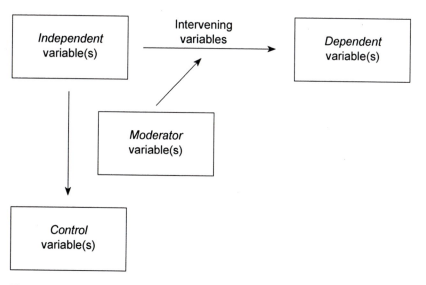

Figure 2.1 Relationship among variables.

---

1. Adapted from Brown 1988: 13.

3 Parametric versus non-parametric statistics

3.1 Introduction

Frequency lists – of word forms, for example – are never more than a set of hints or clues as to the nature of a text. By examining a list, one can get an idea of what further information would be worth acquiring, or one can make guesses about the structure of the text and so focus an investigation.

Returning to our arts and science sample in Chapter 1, let us suppose now that we are interested in examining how modal verbs are distributed in both sublanguages and comparing how they are used. The first thing to do is simply to count each of these verbs in the two corpora. Having done this, we arrive at the following frequencies:

Table 3.1 Modal verbs in arts and science texts.

	Arts	Science
Can	265	778
Could	296	307
May	187	547
Might	157	113
Must	130	236
Ought to	12	6
Shall	18	44
Should	98	159
Will	174	593
Would	421	485

A quick look at these figures reveals whether modal verbs are more frequently used in scientific communication than in arts. But with what degree of certainty can we infer that this is a genuine finding about the two corpora rather than a result of chance? From these figures alone we cannot decide; we need to take some decisions and perform further calculations in order to determine how high or low the probability is that the difference between the two corpora on these features is due to mere chance.

To answer this statistical question, the question has to be translated into a *hypothesis* – a statement which can be subjected to testing. Depending on the decisions and results of the further tests, the hypothesis may be *accepted* or *rejected*.

There are two types of statistical inferences:[1] estimation of population parameters and hypothesis testing. Hypothesis testing is one of the most important tools in the application of statistics to real-life problems. Most often, decisions need to be made concerning populations on the basis of sample information. Statistical tests are used in arriving at these decisions.

Hypothesis testing is the use of statistics to determine the probability that a given hypothesis is true. The usual process of hypothesis testing consists of four steps.

1. Formulate the null hypothesis H_0 (commonly, that the observations are the result of pure chance) and the alternative hypothesis H_1 (commonly, that the observations show a real effect combined with a component of chance variation).
2. Identify the test statistics that can be used to assess the truth of the null hypothesis H_0.
3. Compute the p-value, which is the probability that a test statistic at least as significant as the one observed would be obtained assuming that the null hypothesis H_0 were true. The smaller the *p*-value, the stronger the evidence against the null hypothesis.
4. Compare the *p*-value to an acceptable significance value α (sometimes called an alpha value, critical value or level of significance). If $p \leq \alpha$, then the observed effect is statistically significant, the null hypothesis is ruled out, and the alternative hypothesis is valid.

As seen above, statistical inference means drawing conclusions based on data. The two main contexts for inference are the parametric model and non-parametric model. The parametric model assumes that the population fits any parameterized distributions – most typically the normal distribution. That is, parametric inferential statistical methods are mathematical procedures for statistical hypothesis testing which assume that the distributions of the variables being assessed belong to known parameterized families of probability distribution. In this case we speak of a parametric model.

In contrast, non-parametric statistics is a branch of statistics concerned with non-parametric statistical models and non-parametric inference, including non-parametric statistical tests. Non-parametric methods are often referred to as *distribution-free* methods as they do not rely on assumptions that the data are drawn from a given probability distribution (i.e. normal distribution), in contrast to parametric statistics. Specifically, non-parametric methods are used in cases when the researcher knows nothing about the parameters of the variable of interest in the population. In more technical terms, non-parametric methods do not rely on the estimation of parameters (such as the mean or the standard deviation) describing the distribution of the

---

1. Statistical inference means drawing conclusions based on data.

variable of interest in the population. Therefore, these methods are also sometimes called *parameter-free* methods or *distribution-free* methods.

Basically, there is at least one non-parametric equivalent for each parametric general type of test. In general, these tests fall into the following categories:

- tests of differences between groups (independent samples)
- tests of differences between variables (dependent samples)
- tests of relationships between variables.

Differences between independent groups: usually, when we have two samples that we want to compare concerning their mean value for some variable of interest, we would use:

- parametric statistics: the *t-test for independent samples*
- non-parametric alternatives: the *Wald–Wolfowitz runs test*, the *Mann–Whitney U-test*, and the *Kolmogorov–Smirnov two-sample test*.

If we have multiple groups, we would use:

- parametric statistics: *analysis of variance* (ANOVA)
- non-parametric equivalents: the *Kruskal–Wallis analysis of ranks* and the *median test*.

Differences between dependent groups: if we want to compare two variables measured in the same sample we would customarily use:

- parametric statistics: the *t-test for paired samples*
- non-parametric alternatives: the *sign test* and *Wilcoxon's matched pairs test*.

Relationships between variables: to express a relationship between two variables one usually computes in:

- parametric statistics: the *Pearson correlation coefficient*
- non-parametric statistics: *Spearman rank correlation coefficient, Kendall Tau*, and *coefficient Gamma*.

If the two variables of interest are categorical in nature (e.g. "yes" versus "no" by "male" versus "female"), appropriate non-parametric statistics for testing the relationship between the two variables are the *chi-square test*, the *Phi coefficient* and the *Fisher exact test*.

We do not intend to offer here an exhaustive presentation of all statistical techniques available to linguists, but to offer, illustrate and demonstrate the contribution that statistics can and should make to linguistic studies. We shall present in this book one parametric test and its non-parametric test equivalent for each of the three statistical modelling categories presented above (see Table 3.2), namely:

- tests of differences between groups
- tests of differences between variables
- tests of relationships between variables.

Table 3.2 Statistical tests described.

	Tests of differences between groups (independent samples)		Tests of differences between variables (dependent samples)	Tests of relationships between variables
	Two groups	Multiple groups		
Parametric statistics	*t-test for independent samples* §3.2.1	*ANOVA* §3.2.3	*t-test for paired samples* §3.2.2	*Pearson correlation coefficient* §3.2.4
Non-parametric statistics	*Mann–Whitney U-test* §3.3.1	*Median test* §3.3.4	*Sign test* §3.3.2	*Spearman rank correlation coefficient* §3.3.5
				Chi-square test §3.3.3

3.2 Parametric tests

Parametric statistics are statistics where the population is assumed to fit any parameterized distributions. This branch of statistical inference makes assumptions about the underlying mathematical distributional form of observed variables.

Parametric inferential statistical methods, as we have already mentioned, are mathematical procedures for statistical hypothesis testing which assume that the distributions of the variables being assessed belong to known parameterized families of probability distributions. In this case we speak of a parametric model. The most familiar of these hypothetical mathematical distributions is the normal distribution. Binomial and Poisson distributions are also widely used.

In parametric tests, we assume that the dependent variable(s) is/are interval or rational scored. Additionally, the data need to be somehow distributed. The most typical distribution is the normal distribution, which implies that the mean and standard deviation are appropriate measures of central tendency and dispersion. In parametric techniques we also assume that the observations are independent, that is, the score of one case does not bias the score of any other case.

Some linguists and statisticians believe that these models are inappropriate to language studies, since they rest on assumptions that are violated by much linguistic data, and prefer instead to rely on non-parametric statistics.

3.2.1 *t*-test for independent samples

A *t*-test for independent samples is a very common parametric test, used to compare two small sets of quantitative data when samples are collected independently of each other. That is, when we randomly take replicate measurements from a population, then we are collecting an independent sample.

Suppose we are interested in examining the use of specific vocabulary (medical English) in students of English as a foreign language and compare the population means on the basis of two samples. Students are divided into two groups, ten students in each group. One group (group A) is taught using authentic materials only (medical journals and periodicals), while the other group (group B) uses a standard specific English medical textbook. The instruction period is one academic semester for each group. Our aim is to investigate which teaching material proves better in relation to specific vocabulary acquisition. The data used for this purpose are from a corpus containing twenty equally long essays. Each essay is produced by one of the twenty students. Next, we extract the specific vocabulary from each essay. The data obtained are displayed in Table 3.3.

Table 3.3 Use of medical terms in group A versus group B.

Group A	Group B
22	15
16	12
21	14
18	16
14	14
19	20
20	19
17	11
24	10
15	14

The mean use of medical terms in group A (taught by means of authentic materials) is 18.6, with a standard deviation of 3.204. In contrast, students in group B use an average of 14.5 medical items, with a standard deviation of 3.205. Thus the sample mean of the authentic material group is higher than that of the textbook users. Does this mean that the teaching materials used in group A are superior to those in group B for acquiring more specific English medical vocabulary? Or is this just accidental? In other words, we need to check whether the resulting data of groups A and B are due to chance or due to something else: the teaching material used. Note that for practical reasons, we are deliberately skipping some control and moderator variables, such as students' pre-test scores, academic background, age and so on. We shall just assume that students in both groups had exactly the same pace in learning/acquiring English medical vocabulary.

A positive answer to the questions above can be obtained by applying the *t*-test. This statistic technique tests the difference between two groups. However, it is important to note that the application of this test assumes that the data of both groups:

- are normally distributed,
- have equal or very similar variance, and
- have interval scores.

Actually, when applying statistical tests, what we wish to test is whether there is a significant difference between the data samples and if so, whether this difference is merely due to chance (the *null hypothesis*), or whether it is significant (the *alternative hypothesis*). The purpose of statistical techniques is to give us some confidence in claims about the data and to draw a conclusion about the effect of changes in the values of predictors or independent variables on response or dependent variables.

Returning to our example above, the null hypothesis, which is taken as a starting point and which it is often hoped will be refuted, states that there is no difference between the mean use of real medical materials (journals and periodicals) in group A compared with the traditional medical English textbooks used in group B, or at least, that the difference, although existent, is statistically not significant or merely due to chance. Notationally, the null hypothesis would be stated in the following way:

$$H_0 : \bar{x}_1 = \bar{x}_2$$

where $\bar{x}_1$ stands for the mean of group A and $\bar{x}_2$ for the mean of group B. So the null hypothesis is true whenever the two means (group A and B) on medical English vocabulary acquisition/learning are equal or very much alike. Similarly, the alternative hypothesis would be:

$$H_1 : \bar{x}_1 \neq \bar{x}_2$$

which states that the two means are sufficiently distinct. Now, to discover if the null hypothesis is true, we need to determine how far the mean of group A $(\bar{x}_1)$ is from that of group B $(\bar{x}_2)$. The unit by which this difference between means is evaluated is the *t*-value:

$$t = \frac{\bar{x}_1 - \bar{x}_2}{\sqrt{\dfrac{s_1^2}{n_1} + \dfrac{s_2^2}{n_2}}}$$

where $\bar{x}_1$ stands for the mean of group A and $\bar{x}_2$ for the mean of group B, s_1 for the standard deviation of group A, s_2 for the standard deviation of group B, n_1 for the sample size of group A, and n_2 for the sample size of group B. Thus,

$$t = \frac{\bar{x}_1 - \bar{x}_2}{\sqrt{\dfrac{s_1^2}{n_1} + \dfrac{s_2^2}{n_2}}} = \frac{18.6 - 14.5}{\sqrt{\dfrac{3.204^2}{10} + \dfrac{3.205^2}{10}}} = \frac{4.1}{1.433} = 2.861$$

The resulting t-value for groups A and B above is 2.861. Before we can come to any preliminary conclusion, we need two further things:

1. As t-values vary significantly according to sample size, it is necessary to determine the degrees of freedom (df) for each comparison. The df is the number of values of the variable which are free to vary. The number of the df is calculated straightforwardly with the formula $n - 1$, where n stands for the size of the sample. In a two-sample comparison like ours above, we need to subtract 1 from each sample:

   $df = (n_1 - 1) + (n_2 - 1)$

   or straightforward:

   $n_1 + n_2 - 2 = 10 + 10 - 2 = 18$

   where n_1 = sample size of group A, and n_2 = sample size of group B.

2. Whenever we use statistics on a sample, there is always a probability of error, that is, cases where a sample does not fully represent the population it has been extracted from. In other instances, we might be interested in knowing the probability that rejecting the null hypothesis will be an error. In language and linguistics research it is customary to take an *alpha* decision level of 5 per cent ($p < 0.05$). This means that there is less than 5 per cent probability that rejecting the null hypothesis will be an error. Consequently, our decision level will be $p < 0.05$.

Once we have the t-value (2.861), the df (18) and an *alpha* decision level ($p < 0.05$), we just need to check the appropriate table (see Appendix 3), where the decision levels are given across the top of the table and the degrees of freedom in the first column. The critical t-value needed to reject the null hypothesis is found by finding the intersection of the column for the appropriate probability decision level and the row of the corresponding df. Whenever our estimated t-value is equal to or greater than the value given in the table (critical value), the null hypothesis may be rejected with confidence and we conclude that the difference between the samples is statistically significant. Regarding our example, consultation of Appendix 3 reveals that the critical t-value is 2.101 (for $p < 0.05$; $df = 18$); as our estimated t-value = 2.861 is greater than the critical t-value, we conclude that using authentic medical materials for teaching during one semester is more efficient than medical English textbooks in order to acquire specific English medical vocabulary.

Note that some statistics books give two different tables with the probability decision levels for *t*-tests: a one-tailed (directional) level and two-tailed (non-directional) one. The level we have considered is the two-tailed one. A one- or two-tailed *t*-test is determined by whether the total area of *alpha* is placed in one tail or divided equally between the two tails of the distribution. One-tailed *t*-tests are performed if the results are only interesting in a particular direction. That is, taking our above example, we would perform a one-tailed *t*-test if we had hints or some evidence that using authentic materials is more productive than using textbooks in order to acquire specific vocabulary. In other words, what we want to explore is whether group A performed better than group B (directional), and not vice versa. We have evidence that students taught with authentic materials acquire significantly more vocabulary. In that case, that critical *t*-value would be 1.734 (for $p < 0.05$; $df = 18$) instead; our estimated *t*-value $= 2.861$ is still greater than the critical *t*-value and the conclusions would have been the same. In contrast, two-tailed *t*-tests are performed if the result would be interesting in either direction. Again, take our example; as we had no hints which teaching method is better for acquiring language specific vocabulary, we could not state beforehand which group was going to perform better. Consequently, we performed a two-tailed *t*-test (non-directional) with identical results, although two-tailed *t*-tests (non-directional) are more sensitive and greater *t*-values are needed to be statistically significant.

One further consideration: the values we obtain from a *t*-test have a *t*-distribution. This has a symmetric histogram like the normal distribution or *z*-distribution (see section 1.6.1). The difference between both distributions is that the normal distributions or *z*-statistics require large samples, while *t*-tests do not. This explains why for large samples the *t*-distribution is virtually indistinguishable from the *z*-distribution. In small samples, the *t*-distribution has a larger variance than the *z*-distribution or normal distribution. This gives a flatter and more widely spread histogram. Additionally, as the *t*-test does not require large samples, it can be applied regardless of size, and is therefore much more commonly used than *z*-statistics; this is an important advantage for language and linguistics research.

The situation of our example above is that the two sets of scores come from different or independent samples (group A and B). This was the reason for using a *t*-test for independent samples. Otherwise, in situations in which both sets of scores came from the same group of subjects, we would perform a *t*-test for paired samples.

3.2.2 *t*-test for paired samples

This test compares correlated or paired means coming from the same sample or group, for example when a feature in a study has been observed under two different conditions. The statistical requirements are the same as those demanded by the *t*-test for independent samples:

- normally distributed data sets,
- equal variance, and
- interval scores.

Imagine the following case where the scores of a group of students' answers to two questionnaires are analysed. Both questionnaires were completed by the same eight students. Table 3.4 shows the scores, along with their differences and the squares of their differences.

Table 3.4 Answers to questionnaires 1 and 2, differences and squares differences.

Student	Questionnaire 1	Questionnaire 2	Difference	Difference²
1	30	23	7	49
2	17	17	0	0
3	20	14	6	36
4	27	21	6	36
5	17	13	4	16
6	24	17	7	49
7	15	15	0	0
8	27	24	3	9
			$\Sigma d = 33$	$\Sigma d^2 = 195$

Actually, what we examine here is the same group on two measures, which is different from what we did above (see section 3.2.1), where we analysed two different groups on one measure. So we need to change slightly the original *t*-test formula for independent samples into:

$$t = \frac{\Sigma d}{\sqrt{\dfrac{N\Sigma d^2 - (\Sigma d)^2}{N - 1}}}$$

where d stands for the difference between each pair of scores and N is the number of observed pairs. Using this formula we obtain for our example:

$$t = \frac{33}{\sqrt{\dfrac{(8 \times 195) - (33)^2}{8 - 1}}}$$

The critical value for a *t*-distribution with 7 *df* ($N - 1$) at the 5 per cent level ($p < 0.05$) is for a two-tailed *t*-test (non-directional) 2.365 (see Appendix 3). Since the observed value of *t* (4.02) is greater than the critical value, we reject the null hypothesis and state that students scored significantly higher in one of the two questionnaires. To elucidate in which of the two questionnaires students scored better, we just have to look at the sum of the differences between the scores in questionnaire 1 and questionnaire 2: $\Sigma d = 33$. As the difference was calculated by subtracting the individual scores of questionnaire 2 from those of questionnaire 1, a positive figure indicates that students did better in questionnaire 1. A negative figure would have shown the opposite: better performance in questionnaire 2.

It is important to note that when applying *t*-tests, one cannot cross-compare groups. A parametric test for the comparison of three or more groups such as ANOVA should be used for such comparisons.

3.2.3 Analysis of variance (ANOVA)

The *t*-tests, as discussed above, have been used to make comparisons between only two means. However, there are many cases where we need to compare more than two means across groups. For example, suppose we have groups A, B, C and D, and we would like to compare them. A logical approach would be to compare group A with B, A with C, A with D, B with C and so on and so forth by means of *t*-tests. However, this would geometrically increase the number of *t*-tests needed and would make it artificially easy to reject the null hypothesis. So it is desirable to perform a lower number of hypothesis tests in order to reduce erroneous null hypothesis rejections. The analysis of variance (ANOVA) method of testing performs this function.

Imagine an investigator is interested in the effectiveness of various teaching methods: direct method (DM), traditional method (TM), audiolingual method (ALM), audiovisual method (AVM) and communicative method (CM). She wants to discover the difference, if any, in the level of Spanish proficiency between groups being taught by different teaching methods. Eight students were randomly assigned to each group, taken from five different populations (secondary schools). After a two-semester teaching period, a standardized Spanish language proficiency test was administered. The scores obtained are in Table 3.5.

Table 3.5 Scores on different teaching methods, means, SDs and variances.

	DM	TM	ALM	AVM	CM
	32	21	24	30	34
	12	22	28	26	35
	23	25	23	15	40
	31	25	27	29	35
	25	30	29	31	35
	22	14	17	34	31
	29	27	33	36	37
	23	28	32	32	35
Total	197	192	213	233	282
Mean	24.63	24.00	26.63	29.13	35.25
SD	6.39	5.01	5.21	6.47	2.55
Variance	40.84	25.14	27.13	41.84	6.5

Our aim is to test the null hypothesis against the alternative. The null hypothesis is stated as:

$$H_0 : \overline{x}_1 = \overline{x}_2 = \overline{x}_3 = \overline{x}_4 = \overline{x}_5$$

where $\bar{x}_1, \bar{x}_2, \bar{x}_3, \bar{x}_4$ and $\bar{x}_5$ stand for the means of the DM-group, the TM-group, the ALM-group, the AVM-group and the CM-group respectively. The null hypothesis states that all means are equal or that the differences found among them are not statistically significant but due to chance, whereas the alternative hypothesis states that not all $\bar{x}_i$ have the same value and that their different values are not due to chance.

The five different variances above are five independent estimates and can be combined into a single value. This is done by means of the following formula:

$$\frac{(n_1 - 1) \times v_1 + (n_2 - 1) \times v_2 + (n_3 - 1) \times v_3 + (n_4 - 1) \times v_4 + (n_5 - 1) \times v_5}{n_1 + n_2 + n_3 + n_4 + n_5 - 5}$$

where n_i stands for the number of subjects in i-th group and v_i for the variance of i-th group. In our case, we have five groups, hence $n_1...n_5$ and $v_1...v_5$. The dividend is calculated by multiplying each group's variance by its df (degrees of freedom = $n_i - 1$) and summing the products of all groups, and the divisor is the sum of the df of all the samples. This common estimation is known as the *within-samples*[2] *estimate of variance* (v_w). This gives for our example:

$$v_w = \frac{(7 \times 40.84) + (7 \times 25.14) + (7 \times 27.13) + (7 \times 41.84) + (7 \times 6.5)}{35} = 28.29$$

If we now take the five sample means: 24.63 (DM), 24 (TM), 26.63 (ALM), 29.13 (AVM) and 35.25 (CM) and treat them as random samples of five observations, we get a common mean value of 27.93. So all five means are observed cases of a normal distribution with:

Mean = 27.93

Variance = 20.76

SD = 4.55

Multiplying the variance by the sample size (which is 8 in all groups), we get a new estimate: the *between-groups*[3] *estimate of variance*. This index measures the variation across the five sample means and its formula is:

$$v_b = v \times n$$

where v is the variance and n the sample size. The between-groups estimate of variance for our example is:

$$v_b = 20.76 \times 8 = 166.08$$

---

2. In a within-sample design you compare the responses for several variables for everyone in a single group.
3. Between-sample designs compare the scores of a single variable among several groups.

Once we have both estimates: v_w (the within-samples estimate of variance) and v_b (the between-groups estimate of variance), we are in a position to check whether H_0 is true or not. This is done by means of the *F-ratio*:

$$F = \frac{v_b}{v_w}$$

The *F*-ratio is a measure of how different the estimates are relative to the variability within each sample. In an ANOVA, the *F*-ratio is the statistic used to test the hypothesis that the effects are real. The larger the ratio, the greater the likelihood that the differences between the measures are due to something other than chance, namely real effects (in our case the teaching method). If the *F*-ratio is close to 1, then the between-groups variance is very similar to the within-groups variance and H_0 holds. This means that the groups do not differ significantly from each other. However, if the *F*-ratio is greater than 1, then the effects might be significant; whether or not the samples differ significantly may be determined by consulting the significance table of the *F*-ratio. Regarding our study, we get this *F*-ratio:

$$F = \frac{166.08}{28.29} = 5.87$$

To consult the significance table of the *F*-ratio obtained, we need first to determine the *df*, which is in our study 7 and 35 *df*, since we have eight observations in each group (between-groups): $8 - 1 = 7$ *df*; and forty total observation distributed in five groups (within-groups): $40 - 5 = 35$. Since the 5 per cent critical value ($p < 0.05$) for an *F* with *df*1=7 and *df*2=35 is approximately 2.29 (see Appendix 4), and consequently smaller than our *F*-ratio (5.87), we conclude that the value obtained from the data is significant and we have some grounds for claiming that different language teaching methods produce differences in students' language proficiency.

The ANOVA procedure gives us a single score and a single probability value. This statistical method involves a two-stage process. First, we need to investigate whether there is a difference in the means, either among variables (within-groups) or among groups (between-groups), and then we try to locate where these differences are. In those cases of significant effects, that is, whenever the H_0 can be rejected, it is plausible to state that at least two of the individual means are significantly different from each other. The results in an ANOVA table serve only to indicate whether means differ significantly or not. They do not indicate which means differ from another. A first approach can be simply examining the means in order to determine the nature of the effects. A graphical display of the means can be most useful to assist the analysis. So for our study above, we get the following mean value graph (Figure 3.1).

So, in the preceding analysis of the graphical data (Figure 3.1), the audiovisual method and communicative method seem to be the most effective ones with a mean improvement between, approximately, 30 to 35. However, this is just a tentative approach. To report which pairs of means differ significantly, you might think of

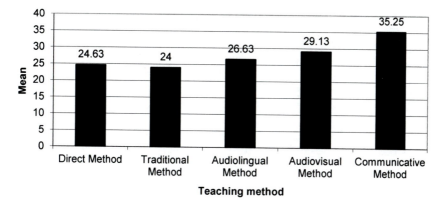

Figure 3.1 Mean scores.

computing a two-sample *t*-test for each pair; however, do not do this. The probability associated with the two-sample *t*-test assumes that only one test is performed. When several means are tested pairwise, the probability of finding one significant difference by chance alone increases rapidly with the number of pairs. If you use a 0.05 significance level to test that the means of methods A and B are equal and to test that the means of methods C and D are equal, the overall acceptance region is now 0.95×0.95 or 0.9025. Thus, the acceptance region for two independent comparisons carried out simultaneously is about 90 per cent, and the critical region is 10 per cent (instead of the desired 5 per cent). For six pairs of means tested at the 0.05 significance level, the probability of a difference falling in the critical region is not 0.05 but $1 - (0.95)^6 = 0.265$. For ten pairs, this probability increases to 0.40. The result of following such a strategy is to declare that differences are significant when they are not. Instead, follow-up or post-hoc analyses can be conducted, only after obtaining a significant *F* value. Then we look at all possible pairwise comparisons in order to determine which individual pairs are statistically different. Among these follow-up or post-hoc comparison tests we have *Newman–Keuls's* test, *Tukey's* tests (A and B), *Dunn's* test, *Scheffe's* test or *Duncan's multiple range* test.[4] Tables 3.6 and 3.7 show the teaching method data above for the two post-hoc tests: Newman–Keuls's test and Duncan's multiple range test.[5]

Now we are in a position to state, with some confidence, which means differ significantly from each other. Both post-hoc tests (Newman–Keuls's test and Duncan's multiple range test) output the same data: clearly, the only statistically significant differences between means are found between the mean of teaching method 5 (Communicative Method) and all other teaching method means. There is no statistical significance between teaching methods 1 and 2, 1 and 3, 1 and 4, 2 and

---

4. Any of these tests can be easily computed using commercial statistical software: STATISTICA (www.StatSoft.com) and SPSS (www.spss.com), among others.
5. 1 = Direct Method (DM); 2 = Traditional Method (TM); 3 = Audiolingual Method (ALM); 4 = Audiovisual Method (AVM) and 5 = Communicative Method (CM).

Table 3.6 Newman–Keuls's test.

Comparison	Difference	Critical value	p	Significant
2 vs 5	−11.250	2.875	0.001	Yes
2 vs 4	−5.125	2.697	0.235	No
2 vs 3	−2.625			No
2 vs 1	−0.625			No
1 vs 5	−10.625	2.697	0.002	Yes
1 vs 4	−4.500	2.447	0.222	No
1 vs 3	−2.000			No
3 vs 5	−8.625	2.447	0.007	Yes
3 vs 4	−2.500	2.030	0.354	No
4 vs 5	−6.125	2.030	0.027	Yes

Table 3.7 Duncan's multiple range test.

Comparison	Difference	Critical value	p	Significant
2 vs 5	−11.250	2.251	0.001	Yes
2 vs 4	−5.125	2.202	0.235	No
2 vs 3	−2.625			No
2 vs 1	−0.625			No
1 vs 5	−10.625	2.202	0.002	Yes
1 vs 4	−4.500	2.134	0.222	No
1 vs 3	−2.000			No
3 vs 5	−8.625	2.134	0.007	Yes
3 vs 4	−2.500	2.030	0.354	No
4 vs 5	−6.125	2.030	0.027	Yes

3, 2 and 4, and 3 and 4. So, we can conclude that the differences between method 5 and all the other methods are not due to chance but due to something else: is it likely to be a more efficient teaching approach?

The ANOVA is an extension of the independent group *t*-test where you have more than two groups. It is used to compare the means of more than two independent groups, more precisely, when there is one interval-scale dependent variable and one nominal-scale independent variable. This is also called a one-way analysis of variance. Thus, the example above is a one-way analysis of variance, where the nominal-scale independent variable is the teaching method: direct method (DM), traditional method (TM), audiolingual method (ALM), audiovisual method (AVM) and communicative method (CM); and the interval-scale dependent variable is the score obtained in the standardized Spanish language proficiency test. The advantage of the one-way ANOVA is that it can be applied when there are more than two groups in the independent variable. So the means of three, four or more groups on a dependent variable can be tested simultaneously for statistically significant differences.

In addition to being able to analyse an experiment with one independent variable, the ANOVA can be used for designs which employ more than one independent variable. Note that, in this context, an independent variable is often referred to as a *factor*. The factorial design is very popular in science. It has a few advantages over single variable designs (i.e. one-way ANOVA). The most important of these is that it can provide some unique and relevant information about how variables interact or combine in the effect they have on the dependent variable.

So, whereas one-way ANOVA tests measure significant effects of one factor only, two-way ANOVA tests (also called two-factor ANOVA) measure the effects of two factors simultaneously. For example, an experiment might be defined by two parameters, such as teaching method effect and age. One-way ANOVA tests would be able to assess only the teaching method effect or the age effect. Two-way ANOVA on the other hand would not only be able to assess both teaching method and age in the same test, but also whether there is an interaction between the parameters. A two-way test generates three *p*-values, one for each parameter independently, and one measuring the interaction between the two parameters. To illustrate this, let us consider the following fictional data (Table 3.8): altogether we have sixteen students from the Netherlands (1), Spain (2), Italy (3) and Mexico (4), as well as their age and the scores on the same English listening test.

Table 3.8 Students' data: nationality, age and scores on a listening exam.

Student	Nationality	Age	Score	Student	Nationality	Age	Score
1	1	12	44	9	3	15	30
2	1	12	46	10	3	15	33
3	1	13	52	11	3	16	31
4	1	12	48	12	3	15	32
5	2	12	32	13	4	12	38
6	2	13	31	14	4	12	37
7	2	13	30	15	4	13	36
8	2	13	31	16	4	12	35

Our aim is to find out if there is any interaction between nationality and age that might somehow determine the score on a standardized English listening exam. We perform a two-way ANOVA test to measure the effects of two factors simultaneously: nationality and age. The two-way test generates three *p*-values: one each for nationality and age independently, and one measuring the interaction between nationality and age (Table 3.9).

Here are three sets of hypotheses with the two-way ANOVA. The null hypotheses for each of the sets are given below:

1. The score distributions among the different nationalities are equal.
2. The age means of the second factor are equal.
3. There is no interaction between the two factors.

Table 3.9 Two-way ANOVA (factors: nationality and age).*

Source	Sum of squares	df	Square mean	F	p
Nationality	497.556	2	248.778	110.568	0.000
Age	4.333	2	2.167	0.963	0.422
Nationality × Age	24.667	2	12.333	5.481	0.032

*This two-way ANOVA was obtained using SPSS (www.spss.com).

If we now examine the *p*-values for each of the factors and their interaction, we realize that students belonging to different nationalities score differently in the English listening exam ($p = 0.000$, below the critical value 0.05), whereas age does not seem to be a determining factor in the English listening exam ($p = 0.422$, clearly above the critical 5% value). Finally, the data reveals that the interaction between nationality and age is also determining. Consequently, we can reject null hypotheses 1 and 3 above. As we did with the above example on teaching method efficiency, we could now continue with the second-stage process in order to try to locate precisely where the differences lie, that is, which nationalities score better and which interaction between nationality and age produces better results in the English listening exam.

The two-way ANOVA is an extension of the one-way ANOVA. There are two independent variables (hence the name two-way). It should be noted that exactly the same logic can be extended to three-way designs, four-way designs, and so on.

3.2.4 Pearson correlation coefficient

Suppose that a group of ten foreign language learners were administered two placement tests: one on writing skills and another on oral fluency, with a maximum score of 100 on each. The individual scores on both tests are labelled *written test* and *oral test* (see Table 3.10).

Table 3.10 Students' scores in written and oral tests.

Student	Written test	Oral test
1	86	78
2	72	58
3	54	47
4	65	52
5	83	77
6	67	53
7	49	39
8	91	81
9	38	27
10	42	31

A quick glance reveals a sort of relationship between the two variables: high scores in one test result in high scores in the second one. In other words, if a student scores highly in the written test, then it is also expected that he will do the same in the oral test. This means that the score in one test is related to the score in the other, and, of course, vice versa. To illustrate this in a much neater way, let us order the data according to the written scores (Table 3.11).

Table 3.11 Scores ordered according to the written test scores.

Student	Written test	Oral test
8	91	81
1	86	78
5	83	77
2	72	58
6	67	53
4	65	52
3	54	47
7	49	39
10	42	31
9	38	27

Now it becomes evident that high scores in the written test are related to high scores in the oral one and vice versa. So what we want is to establish the strength of the relationship between these two continuous variables. If we visualize the two experimental variables against each other on a graph, where the written test scores are assigned to the x-axis and the oral test scores to the y-axis, we get a scatter plot (Figure 3.2).

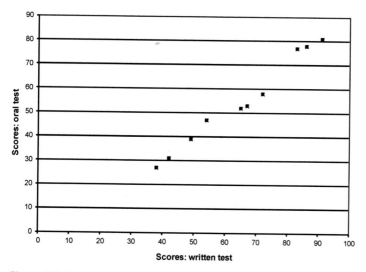

Figure 3.2 Scatter plot.

The strength of relationship between the two variables can be expressed numerically by means of a correlation coefficient. The correlation coefficient is a kind of measure of the degree of linear relationship between the variables. The correlation coefficient used for interval and rational scales is the Pearson correlation coefficient, or simply *r*, and takes on any value between plus and minus one:

$$-1 \leq r \leq +1$$

A value of *r* = +*1* is obtained when high values of one variable are associated with high values of the second variable; if the value of one variable increases, the value of the other increases too. A value of −1 indicates a perfect negative correlation; high values in one variable are associated with low values in the second or vice versa. If we return to our example above (see Figure 3.2), we get a positively related correlation, as the scores depicted move up from bottom left to top right, meaning that the better a student's scores in the written test, the better her scores will be in the oral one, and vice versa.

The values +1 and −1 are the absolute values for a perfect correlation. However, this is not the normal case. To observe the strength of relationship between two variables we can add the regression line to our scatter plot. The regression line is a straight line that shows the perfect correlation between the two variables. If all the points fell on that line then we would get *r* = +*1*. In our example, the points fall on or very close to the regression line, and this, in turn, indicates a strong relationship between the variables (Figure 3.3).

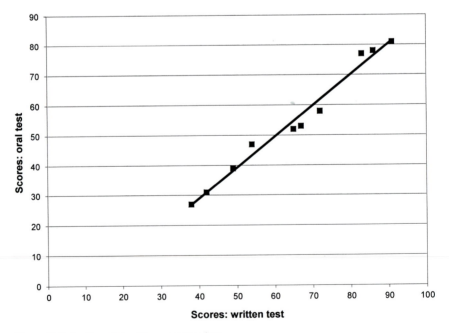

Figure 3.3 Scatter plot with regression line.

So by simply looking at the ordered data, scatter plot and regression line, we can see that the two variables are related, or more accurately, are correlated. But can we make any statement such as "these variables are related to one another" or "these two variables are strongly correlated"? To do this, we first need to know the correlation coefficient of the two variables. An appropriate statistical technique for this purpose is the Pearson product-moment correlation coefficient. To obtain the Pearson product-moment correlation coefficient we need to calculate:

1. the sum of all values of variables X and Y (Σx and Σy)
2. the sum of all square values of variables X and Y (Σx^2 and Σy^2)
3. the sum of all products of XY (Σxy).

Table 3.12 Calculating the Pearson product-moment correlation coefficient.

Student	X (written test)	Y (oral test)	X^2	Y^2	XY
1	86	78	7,396	6,084	6,708
2	72	58	5,184	3,364	4,176
3	54	47	2,916	2,209	2,538
4	65	52	4,225	2,704	3,380
5	83	77	6,889	5,929	6,391
6	67	53	4,489	2,809	3,551
7	49	39	2,401	1,521	1,911
8	91	81	8,281	6,561	7,371
9	38	27	1,444	729	1,026
10	42	31	1,764	961	1,302
Total	647	543	44,989	32,871	38,354

The correlation coefficient is then computed using the formula:

$$r = \frac{N\Sigma xy - \Sigma x \Sigma y}{\sqrt{\{N\Sigma x^2 - (\Sigma x)^2\}\{N\Sigma y^2 - (\Sigma y)^2\}}}$$

Now, we simply have to insert the values from Table 3.12 into the formula and we get:

$$r = \frac{(10 \times 38,354) - (647 \times 543)}{\sqrt{\{(10 \times 44,989) - 418,609\} \times \{(10 \times 32,871) - (294,849)\}}}$$

$$r = \frac{32,219}{32,545} = 0.98$$

Two variables which are mutually independent would have correlation coefficients that are equal to or close to 0. Similarly, correlation coefficients that are equal to or close to +1 or −1 would reveal a very high correlation. Thus, the data of our example show that there is a very strong positive relationship between the written and the oral placement tests applied to our students, $r = 0.98$. To follow the general procedure for testing a statistical hypothesis, we need a null hypothesis (H_0), an alternative hypothesis (H_1), a test statistic (the Pearson product-moment correlation coefficient), and the appropriate table for the critical values of that test statistic. Here we have:

$$H_0 : r = 0$$

$$H_1 : r \neq 0$$

A look at the data and at the appropriate table (Appendix 5) reveals that as our study consists of ten subjects ($N = 10$), in order to show significance at the 0.05 level, r has to be greater than 0.549, and since our calculated coefficient is 0.98, we conclude that the correlation between the variables x (score in the written test) and y (score in the oral test) is significant at the 5 per cent level. Consequently, we reject the H_0 and state that the positive correlation between the scores in the written and oral placement tests is not due to chance, but due to a strong relationship between students' performance in written and oral skills/communication.

The Pearson product-moment correlation coefficient can be used if the following conditions are met, although critical values will depend on the sample size.

- the scales of the two variables x and y are interval or rational,
- x and y are independent variables,
- the relationship between x and y is linear, and
- the data are normally distributed.

To know whether a correlation is significantly different from zero you must know the sample size. A correlation of $r = 0.1$ is significant with five hundred people at the 0.05 level (even though $r^2 = 0.01$ and therefore only 1 per cent of the variance of y is accounted for by x), but not significant with three hundred people. Alternatively, a correlation of $r = 0.4$ (16% shared variance) is not significant at the 0.05 level when there are only twenty people, but it is when there are thirty people. Apart from looking at the tables for significance levels of r, we can also use a transformation that allows significance to be tested using the t table. To test the hypothesis $r = 0$, we use the following equation:

$$t = r \sqrt{\frac{n-2}{1-r^2}}$$

and evaluate the result using *t* tables with $n-2$ degrees of freedom.[6] Applying this to the above example, we get:

$$t = 0.98 \sqrt{\frac{10-2}{1-0.9604}} = 13.929$$

We look up this value, as we did for the *t*-values above (Appendix 3). With eight *df*, the absolute value for *t* exceeds the critical value for $\alpha = 0.05$, which is 2.306. Therefore, we would conclude that the two variables are significantly correlated.

When we have large samples, it is important to distinguish between statistical significance, which says a relationship has been detected, and substantial significance, meaning that the effect is large enough to be of importance.

3.2.5 Simple regression

In the previous section we proposed a technique that tells us the degree to which two variables are related, that is, correlation. The relationship discussed is of a specific type, namely linear. That is, if we represent the data graphically, joining the various different items with a line, we are likely to get a more or less straight line (Figure 3.4).

In this section we shall go further and use the linear relationship in order to create a model that might allow us to estimate and predict the expected hypothetical value of a variable not observed in our experiment.

Let us return to our previous example of the relationship between students' scores in two different placement tests, where we found a very strong positive relationship between the written and the oral placement tests applied to the ten students in our experiment ($r = 0.98$). From Appendix 4, the H_0 can be rejected with $p < 0.05$ and we are quite confident that there is some linear relationship between the oral and the written placement test. With this data, the simple linear regression technique might allow us to construct a model to calculate the expected oral or written scores on these placement tests, given students' written or oral scores.

To start, take the graphical representation of the observed students and the regression line, that is, the linear representation that best fits the whole data set (Figure 3.3). To express the relationship mathematically, we need to extend the regression line and see where it passes through the *y*-axis (oral test score); this value is known as the independent value or intercept. Next we need to determine the slope or gradient of the line. This tells us how much change to expect in the value of *y* (oral test score) corresponding to the unit change in *x* (written test score). In general, we can express this in an algebraic relation of the form:

$$y = \alpha + \beta x$$

---

6. The number of *df* is the number of cases minus the total number of parameters estimated. In the example above (Table 3.12) two parameters are estimated: written and oral exam scores.

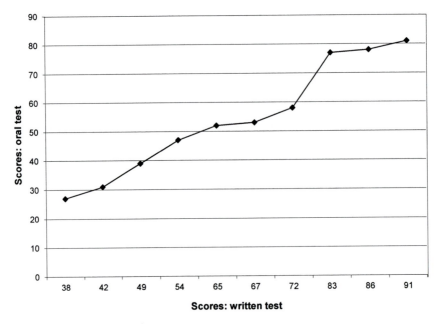

Figure 3.4 Linear relationship.

where y stands for the oral test score, α for the independent value (passing of the regression line through y), β the slope and x the written test score. Figure 3.5 shows an extended regression line, passing through the y-axis at approximately -12, giving $\alpha = -12$. Figuring out the slope is less evident from our graph as it is not very accurate, but we observe that for approximately every ten x units (written test score units) we get ten y units (oral test score units), giving a slope of:

$$\beta = \frac{10x}{10y} = 1$$

And our final mathematical representation gives us:

$$y = -12 + x$$

If we substitute y for the oral test score and x for the written one, we get:

oral test score $= -12 +$ *written test score*

In other words, the model predicts that on average, students will score twelve units or points more in the written test than in the oral one. In other words, once we know the score on the written test, we can predict the student's score on the oral test and vice versa. So a student with an oral test score of 50 is likely to score 62 in the written counterpart:

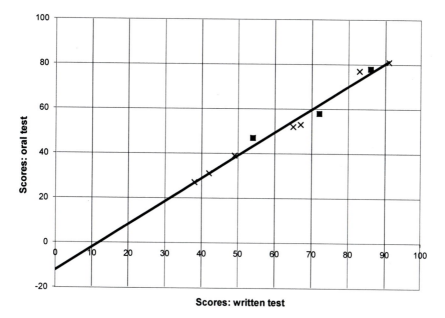

Figure 3.5 Regression line and its interception on the *y*-axis.

$50 = -12 + written\ test\ score$

written test score = 62

Of course, the method seen so far to model the regression line is not very accurate and is not always applicable. Recall that it relies on simple graph observations and on a known regression line, from a previous correlation analysis. But suppose we just had the students' data based on their performance in both tests and we wanted to construct a regression model and express it mathematically. To do this most efficiently we need to have a method that allows us not just to solve the parameter values *α* and *β* but also to get the optimal parameter values for *α* and *β*. Take the data we had for the correlation example, that is, the scores of the ten students on the two placement tests, a written and an oral one. The resulting model needs to ensure that the oral/written scores assigned by it will be close to those actually observed. If the difference between the observed and the predicted value is zero, then the model will be perfect as the regression line will pass exactly through the observed data. So our aim is to construct a model whose regression line passes close to all or most observed points. The more observed points fall on the regression line or the closer the points fall to it, the better the model will be. The difference between the observed (*y*) and the predicted values (*y′*) is known as the residual (r_e):

$r_e = y - y'$

So the residual can be positive, whenever the observed value is greater than the pre-dicted one, or negative, when the predicted value is greater, and as all the residuals add up to zero, we square the sum of all residuals (similar to the way we calculate the variance and standard deviation). The sum of squared residuals for our above model ($y = -12 + x$) is given in Table 3.13.

Table 3.13 Sum of squared residuals.

Student	X (written test)	Y (oral test)	Y' ($y = -12 + x$)	$Y - Y'$	$(Y - Y')^2$
1	86	78	74	4	16
2	72	58	58	0	0
3	54	47	42	5	25
4	65	52	53	−1	1
5	83	77	71	6	36
6	67	53	55	−2	4
7	49	39	37	2	4
8	91	81	79	2	4
9	38	27	26	1	1
10	42	31	30	1	1
Total					94

Of course, in the above model we did it roughly "by eye", without an accurate methodology, and what we attempt to do here is to get the optimal estimate, that is the best model, so that the resulting sum of squared residual is the lowest one: the least squares line of linear regression of *x* on *y*. And this is why the mathematical method used to achieve this goal is called the *least squares criterion*.

At this point we shall ask the mathematically less sophisticated reader to "believe". The calculation needed to obtain β and α is:

$$\beta = \frac{N\sum XY - \sum X \sum Y}{N\sum X^2 - (\sum X)^2}$$

and

$$\alpha = \bar{Y} - \beta \bar{X}$$

Let us now take the above data and calculate X^2 and XY for any *i*-th value, and the sums of X, Y, X^2 and XY (Table 3.14).

We have:

$N = 10$

$\sum X = 647$

Table 3.14 Sums of X, Y, X^2 and XY.

Student	X (written test)	Y (oral test)	X^2	XY
1	86	78	7,396	6,708
2	72	58	5,184	4,176
3	54	47	2,916	2,538
4	65	52	4,225	3,380
5	83	77	6,889	6,391
6	67	53	4,489	3,551
7	49	39	2,401	1,911
8	91	81	8,281	7,371
9	38	27	1,444	1,026
10	42	31	1,764	1,302
Total	647	543	44,989	38,354

$\sum Y = 543$

$\sum X^2 = 44,989$

$\sum XY = 38,354$

The result of these calculations gives a regression model of:

$$\beta = \frac{N\sum XY - \sum X \sum Y}{N\sum X^2 - (\sum X)^2}$$

$$\beta = \frac{(10 \times 38,354) - (647 \times 543)}{(10 \times 44,989) - (647 \times 647)}$$

$$\beta = \frac{383,540 - 351,321}{449,890 - 418,609}$$

$$\beta = \frac{32,219}{31,281} = 1.029$$

To solve the remaining parameter α, we first need $\bar{X}$ and $\bar{Y}$, which are 64.7 and 54.3 respectively, giving:

$\alpha = \bar{Y} - \beta \bar{X}$

$\alpha = 54.3 - (1.029 \times 64.7)$

$\alpha = 54.3 - 66.57 = -12.27$

This produces the following "optimal" regression model:

$$y = -12.27 + 1.029x$$

Table 3.15 Sum of squared residuals for optimal model.

Student	X (written test)	Y (oral test)	Y' ($y = -12.27 + 1.029x$)	Y − Y'	(Y − Y')²
1	86	78	76.224	1.776	3.154
2	72	58	61.818	−3.818	14.577
3	54	47	43.296	3.704	13.720
4	65	52	54.615	−2.615	6.838
5	83	77	73.137	3.863	14.923
6	67	53	56.673	−3.673	13.491
7	49	39	38.151	0.849	0.721
8	91	81	81.369	−0.369	0.136
9	38	27	26.832	0.168	0.028
10	42	31	30.948	0.052	0.003
Total					69.591

Clearly, the optimal model fits the data much better with a sum of squared residuals of 69.59 compared with 94 in our initial model. We are now able to use the equation:

$$y = -12.27 + 1.029x$$

and predict the oral score of any student given his written score or vice versa. Of course, the predictions will not be perfect, but they will be the best available, given the data and the form of the model.

A good indicator to evaluate whether a given model fits the data well or not is the Pearson product-moment correlation coefficient (see above) on observed data. High correlation might indicate that the data are very likely to be modelled into a simple regression with good prediction power.

Another evaluation estimate is the standard error. This is the measure of error in prediction and is defined by the formula:

$$S_{YX} = \sqrt{\frac{\sum_{i=1}^{N}(Y_i - Y_i')^2}{N-2}}$$

S_{YX} stands for the standard deviation of Y given that the value of X is known. It is a kind of mean deviation of the prediction from the observed values of Y; and the denominator, $N - 2$, is the *df* for the regression (−2, one for each parameter: α and β). As the numerator has already been calculated (sum of square residual), the standard error of estimate for our optimal model above is:

$$S_{YX} = \sqrt{\frac{69.591}{10-2}} = \sqrt{\frac{69.591}{8}} = \sqrt{8.69} = 2.94$$

The larger the value, the less well the regression models fits the data, and the worse the prediction. To demonstrate this, compare the standard error of estimate of our optimal model with our rough model now:

$$S_{YX} = \sqrt{\frac{94}{10-2}} = \sqrt{\frac{94}{8}} = \sqrt{11.75} = 3.42$$

Clearly, the regression model with the standard error of estimate 2.94 fits the data better and predicts much better than the rough one.

3.3 Non-parametric tests

In contrast to parametric tests, non-parametric statistics operate on frequencies (nominal scores) and ordinal scales, and the data do not need to be normally distributed. Non-parametric procedures can also deal with interval or rational scores, whenever no distributional assumptions are to be made.

3.3.1 Mann–Whitney *U*-test or Wilcoxon rank sums test

The Mann–Whitney *U*-test (also known as the Wilcoxon rank-sum test) is a non-parametric alternative to the *t*-test for independent samples and is based solely on the order in which the observations from the two samples fall. Similar to the chi-square test, the Mann–Whitney *U*-test does not make any assumptions about the distribution of the data. Succinctly, this technique compares two samples by means of ranking the occurrences of a specific event within these samples and adding the counts of the smaller sample.

To illustrate this, imagine we are interested in knowing how two different translators have used the definite article *the* when translating the same Spanish novel. We start by dividing the novel into its five different chapters. Next, the number of occurrences of the definite article *the* is directly compared across the chapters in the two translations (T1 and T2) (see Table 3.16).

Table 3.16 Distribution of the definite article *the* throughout the translated chapters.

	Chapter 1	Chapter 2	Chapter 3	Chapter 4	Chapter 5
T1	23	34	128	3	99
T2	67	2	78	37	188

Unfortunately we cannot say much about the distributions as the samples are too small. However, there do seem to be differences. But are the two distributions similar in shape? This is hard to say with such small samples.

In order to apply the Mann–Whitney test, the raw data from samples T1 and T2 must first be combined into a set of elements, which are then ranked from lowest to highest. These rankings are then re-assigned to the two separate samples T1 and T2. We now rank the occurrences of the definite article *the* according to samples T1 and T2, and add the two ranks (Σ) (see Table 3.17).

Table 3.17 Ranked distribution of the definite article *the* according to the two translators.

Counts	2	3	23	34	37	67	78	99	128	188	Σ
Translation	T2	T1	T1	T1	T2	T2	T2	T1	T1	T2	
Rank (T1)		2	3	4				8	9		27
Rank (T2)	1				5	6	7			10	29

The sum of the ranks found are:

$$\Sigma T1 = 2 + 3 + 4 + 8 + 9 = 27$$

$$\Sigma T2 = 1 + 5 + 6 + 7 + 10 = 29$$

So the smaller of the two samples is translation 1 (T1), 27 compared with 29 for T2. The sum of ranks of the smaller sample is assigned to the variable R; N_1 is the sample size of the smaller sample and N_2 the sample size of the other sample. Now we calculate the two statistics, U_1 and U_2, by use of the following two formulae:

$$U_1 = N_1 N_2 + \frac{N_1(N_1 + 1)}{2} - R$$

$$U_2 = N_1 N_2 - U_1$$

We get:

$$U_1 = 5 \times 5 + \frac{5(5 + 1)}{2} - 27 = 25 + \frac{30}{2} - 27 = 13$$

$$U_2 = 5 \times 5 - 13 = 12$$

The smaller of the values U_1 and U_2 is the U-value; 12 in our case. We then need to refer to the corresponding value given in Appendix 6 (U-distribution at 5% signifi-cance level for the Mann–Whitney test). The calculated U-value is significant if it is smaller than or equal to the critical value tabulated. However, since our U-value (12) is greater than the tabulated value of 2, we do not reject the null hypothesis and conclude that both translators resorted to the definite article *the* in their translations in a similar way.

The Mann–Whitney *U*-test neutralizes very high or low counts, such as 188 and 2 (see example above), which have only limited impact on the statistics, as it compares ordinal rating scales rather than interval type scores. This is a main difference with chi-square, and to some extent a desired behaviour for our purposes here, as it is of little interest for us if a single chapter in a specific translation has very many occurrences of the article *the*; we are much more interested in an overall comparison.

For samples with twenty or more observations, the *U*-distribution becomes relatively normal and the sum of rank R_1 can be used with the following formula to create a different test statistic:

$$z = \frac{2R_1 - N_1(N + 1)}{\sqrt{\dfrac{(N_1)(N_2)(N + 1)}{3}}}$$

The resulting values can be compared with critical values of standard normal distribution (see Appendix 1).

Suppose we circulate a questionnaire to fifty-three students who use either computer-based language learning tools (25) or non-computer-based language learning tools (28). The questions are related to students' motivation, ranging from "completely agree" (5 points) to "completely disagree" (1 point). The preliminary data are shown in Table 3.18.

Table 3.18 Distribution of students' motivation score.

Computer-based language learning N = 25				Non-computer-based language learning N = 28			
Student	Score	Student	Score	Student	Score	Student	Score
1	4.2	14	4.7	1	3.5	15	3.9
2	3.8	15	4.3	2	3	16	2.9
3	4.1	16	4.2	3	3.4	17	3
4	4	17	4	4	4	18	4
5	4.5	18	4.1	5	3.2	19	3.2
6	4.1	19	3.8	6	3.5	20	3.1
7	3.9	20	3.9	7	2.8	21	3.5
8	3.7	21	3.6	8	4.2	22	3.1
9	4.6	22	4	9	3	23	3
10	4	23	4.1	10	3.5	24	3.2
11	4.6	24	4	11	3.7	25	3.3
12	4	25	4.2	12	3.2	26	3.5
13	3.2			13	3	27	3
				14	3.5	28	2

The sum of ranks for the two groups are:

$\sum Computer\_based\_learning = 968$

$\sum Non\_computer\_based\_learning = 463$

The sum of ranks found in the smaller group is assigned to the variable R_1. Now we need to calculate z, by use of the following formula:

$$z = \frac{2R_1 - N_1(N + 1)}{\sqrt{\dfrac{(N_1)(N_2)(N + 1)}{3}}} = \frac{(2 \times 463) - 25(54)}{\sqrt{\dfrac{25 \times 28 \times 54}{3}}} = 3.77$$

Consulting the critical values for z in Appendix 1, and looking up the value $z = -3.7$, we find a probability of 0.00011, which is clearly smaller than the 5 per cent significance level. Since the p-value of z obtained in the experiment is smaller than 0.05, the null hypothesis can be rejected and we can, with some degree of certainty, claim that computer-based language learning increases students' motivation, compared with non-computer-based language learning.

3.3.2 Sign test

The t-test is the standard test for testing that the population means for two paired samples are equal. If the populations are non-normal, particularly for small samples, then the t-test may not be valid. The sign test is an alternative that can be applied when distributional assumptions are suspect.

The sign test is one of the simpler tests available to the researcher; it is a non-parametric test used to compare two related groups with a given value. This test could be used as an alternative to the t-test for paired samples. Unlike the t-test, the sign test can work with non-normal distributions.

The sign test has only one requirement: scale of measurement should be ordinal, interval or ratio (i.e. the test could not be applied to nominal variables). This is the only restriction. On the one hand, this makes the test as widely applicable as possible. On the other hand, this lowers its effectiveness, because the test cannot use any assumptions about distribution properties. This non-parametric test may be of use when it is only necessary (or possible) to know if observed differences between two conditions are significant. That is to say, with appropriate use of the sign test, it would be possible to determine if X is really "more" than Y, or however the conditions are arranged.

The sign test is not very powerful on small samples. This is because the test uses only information about element positions relative to the assumed median: to the left or to the right. The test does not use information about their values. It is structured so that plus (+) and minus (−) "signs" are used to denote change in magnitude, as opposed to any attempt at quantitative measurement. The test statistic is computed by simply noting the direction of the difference between the pairs of scores.

To illustrate how the sign test performs, imagine the following example: ten students were randomly selected to test the effectiveness of a revolutionary language learning methodology. Prior to any teaching instruction students were given a language pre-test in order to know their language proficiency before any effect of the teaching method. After the teaching instruction period, a second test was administered (post-test). This final test might allow the researcher to know the effectiveness of the teaching method. The performance in the pre- and post-test is shown in Table 3.19.

Table 3.19 Students' scores in the pre- and post-test.

	Pre-test	Post-test
Student 1	2	6
Student 2	3	5
Student 3	2	4
Student 4	3	5
Student 5	1	6
Student 6	2	5
Student 7	3	3
Student 8	2	5
Student 9	3	4
Student 10	4	3

The null hypothesis would be that there is no difference between the scores obtained in the pre-test and in the post-test. The sign test would take into account whether a score is rated higher in the pre-test as opposed to the post-test, without taking into account the magnitude of the difference between the scores. It is simply denoted with a plus sign (+) whenever the post-test score is greater than its pre-test score counterpart, and a minus (−) sign whenever the opposite occurs (see Table 3.20). Note that magnitude is not considered.

Table 3.20 Differences for students' scores in the pre- and post-test.

	Pre-test	Post-test	Sign of difference
Student 1	2	6	+
Student 2	3	5	+
Student 3	2	4	+
Student 4	3	5	+
Student 5	1	6	+
Student 6	2	5	+
Student 7	3	3	0
Student 8	2	5	+
Student 9	3	4	+
Student 10	4	3	−

If the null hypothesis were true, we would expect the number of positive differences to be roughly equal to the number of negative differences. In total we have eight positive differences, one negative difference and a draw. To determine the critical value of our sign test, we need to follow these steps:

1. Count the number of students whose scores were not the same (all students with a + or −) and assign it N.
2. Count the number of pluses.
3. Count the number of minuses.
4. Which number is smaller? Assign that number to X.
5. Using the N and the X, refer to a sign test table to determine the probability.
6. Determine if the number on the sign test table is greater than or less than the critical value ($p = 0.05$).
7. If less than 0.05, the scores are significantly different and we reject the H_0 and accept H_1; otherwise, the H_0 cannot be rejected as the scores are not significantly different.

In our example experiment above, these are the data we obtain:

- Count the number of students whose scores were not the same; we get $N = 9$.
- The smallest number is for minuses, thus we get $X = 1$.
- We set the critical value at $p = 0.05$ and refer to a sign test table (Appendix 7).

Appendix 7 shows only statistically significant distributions less than or equal to $p = 0.05$. It is important that the value obtained for X in the research should be less than or equal to X for N in the sign test table. So, in our experiment we get $N = 9$ and $X = 1$. Looking at the sign test table (Appendix 7) for $N = 9$, we find that the least significant distribution at $p = 0.05$ requires $X = 2$. However, since the value for X in our experiment is less than 2, we can reject the null hypothesis and conclude that there is a significant difference between the pre- and post-test under comparison and state, with 95 per cent certainty, that, indeed, this revolutionary language learning methodology is effective.

Obviously, if all the scores in one group are larger than all the scores in the other group, then, provided the groups are of a reasonable size, it is very likely that the difference between the groups is significant. The difficulty starts when only a proportion of the scores in one group is larger than the other; some scores may also be equal, of course. The sign test calculates the probability associated with these different proportions.

To sum up, the sign test is a very crude and insensitive test. It is also the most convincing and easiest to apply. The level of significance can often be estimated without the help of a calculator. Note that, if the sign test indicates a significant difference, and another test does not, you should seriously rethink whether the other test is valid.

3.3.3 Chi-square test

One of the most common and useful ways to look at information about (applied) linguistics is in the format of a table. Say, for example, we want to know whether the use of the modal verbs *can* and *could* in arts and scientific written communication differs in any way. There are many ways we might show information related to this question, but perhaps the most frequent and easiest to comprehend is in a table, as shown in Table 3.21.

Table 3.21 Distribution of *can* and *could* in arts and science texts.

	Arts	Science
Can	265	778
Could	296	307

This example is relatively straightforward in that we can fairly quickly tell that *can* is more frequently used in scientific communication than in arts and that *could* is more or less equally used. Calculating percentages, we find that

$$can_{ARTS} = \left(\frac{265}{265 + 778}\right) \times 100 = 25.41\%$$

$$can_{SCIENCE} = \left(\frac{778}{265 + 778}\right) \times 100 = 74.59\%$$

$$could_{ARTS} = \left(\frac{296}{296 + 307}\right) \times 100 = 49.09\%$$

$$could_{SCIENCE} = \left(\frac{307}{296 + 307}\right) \times 100 = 50.91\%$$

That is, 25.41 per cent of the occurrences of *can* are in arts written communication, whereas scientific writing accounts for 74.59 per cent: nearly three times more. As compared with *could*, both written sublanguage varieties make more or less equal use of it; arts 49.09 per cent and science 50.91 per cent. These figures are a good start to examining our hypothesis on the use of the modal verbs *can* and *could* in arts and scientific communication; however, the figures in the table are only descriptive. To examine our hypothesis, we need to employ a statistical test that allows us to investigate whether distributions of categorical variables differ from one another. There are a number of features in (applied) linguistics we characterize through categorical or nominal variables: parts-of-speech, sex, nationality, students' preferences, and so on. To examine hypotheses using such variables, use the chi-square test.

  Among the various non-parametric significance tests available to linguists, the chi-square test is probably the most commonly used, as it has numerous advantages for linguistic purposes:

- It is more accurate than, for example, the *t*-test.
- It does not assume that the data are normally distributed (linguistic data are quite frequently not normally distributed).
- It is easy to calculate, even without a computer statistics package, and disparities in the data are unimportant.

At first glance, Table 3.21 would appear to give strong evidence that there are, indeed, differences in use of the modal verbs *can* and *could* depending on whether they are used in arts or scientific contexts. There are more *can*s and *could*s in scientific writing than expected. However, it is possible that such differences occurred by chance. The chi-square test can be used to estimate the likelihood that the values observed occurred by chance.

The key idea of the chi-square test is a comparison of the difference between the actual observed frequencies in the texts, and those frequencies that we would expect if the only factor operating had been chance. The closer the expected frequencies are to the observed frequencies, the more likely it is that the observed frequencies are a result of chance. However, if the difference between the observed frequencies and the expected ones is greater, then it is more likely that the observed frequencies are being influenced by something other than chance: for instance, stylistic features that influence the use of the modal verbs *can* and *could* in arts and scientific written communication. A significant difference between the observed frequencies and the expected ones of *can* and *could* would mean a true difference in the grammar or style of the two domain languages: arts and science.

The first step is to determine the significance level or threshold of tolerance for error. In linguistic issues, it is common to fix the probability of error threshold at 1 in 20, or $p < 0.05$. Remember that chi-square compares what actually happened to what hypothetically would have happened if all other things were equal. The first thing to do is to calculate the column and row totals, as shown in Table 3.22.

Table 3.22 Distribution of *can* and *could*: partial and total sums.

	Arts	Science	Total
Can	265	778	1,043
Could	296	307	603
Total	561	1,085	1,646

Next, the expected frequencies (*E*) are calculated. This is done by multiplying the cell's row total by the cell's column total, divided by the sum total of all observations (all cells).

$$E = \frac{\sum row \times \sum column}{\sum cells}$$

Therefore, to derive the expected frequency of the modal verb *can* in the arts corpus, we multiply its cell row total (1,043) by its cell column total (561) and divide that product by the sum total (1,646):

$$can(expected) = \frac{1,043 \times 561}{1,646} = 355.48$$

All the calculations of the expected frequencies of each cell are shown in Table 3.23.

Table 3.23 Observed and expected frequencies of *can* and *could*.

	Arts	Science	Total
Can (observed)	265	778	1,043
Can (expected)	355.48	687.52	
Could (observed)	296	307	603
Could (expected)	205.52	397.48	
Total	561	1,085	1,646

Note that the row totals, the column totals and the cell totals remain unaltered.

Next, we need to measure the size of the difference between the pair of observed and expected frequencies in each cell. This is done with the formula (note that squaring the difference ensures positive numbers):

$$\frac{(O - E)^2}{E}$$

where O = observed frequency and E = expected frequency. So, for instance, the difference measure for *can* (in the arts corpus) is:

$$can \left[\frac{(O - E)^2}{E} \right] = \frac{(265 - 355.48)^2}{355.48} = 23.02$$

Next, we calculate the difference measure for all cases (*can* in the art corpus, *can* in the science corpus, *could* in the art corpus and *could* in the science corpus; Table 3.24).

And finally we add all these measures up. The value of chi-square is the sum of all these calculated values. Thus, the formula for chi-square is as follows:

$$\chi^2 = \Sigma \frac{(O - E)^2}{E}$$

For our data above, this results in a total chi-square value of 95.38.

Finally, to determine the significance level we need to know the "degrees of freedom". The number of degrees of freedom is very simple to work out:

Table 3.24 Difference calculations of observed versus expected frequencies.

	Arts	Science	Total
Can (*O*)	265	778	
Can (*E*)	355.48	687.51	1,043
Can $\left(\dfrac{(O-E)^2}{E}\right)$	23.03	11.91	
Could (*O*)	296	307	
Could (*E*)	205.51	397.48	603
Could $\left(\dfrac{(O-E)^2}{E}\right)$	39.84	20.60	
Total	561	1,085	1,646

df = (*number of columns in the table* − 1) × (*number of rows in the table* − 1)

For our case:

df = (2 −1) × (2 −1) = 1

Therefore, the number of degrees of freedom is one.

The next step is to compare the value calculated in the formula above to a standard set of tables. We now look in the table of chi-square values (Appendix 8) in the row for the relevant number of degrees of freedom (1 *df*) and the appropriate column of significance level (0.05 in linguistics). Returning to our example, we have a *chi*-value of 95.38 with *df* = *1*, so according to the distribution table, we would need our *chi*-value to be equal to or greater than 3.84 (see Appendix 8), which it is. This means that the difference found between the two sublanguages regarding the use of *can* and *could* is statistically significant at *p* < 0.05, and we can therefore, with quite a high degree of certainty, reject the null hypothesis and conclude that the differences are not due to chance, but due to a true reflection of variation in the use of *can* and *could* in the two sublanguages.

To recap the steps used in calculating a chi-square test, we need to:

1. Establish hypotheses.
2. Calculate expected values for each cell of the table.
3. Calculate the chi-square statistic; doing so requires that we know:
   (a) the number of observations
   (b) observed values.
4. Assess the significance level; doing so requires that we know the number of degrees of freedom.
5. Finally, decide whether to accept or reject the null hypothesis.

The chi-square test is by far the most common type of significance test. It can be used even with nominal data. Note that chi-square is more likely to establish significance to the extent that (1) the relationship is strong, (2) the sample size is large, and/or (3) the number of values of the two associated variables is large. A chi-square probability of 0.05 or less is commonly interpreted by linguists as justification for rejecting the null hypothesis that the row variable is unrelated – that is, only randomly related – to the column variable.

The chi-square test also assumes adequate cell sizes. A common rule is a count of five or more in all cells of a two-by-two table, and a count of five or more in 80 per cent of cells in larger tables, but no cells with zero count. When this assumption is not met, Yates's correction is applied. This correction is an arbitrary, conservative adjustment to chi-square when applied to tables with one or more cells with counts lower than five. It is only applied to two-by-two tables. Some statisticians also apply it to all two-by-two tables since the correction gives a better approximation to the binomial distribution. Yates's correction is conservative in the sense of making it more difficult to establish significance.[7] The calculation of Yates's correction is the same except that for each cell, an additional 0.5 is subtracted from the difference $O - E$, prior to squaring and then dividing by E.

$$x^2 = \sum \frac{((O - E) - 0.5)^2}{E}$$

If we apply Yates's correction to our example above, we get the results shown in Table 3.25.

Table 3.25 Chi-square with Yates's correction.

	Arts	Science	Total
Can (O)	265	778	
Can (E)	355.48	687.51	1,043
Can $\left(\frac{((O-E)-0.5)^2}{E}\right)$	23.29	11.78	
Could (O)	296	307	
Could (E)	205.51	397.48	603
Could $\left(\frac{((O-E)-0.5)^2}{E}\right)$	39.41	20.82	
Total	561	1,085	1,646

---

7. Some computer packages label Yates's correction as continuity corrected chi-square in their output.

Which leads to a very similar chi-square value:

$$x^2 = \sum \frac{((O - E) - 0.5)^2}{E} = 95.30$$

This *chi*-value of 95.30 with $df = 1$ is clearly greater than the expected critical value of 3.84 (see Appendix 8). Consequently, the difference found between the two sublanguages regarding the use of *can* and *could* is statistically significant at $p < 0.05$, and we can reject the null hypothesis.

Yates's correction reduces the size of the calculated chi-square value, making a finding of significance less likely – a penalty deemed appropriate for tables with low counts in some cells.

3.3.4 Median test

The median test is a non-parametric test that is used to test the equality of medians from two or more populations. Therefore, it provides a non-parametric alternative to the parametric one-way ANOVA.

The median test assumes that the samples are randomly and independently drawn from populations that have the same shape. It tests the null hypothesis that the medians of the populations from which two or more samples are drawn are identical. The data in each sample are assigned to two groups, one consisting of data whose values are higher than the median value in the two or more samples combined, and the other consisting of data whose values are at the median or below. A contingency table is constructed and a chi-square test is then used to determine whether the observed frequencies in each group differ from the expected frequencies derived from a distribution combining the two or more groups.

Let us illustrate this technique based on the following example. Suppose we want to know whether there is any difference in teachers' perceptions in four different European countries on the usefulness of the computer as a teaching aid. Samples of twenty teachers were randomly selected for each country: Spain, France, Italy and Germany. All teachers were administered a ten-item Likert test where the respondents were asked to evaluate their agreement or disagreement with the statement that the computer is a useful teaching aid. A five-ordered response level was used with format:

1. Strongly disagree
2. Disagree
3. Neither agree nor disagree
4. Agree
5. Strongly agree

After the questionnaire was completed, each item was given a value, ranging from 1 (*strongly disagree*) to 5 (*strongly agree*). Finally, item responses were added to create a total and the means for each teacher were calculated; these were the preliminary results (see Table 3.26).

Table 3.26 Scores for teachers' perceptions of the usefulness of computers as a learning aid.

Country	Teacher	Mean score	Country	Teacher	Mean score
Spain	1	3.03	Italy	1	2.79
Spain	2	2.54	Italy	2	2.28
Spain	3	3.11	Italy	3	2.56
Spain	4	3.04	Italy	4	2.44
Spain	5	3.02	Italy	5	3.13
Spain	6	3.26	Italy	6	2.75
Spain	7	2.88	Italy	7	2.24
Spain	8	2.44	Italy	8	2.53
Spain	9	2.38	Italy	9	2.46
Spain	10	2.96	Italy	10	3.27
Spain	11	2.23	Italy	11	2.59
Spain	12	3.01	Italy	12	2.78
Spain	13	2.43	Italy	13	2.17
Spain	14	3.12	Italy	14	3.07
Spain	15	2.28	Italy	15	3.26
Spain	16	2.25	Italy	16	2.55
Spain	17	1.92	Italy	17	3.03
Spain	18	2.71	Italy	18	2.32
Spain	19	3.16	Italy	19	2.61
Spain	20	3.04	Italy	20	2.21
France	1	3.24	Germany	1	3.63
France	2	3.63	Germany	2	3.81
France	3	3.82	Germany	3	3.71
France	4	2.81	Germany	4	2.88
France	5	2.78	Germany	5	3.96
France	6	3.25	Germany	6	3.65
France	7	3.44	Germany	7	3.84
France	8	3.22	Germany	8	3.63
France	9	2.71	Germany	9	3.83
France	10	2.99	Germany	10	2.72
France	11	3.16	Germany	11	3.61
France	12	3.54	Germany	12	3.81
France	13	3.23	Germany	13	2.53
France	14	3.22	Germany	14	3.73
France	15	2.52	Germany	15	2.42
France	16	3.24	Germany	16	3.61
France	17	2.88	Germany	17	3.81
France	18	3.64	Germany	18	3.68
France	19	2.12	Germany	19	2.96
France	20	3.03	Germany	20	3.75

We now need to determine the median out of the scores above. As we already know, the median is the middle point with half of the scores falling above and half falling below. As there is an even number of scores (80), the median is the midpoint between the two middle scores (40 and 41), that is, 3.02 and 3.03; which is calculated by adding the two middle scores and dividing by 2:

$$Median = \frac{3.02 + 3.03}{2} = 3.025$$

We now construct a contingency table showing the scores above and below the median (3.025) grouped by countries (see Table 3.27).

Table 3.27 Contingency table for teachers' perception.

Country	Above median	Below median	Total
Spain	7	13	20
Italy	5	15	20
France	13	7	20
Germany	15	5	20
Total	40	40	80

Finally, a chi-square test (see section 3.3.3) was used to determine whether the observed frequencies in each group differ from the expected frequencies derived from a distribution combining all groups. We get a chi-square value of 13.6 for 3 *df*; so according to the distribution table, we would need our *chi*-value to be equal to or greater than 7.82 for *p* = 0.05 (see Appendix 8), which it is. This means that the difference found between teachers' perception of the usefulness of the computer as a teaching aid in Spain, France, Italy and Germany is statistically significant at *p* < 0.05, and we can therefore, with quite a high degree of certainty, reject the null hypothesis:

$$H_0 : median_{Spain} = median_{France} = median_{Italy} = median_{Germany}$$

accept the alternative hypothesis:

$$H_1 : median_{Spain} \neq median_{France} \neq median_{Italy} \neq median_{Germany}$$

and conclude that the differences in the perception of this teaching aid are not due to chance.

As an alternative to the chi-square test, for two groups under investigation, we can also use the following formula:

$$t = \dfrac{\dfrac{A}{N_1} - \dfrac{B}{N_2}}{\sqrt{p(1-p)\left[\dfrac{1}{N_1} + \dfrac{1}{N_2}\right]}}$$

where $N_1 = A + C$, $N_2 = B + D$ and $p = \dfrac{A+B}{N_1 + N_2}$

Going back to our previous research and comparing only two groups (countries), say Spain and France, we need to construct a contingency table for the median with the conditions (see Table 3.28).

Table 3.28 Contingency table for the median test.

	Above median	Below median
Group 1	A	C
Group 2	B	D

We insert the above data for Spain and France and obtain the results shown in Table 3.29.

Table 3.29 Contingency table for Spanish versus French teachers' perception.

	Above median	Below median
Spain	7	13
France	13	7

Using the alternative formula for the two groups above, we get:

$$t = \dfrac{\dfrac{A}{N_1} - \dfrac{B}{N_2}}{\sqrt{p(1-p)\left[\dfrac{1}{N_1} + \dfrac{1}{N_2}\right]}} = \dfrac{\dfrac{7}{20} - \dfrac{13}{20}}{\sqrt{\left[\left(\dfrac{7+13}{40}\right)\left(1 - \dfrac{7+13}{40}\right)\right]\left[\dfrac{1}{20} + \dfrac{1}{20}\right]}} = -12$$

t-values correspond to z-values, so we have to compare the value obtained with the standard normal distribution of z (Appendix 1). Clearly, as our t-score (-12) is better than the first z-score on the table ($z = -4.0$; $p = 0.00003$), the null hypothesis at the 5 per cent level can be rejected, as $z = -12$ is even below $p = 0.00003$. Thus, we can conclude that the difference found between teachers' perception of the usefulness of the computer as a teaching aid in Spanish and French teachers is statistically significant at $p < 0.05$.

Note that the median test has low efficiency for moderate to large sample sizes. The Mann–Whitney *U*-test should be considered instead. The important difference between the two tests is that the median test only considers the position of each observation relative to the overall median, whereas the Mann–Whitney *U*-test takes the ranks of each observation into account. Thus the latter test is usually the more powerful of the two.

3.3.5 Spearman rank correlation coefficient

Correlation is one of the most common and most useful statistics. A correlation is a single number that describes the degree of relationship between two variables. The type of correlation illustrated earlier (section 3.2.4) is appropriate when both variables are measured on an interval scale. However, there is a wide variety of other types of correlations for other circumstances; for instance, when we have two ordinal variables or when the data are not normally distributed.

Imagine we want to carry out an experiment in order to determine the correlation between text length and lexical density.[8] Text length is the total number of words or tokens a text consists of. To determine the lexical density we calculate the type-token ratio. For example, if a text is 2,000 words long, it is said to have 2,000 tokens. But a lot of these words will be repeated, and there may be only, say, 700 different words in the text. Types therefore are the different words, and the type–token ratio is:

$$\frac{types}{tokens} = \frac{700}{2,000} = 0.35$$

In other words, the ratio between types and tokens in this example would be 35 per cent (0.35×100). However, this ratio varies very widely depending on the length of the text. This is why this ratio is rather meaningless in most cases, and is replaced by the standardized type–token ratio. This statistic is computed every *n* words, that is, the ratio is calculated for the first *n* running words, then calculated afresh for the next *n* words, and so on to the end of the text. An average is computed, which means that you get an average type–token ratio based on consecutive *n*-word pieces of text. This ratio allows us to compare type–token ratios across texts of differing lengths.

Table 3.30 illustrates the text length (tokens) and lexical density (standardized type–token ratio) for eight different texts.

To determine any possible correlation between the text length and the lexical density we can use the Pearson correlation coefficient. However, the use of this technique depends on the assumption that both variables being observed are interval scales and follow a normal distribution. This is an occasion when this assumption is

---

8. The lexical density of a text is a measure of the proportion of the content (lexical) words over the total number of words. Texts with a lower density are more easily understood. As a guide, a lexically dense text has a lexical density of around 60–70 per cent and those which are not dense have a lower lexical density measure of around 40–50 per cent.

Table 3.30 Data on text length and associated lexical density.

Texts	Text length (tokens)	Lexical density (standardized type–token ratio)
T1	1,350,000	40.32
T2	2,000,500	39.23
T3	900,750	38.55
T4	4,000,000	41.23
T5	3,450,000	42.44
T6	3,800,000	41.89
T7	4,250,000	42.31
T8	885,000	39.95

not tenable: the variety of texts and text lengths are so diverse that it would be virtually impossible to talk of any "normal" text(s) or "normal" text length. In such cases there is an alternative technique to determine the correlation or relationship between two variables. This method changes the continuous data into non-continuous data, by means of ranking the values. Table 3.31 shows the ranked data for text length and standardized type–token ratio (STT), where the highest value is given a rank of 1, the next highest value is assigned a rank 2 and so on.

Table 3.31 Ranked data on text length and associated lexical density.

Texts	Text length		Lexical density	
	Tokens	Rank	STT	Rank
T1	1,350,000	6	40.32	5
T2	2,000,500	5	39.23	7
T3	900,750	7	38.55	8
T4	4,000,000	2	41.23	4
T5	3,450,000	4	42.44	1
T6	3,800,000	3	41.89	3
T7	4,250,000	1	42.31	2
T8	885,000	8	39.95	6

A preliminary analysis of the potential relationship between the two variables, without making any assumptions about the data, can be performed by means of visualizing the data.

In Figure 3.6, the horizontal axis (x) plots the rank in *text length*, and the vertical axis (y) plots the rank in *lexical density*. Note that, for instance, the text with the maximum text length (T$_1$ on the x-axis) is ranked second in lexical density (2 on the y-axis), the second longest text is fourth in lexical density, and so forth.

To show whether text length has an effect on lexical density, or vice versa, Spearman's rank correlation is used to test the strength of the relationship between the two variables. The formula for the Spearman rank correlation coefficient is:

$$\rho = 1 - \frac{6\sum D^2}{N(N^2 - 1)}$$

where $\sum D^2$ is the sum of all squares of the rank differences and N the number of samples. So our next step is to calculate:

1. the differences between ranks (D),
2. the squares of these rank differences (D^2), and
3. the sum of all squares of the rank differences: $\sum D^2$.

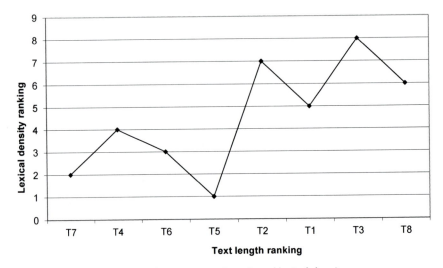

Figure 3.6 Linear correlation between text length and lexical density.

Table 3.32 Rank-ordered data on text length and associated lexical density.

Texts	Text length rank	Lexical density rank
T7	1	2
T4	2	4
T6	3	3
T5	4	1
T2	5	7
T1	6	5
T3	7	8
T8	8	6

Table 3.33 Differences between ranks, squares of rank differences and sum of squares of the rank differences.

Texts	Text length rank	Lexical density rank	Rank difference (D)	D^2
T1	6	5	1	1
T2	5	7	−2	4
T3	7	8	−1	1
T4	2	4	−2	4
T5	4	1	3	9
T6	3	3	0	0
T7	1	2	−1	1
T8	8	6	2	4
Total (Σ)				24

The p-value for our experiment gives:

$$\rho = 1 - \frac{6\sum D^2}{N(N^2 - 1)} = 1 - \frac{6 \times 24}{8 \times (8^2 - 1)} = 0.28$$

If we check the appropriate table (Appendix 9), for eight observations at a 5 per cent significance level, the critical value is 0.619. The p-value we obtained was 0.28, that is, less than the critical value. So we conclude that the relationship found between text length and lexical density is not statistically significant at the 5 per cent level, and we therefore cannot reject the null hypothesis. Although the two variables show some positive correlation, we cannot state that longer texts have on average a higher lexical density than shorter ones.

4 Reducing dimensionality: multivariate statistics

4.1 Introduction

The aim of this chapter is to familiarize the reader with a range of multivariate statistical procedures and their applications to language. It offers a summary of the statistical techniques presented and demonstrates each with examples and illustrations. This is accomplished in two ways, through an introduction to the underlying rationale, and via subsequent applications to a typical set of language. Stress is placed upon the validity of individual procedures in sample empirical contexts and the ability to interpret the results. The chapter is set up to allow the linguist using multivariate statistics to obtain assistance in the choice of which multivariate techniques to use and the state the data must be in to use the particular technique. The four multivariate statistical techniques which will be assessed are:

- cluster analysis
- discriminant function analysis
- factor analysis
- multiple regression.

The word *multivariate* should say it all: these techniques look at the pattern of relationships between several variables simultaneously. Multivariate statistics provide the possibility of analysing complex sets of data. They allow analysis where there are many independent variables and possible dependent variables which correlate with each other to varying degrees. The ready availability of software application programs which can handle the complexity of large sets of multivariate data has increased and popularized the use of this type of statistics.

Multivariate statistics help the researcher to summarize data and reduce the number of variables needed to describe it. Most commonly, multivariate statistics are employed in the following cases:

- to classify data or to develop a system of classification for the data
- to help investigate useful ways to group items or data to generate hypotheses
- to test hypotheses.

In multivariate statistics, we have lots of variables and we want to condense the information they contain in one way or another. The general idea is to look for structure in the data. The problem is that structure is rather easy to find, and all too often it is a feature of that particular data set alone. The real challenge is to find general structure that will apply to other data sets as well. The use of multivariate statistics will allow us to analyse complex sets of data from our set, as it reduces the dimensionality of the data. Reducing dimensionality has some advantages such as a reduction in the costs of data acquisition, a better understanding of the final classification model, and an increase in the efficiency and efficacy of the model itself.

There are many statistical computer software packages that will perform and calculate multivariate statistics. Some examples of statistical computer software packages include SPSS, SAS and Systat, among others. If unsure as to which multivariate statistic to use, try two or more multivariate statistics to see if the results are consistent across multivariate statistics. It is important to get help with multivariate statistics if required. Since there are different types of multivariate statistics, making the correct choice about which multivariate statistic to choose is crucial, as it might affect your results.

4.2 Cluster analysis

We deal with grouping or classification in almost every facet of daily life. A general question facing researchers in many areas of enquiry is how to organize observed data into meaningful structures, that is, how to develop taxonomies.

Cluster analysis is an exploratory method of data analysis for solving classification problems. It is thus a tool of discovery. Cluster analysis, also called segmentation analysis or taxonomy analysis, seeks to identify homogeneous groups of cases in a population. There are countless numbers of examples in which clustering plays an important role. For instance, lexicographers have to organize or typify the various senses of a word before a meaningful description of the differences between the senses is possible. The object of cluster analysis is to sort cases (people, things, events, etc.) into groups, or clusters, so that the degree of association is strong between members of the same cluster and weak between members of different clusters. That is, cluster analysis seeks to identify a set of groups which both minimize within-group variation and maximize between-group variation. Thus, cluster analysis simply discovers structures in data without explaining why they exist. Each cluster thus describes, in terms of the data collected, the class to which its members belong; and this description may be abstracted through use from the particular to the general class or type. It may reveal associations and structure in data which, although not previously visible, are nevertheless sensitive and useful once found. The results of cluster analysis may contribute to the definition of a formal classificatory scheme, such as a taxonomy for related text types, or suggest statistical models with which to describe students' behaviour, or indicate rules for assigning new cases to classes for identification and diagnostic purposes, or they may provide measures of definition, size and change in what were previously only broad concepts, or may reveal exemplars to represent classes.

4.2.1 Dissimilarity matrix

A *dissimilarity matrix* describes pairwise distinctions or distances between subjects. For example, if we tabulate the responses given by four language students in a ten-item multiple choice test on English prepositions, we may obtain the data shown in Table 4.1.

Table 4.1 Students' responses in multiple choice test.

Student	Item									
	1	2	3	4	5	6	7	8	9	10
1	A	C	D	A	B	D	D	C	C	B
2	A	C	D	B	B	C	C	C	C	A
3	A	C	B	A	A	D	D	C	C	A
4	A	B	C	D	C	A	A	B	B	C

Now, to calculate the corresponding dissimilarity matrix we need to estimate the distances or dissimilarities for every pair of subjects. To do this we can count the number of cases where two subjects diverge; for example, take students 1 and 2; the students differ in the responses given to questions 4, 6, 7 and 10. That is, in four out of ten responses:

$$dissimilarity_{Student1-Student2} = \frac{4}{10} = 0.4$$

The results of all dissimilarities among all four subjects are then displayed in a square symmetrical matrix (Table 4.2).

Table 4.2 Dissimilarity matrix for students' responses.

	Subject			
	1	2	3	4
1	0			
2	0.4	0		
3	0.3	0.5	0	
4	0.9	0.9	0.9	0

Looking at Table 4.2, we note that the two least dissimilar, or most similar, students are students 1 and 3 (0.3), followed by the pair of students 1 and 2 (0.4), and the pair formed by students 2 and 3 (0.5). Clearly, student 4 is the most dissimilar one (0.9) to students 1, 2 and 3.

Note that only the bottom half of the matrix is given; the missing half can be ignored since the dissimilarities between student 1 and 2 are the same as the dissimilarities between students 2 and 1. The diagonal elements are not considered and are equal to zero (i.e. the distinction between a subject and herself is postulated as zero).

Of course, it is perfectly possible to construct a dissimilarity matrix from numerical data, not only from categorical variables as we did in the example above (see Table 4.1). For instance, imagine the data on 50 high-school students' performances relative to five academic subjects: English, Mathematics, Biology, History and Music. We might be interested in knowing if there is any sort of similarity in the pattern of performance across the subjects. A first attempt would be to calculate the correlations between the scores of the five subjects. Table 4.3 gives the correlation coefficients for pairs of subjects.

Table 4.3 Correlation matrix for five academic subjects.

	English	Mathematics	Biology	History	Music
English	1				
Mathematics	0.32	1			
Biology	0.47	0.88	1		
History	0.91	0.67	0.79	1	
Music	0.89	0.73	0.61	0.82	1

Correlations of 1 indicate that these academic subjects correlate perfectly with themselves; any different value would be a sign of mismatch or error. To transform the correlation matrix above into a dissimilarity matrix, we would need the opposite of correlation, as correlation coefficients allow us to establish the strength of the relationship between variables. One possibility is to take the inverse of the correlation:

$$dissimilarity = \frac{1}{correlation}$$

Table 4.4 Dissimilarity matrix using the inverse of correlation.

	English	Mathematics	Biology	History	Music
English	1				
Mathematics	3.13	1			
Biology	2.13	1.14	1		
History	1.10	1.49	1.27	1	
Music	1.12	1.37	1.64	1.22	1

The contribution of this data transformation is that low correlation coefficients result in high dissimilarity values and vice versa. The problem, however, is how to interpret these values. When comparing correlation coefficients we know that the values range from 1[1] (two variables vary together exactly) to 0 (two variables are not correlated at all). In Table 4.4 above the data ranges from 1.10 to 3.13 (the diagonal elements are not considered), but we have neither a lower nor an upper limit that would allow accurate interpretation of the data.

An alternative measure of dissimilarity is to transform the data using the formula:[2]

$$dissimilarity = 1 - correlation$$

This has three positive effects:

- It results in a similar inverse correlation coefficient.
- It sets an upper (1) and lower (0) limit.
- Two identical scores would be assigned 0 dissimilarity.

Table 4.5 Dissimilarity matrix using *dissimilarity* = 1 − *correlation*.

	English	Mathematics	Biology	History	Music
English	0				
Mathematics	0.68	0			
Biology	0.53	0.12	0		
History	0.09	0.33	0.21	0	
Music	0.11	0.27	0.39	0.18	0

Table 4.5 gives a dissimilarity matrix using *dissimilarity = 1 − correlation*. Looking at the correlation matrix we find that English and History exhibit the highest correlation (0.91) and, in turn, also the least dissimilarity (0.09); so we could say that English and History form the pair that is most alike. English and Music have the second highest correlation (0.89) and second least dissimilarity (0.11). Since English is linked to both History and Music, we can predict that these three subjects form a group or *cluster*. Similarly, we could continue and say that Mathematics and Biology also form a *cluster*. Hence we would have two clearly distinct clusters: (1) History, English and Music, and (2) Mathematics and Biology.

Probably the most common dissimilarity or distance measure is *Euclidean distance*. In most cases when someone talks about dissimilarities or distances, he is referring to Euclidean distance. Its most positive contribution is that we can calculate the distance between two subjects based on the numerous variables. For example, take the data obtained from four students on their performances in their final exam, relative to English, Mathematics, Biology, History and Music.

---

1. +1 when the two variables vary together exactly or −1 when high values in one variable vary together exactly with low values in the second variable.
2. Other common choices are: *dissimilarity* = 1 − *correlation²* or *dissimilarity* = $\sqrt{(1 - correlation^2)}$.

Table 4.6 Students' scores in five academic subjects (%).

	English	Mathematics	Biology	History	Music
Student 1	85	65	76	65	88
Student 2	66	76	56	84	65
Student 3	75	66	43	75	76
Student 4	61	79	76	63	45

Which students are less dissimilar? How can we cluster them? The Euclidean distance, or simply *distance*, examines the root of square differences between coordinates of a pair of subjects.

$$d_{ab} = \sqrt{\sum_{i=1}^{n} (x_{ia} - x_{ib})^2}$$

where d = distance and a and b are the subjects under comparison; the Euclidean distance between student 1 and student 2 is:

$$d_{Student1-Student2} = \sqrt{(85-66)^2 + (65-76)^2 + (76-56)^2 + (65-84)^2 + (88-65)^2} = 42.09$$

Table 4.7 Euclidean distance matrix for students' scores in five academic subjects.

	Student 1	Student 2	Student 3	Student 4
Student 1	0			
Student 2	42.09	0		
Student 3	37.86	24.33	0	
Student 4	51.23	35.71	50.58	0

The complete Euclidean distance matrix (Table 4.7) reveals how students 2 and 3 are the least dissimilar ones (24.33), forming a cluster. On the opposite side, we find student 4, who is, on the whole, the most dissimilar one from all the others. Finally, student 1 is less dissimilar from students 2 and 3 than from student 4.

These matrices offer interesting exploratory data, as they present valuable information on how dissimilar each student is from all the others. It should be possible to go more deeply into research questions such as whether students' scores are less dissimilar in History, English and Music, or in Mathematics and Biology. There are many ways of using dissimilarity/distance matrices; this section has just been a starting point.

4.2.2 Hierarchical cluster analysis

So far the clustering carried out has been very simple and elementary. What we aim to do in this section is to introduce the reader to a more systematic and analytical procedure in grouping or clustering once we have a dissimilarity/distance matrix.

Hierarchical cluster analysis (or hierarchical clustering) is a general approach to cluster analysis, in which the aim is to group together subjects that are "close" to one another. It starts with each case in a separate cluster and then combines the clusters sequentially, reducing the number of clusters at each step until only one cluster is left. A key component of the analysis is the repeated calculation of distance measures between objects and between clusters once objects begin to be grouped into clusters.

Hierarchical clustering is subdivided into agglomerative methods, which proceed by series of fusions of the objects into groups, and divisive methods, which separate objects into successively finer groupings (see Figure 4.1). Agglomerative techniques are more commonly used.

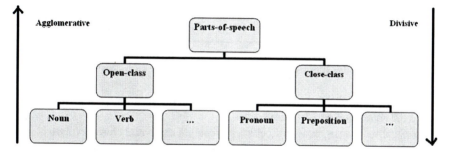

Figure 4.1 Example of hierarchical clustering methods: agglomerative versus divisive.

There is a concept of ordering involved in this approach. The ordering is driven by how many observations can be combined at any one time. The outcome of this hierarchical clustering process can be represented graphically as a *dendogram*.

To illustrate and describe this technique, we shall base it on the extended data from the above example of ten students' academic performance in English, Mathematics, Biology, History and Music.

Table 4.8 Students' scores (%).

	English	Mathematics	Biology	History	Music
Student 1	85	65	76	65	88
Student 2	66	76	56	84	65
Student 3	75	66	43	75	76
Student 4	61	79	76	63	45
Student 5	87	77	65	43	65
Student 6	56	44	44	46	65
Student 7	49	32	65	76	84
Student 8	93	90	91	98	88
Student 9	32	67	52	55	76
Student 10	66	54	69	64	67

First, the Euclidean distance matrix is calculated (Table 4.9).

Table 4.9 Euclidean distance matrix.

	1	2	3	4	5	6	7	8	9	10
1	0.00									
2	42.10	0.00								
3	37.87	23.49	0.00							
4	51.23	35.71	50.59	0.00						
5	35.81	46.95	43.52	40.01	0.00					
6	56.53	52.08	42.52	54.43	50.00	0.00				
7	51.41	52.26	48.80	64.53	70.14	43.53	0.00			
8	44.75	53.62	62.27	66.66	66.60	94.48	80.47	0.00		
9	60.27	47.06	48.28	50.85	59.66	37.03	46.78	88.11	0.00	
10	31.19	32.51	33.21	34.41	37.83	33.96	34.96	64.08	42.14	0.00

The procedure for hierarchical clustering can be typified in the following stages:

1. The two cases that have the smallest Euclidean distance between them are clustered: students 2 and 3 (23.49).
2. Next, the distance measures between all single cases and clusters (there is only one cluster of two cases after the first step) are recalculated.
3. The case(s) and/or cluster(s) with the smallest distance are then combined, yielding either two clusters of two cases (with six cases unclustered) or one cluster of three cases (with seven cases unclustered). This process continues until all cases are clustered into a single group.

To clarify, see Table 4.10, which displays the full agglomeration schedule.[3] We shall focus our explanation on stages 1, 6 and 9:

• At stage 1, case 2 is clustered with case 3. The Euclidean distance between these two cases is 23.49. Neither variable has been previously clustered (see the two zeros under cluster 1 and cluster 2), and the next stage (when the cluster containing case 2 combines with another case) is at stage 3. Note that at stage 3, case-2 cluster (cases 2 and 3) joins case-1 cluster (cases 1 and 10).
• At stage 6, case-1 cluster (previously clustered with case 10 back in stage 2, thus creating a cluster of two cases: 1 and 10; and clustered with case-2 cluster in stage 3: cases 2 and 3) joins the case-4 cluster (clustered cases 4 and 5 back in stage 5). The Euclidean distance between case-1 cluster and case-4 cluster is 42.51, which gives a cluster formed by cases 1, 10, 2, 3, 4 and 5. The next stage

---

3. The *agglomeration schedule* displays the cases or clusters combined at each stage, the distances between the cases or clusters being combined, and the last cluster level at which a case joined the cluster. It is a standard output in most statistical packages, such as SPSS.

when the cluster containing case 1 clusters is at stage 8 (when it combines with the case-6 cluster).

- At stage 9, case-1 cluster (containing cases 1, 10, 2, 3, 4, 5, 6, 9 and 7) joins case 8 (case 8 has not clustered before), thus forming the final cluster of all ten cases. The Euclidean distance between the joined cluster and the case is 70.64.

Table 4.10 Agglomeration schedule.

Stage	Cluster combined		Coefficients	Stage cluster first appears		Next stage
	Cluster 1	Cluster 2		Cluster 1	Cluster 2	
1	2	3	23.49	0	0	3
2	1	10	31.19	0	0	3
3	1	2	36.63	2	1	6
4	6	9	37.03	0	0	7
5	4	5	40.01	0	0	6
6	1	4	42.51	3	5	8
7	6	7	45.18	4	0	8
8	1	6	51.90	6	7	9
9	1	8	70.64	8	0	0

The agglomeration schedule can also be displayed visually by means of an *icicle plot* and/or a dendogram. From Table 4.11, we can see what is happening at each step of the cluster analysis when average linkage between groups is used to link the clusters. This table is called an *icicle plot* because the columns of X's look (supposedly) like icicles hanging from eaves. Each column represents one of the objects we are clustering. Each row shows a cluster solution with different numbers of clusters. You read the figure from the bottom up. The last row, which is not given, is the first step in the analysis. Each of the cases is a cluster unto itself. The number of clusters at that point is ten. The 9-cluster solution arises when cases 3 and 2 are joined into a cluster. Remember they had the smallest distance of all pairs. The 8-cluster solution results from the merging of cases 10 and 1 into a cluster. The 7-cluster solution is the result of combining cases 3, 2, 10 and 1. For the 1-cluster solution, all of the cases are combined into a single cluster.

The branching-type nature of the dendrogram (Figure 4.2) allows us to trace backward or forward to any individual case or cluster at any level. In addition, it gives an idea of how great the distance was between cases that are clustered in a particular step, using a 0 to 25 scale along the top of the chart. While it is difficult to interpret distance in the early clustering phases (the extreme left of the graph), as we move to the right, relative distance becomes more apparent. The bigger the distances before two clusters are joined, the greater the differences in these clusters. To find a membership of a particular cluster, simply trace backwards down the branches to the name.

Table 4.11 Icicle plot.

Number of clusters	8		7		9		6		5		4		3		2		10		1
1	X	X	X	X	X	X	X	X	X	X	X	X	X	X	X	X	X	X	X
2	X		X	X	X	X	X	X	X	X	X	X	X	X	X	X	X	X	X
3	X		X		X	X	X	X	X	X	X	X	X	X	X	X	X	X	X
4	X		X		X	X	X	X	X	X	X		X	X	X	X	X	X	X
5	X		X		X	X	X		X	X	X		X	X	X	X	X	X	X
6	X		X		X	X	X		X	X	X		X	X	X		X	X	X
7	X		X		X	X	X		X		X		X	X	**X**		X	X	X
8	X		X		X		X		X		X		X	X	X		**X**	X	X
9	X		X		X		X		X		X		X	**X**	X		X		X

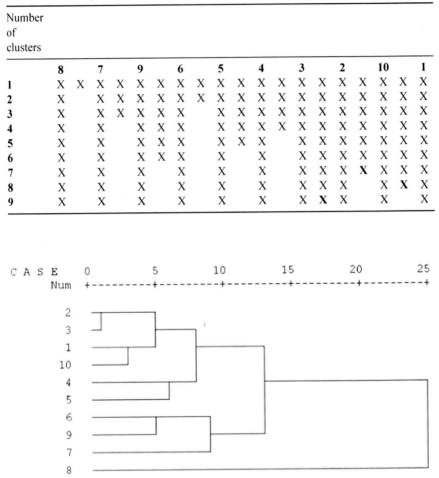

Figure 4.2 Dendogram.

4.2.3 Non-hierarchical clustering

A non-hierarchical clustering method generates a classification by partitioning a sample, giving a set of (generally) non-overlapping groups (clusters) with no hierarchical relationships between them. Each cluster has a centroid or seed point and all objects within a prescribed distance are included in that cluster. Non-hierarchical clustering methods do not possess tree-like structures and new clusters are formed in successive clustering either by merging or splitting clusters.

Partitioning methods, such as the *k-means* procedure, construct *k* clusters from the data under the condition that each cluster *k* consists of at least one object *n* and each *n* must belong to only one *k*. This condition implies that $k \leq n$.

The algorithm is performed in the following way:

1. An initial number k of clusters is fixed.
2. Given a certain threshold, all objects are assigned to the nearest cluster centres.
3. New centres or seeds are computed.
4. Step 3 is repeated until no reclassification is necessary.

Objects can be reassigned in successive steps, optimizing the partioning process. Note also that k is normally determined by the user, so it seems wise to perform several test runs with different ks, in order to choose the best data partitioning. It is also possible in some statistical packages to generate k automatically and then choose the best k-value under certain criteria.

The usefulness of non-hierarchical clustering for research in language and linguistics arises when researchers are interested in detecting clusters or groups in the data, with little or no interest in how the data are structured and/or related. Let us illustrate this with an example. Suppose that fifty-six students (twenty-six native students and thirty non-native ones) have each taken five vocabulary tests. The correct answer means are calculated for each student and the time for completing the tests is measured. Table 4.12 gives the data for each student (1 is assigned to native students and 2 to non-native ones).

Figure 4.3 presents the data graphically. The visual representation of the data allows the experimenter's eye to perceive at least two clusters.

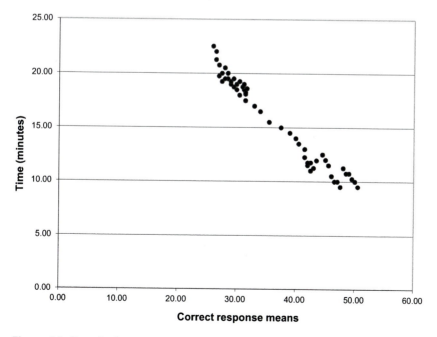

Figure 4.3 Data display.

Table 4.12 Students' data.

Case number	Native vs. Non-native	Correct-answer mean	Time	Case number	Native vs. Non-native	Correct-answer mean	Time	Case number	Native vs. Non-native	Correct-answer mean	Time
1	1	50.50	9.50	20	1	44.50	12.50	39	2	29.50	18.75
2	1	47.50	9.50	21	1	43.50	11.95	40	2	31.25	19.00
3	1	50.00	10.00	22	1	41.50	13.00	41	2	30.00	19.00
4	1	47.00	10.00	23	1	40.50	13.50	42	2	29.00	19.00
5	1	46.50	10.00	24	1	40.00	14.00	43	2	30.50	19.25
6	1	49.50	10.25	25	1	39.00	14.50	44	2	29.00	19.25
7	1	46.00	10.50	26	1	37.50	15.00	45	2	27.50	19.25
8	1	49.00	10.75	27	2	35.50	15.50	46	2	29.50	19.50
9	1	48.50	10.75	28	2	34.00	16.50	47	2	28.50	19.50
10	1	42.50	11.00	29	2	33.00	17.00	48	2	28.00	19.50
11	1	48.00	11.25	30	2	31.50	17.50	49	2	27.00	19.75
12	1	43.00	11.25	31	2	30.50	18.00	50	2	28.50	20.00
13	1	45.50	11.50	32	2	31.50	18.10	51	2	27.50	20.00
14	1	42.00	11.50	33	2	31.50	18.25	52	2	28.00	20.50
15	1	42.50	11.75	34	2	31.25	18.50	53	2	27.00	20.75
16	1	42.00	11.75	35	2	30.00	18.50	54	2	26.50	21.25
17	1	45.00	12.00	36	2	31.75	18.60	55	2	26.50	22.00
18	1	45.00	12.00	37	2	31.00	18.75	56	2	26.00	22.50
19	1	41.50	12.25	38	2	31.00	18.75				

We shall start our non-hierarchical cluster analysis[4] by specifying the number of clusters with an initial value of $k = 2$. Next, the cluster centres[5] are calculated for a two-cluster data partitioning (Table 4.13). Figure 4.4 shows the data with the two cluster centres and their areas.

Table 4.13 Cluster centres.

	Cluster	
	1	2
Correct-answer mean	44.54	29.74
Time	11.61	19.09

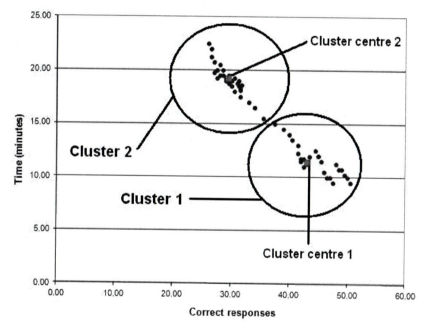

Figure 4.4 Data display with two cluster centres.

Next, the non-hierarchical cluster analysis proceeds to assign each subject to the nearest cluster centre, which produces the cluster membership in Table 4.14.

Altogether, twenty-six cases are assigned to cluster 1 and the rest, thirty cases, to cluster 2 (Table 4.15).

---

4. All calculations were computed using SPSS.
5. We shall only illustrate the *final cluster centres*.

Table 4.14 Cluster membership (two clusters).

Case number	Cluster	Distance	Case number	Cluster	Distance	Case number	Cluster	Distance
1	1	6.33	20	1	0.89	39	2	0.42
2	1	3.64	21	1	1.09	40	2	1.51
3	1	5.69	22	1	3.34	41	2	0.27
4	1	2.94	23	1	4.46	42	2	0.75
5	1	2.54	24	1	5.13	43	2	0.78
6	1	5.15	25	1	6.25	44	2	0.76
7	1	1.84	26	1	7.81	45	2	2.25
8	1	4.54	27	2	6.79	46	2	0.48
9	1	4.05	28	2	4.98	47	2	1.31
10	1	2.13	29	2	3.87	48	2	1.79
11	1	3.48	30	2	2.37	49	2	2.82
12	1	1.58	31	2	1.33	50	2	1.54
13	1	0.97	32	2	2.02	51	2	2.42
14	1	2.54	33	2	1.95	52	2	2.24
15	1	2.04	34	2	1.62	53	2	3.21
16	1	2.54	35	2	0.64	54	2	3.90
17	1	0.60	36	2	2.07	55	2	4.36
18	1	0.60	37	2	1.30	56	2	5.06
19	1	3.10	38	2	1.30			

Table 4.15 Number of cases in each cluster.

Cluster	1	26
	2	30
Valid		56
Missing		0

It is interesting to note how our non-hierarchical cluster model assigned all native-speaker cases to cluster 1 and all non-natives to cluster 2, based on the variables correct-answer mean and time.

We can go further and test on a three-cluster or four-cluster model. Table 4.16 and Figure 4.5 give the cluster membership for four-cluster data partitioning. Examining these new cluster memberships reveals how native speakers are split into two main clusters (1 and 2), whereas nearly all non-natives are clustered together (cluster 4). This is evidence that the data relative to native speakers on correct-answer mean and time is more disperse, in contrast to the same data in non-native speakers. Also interesting is the new cluster 3, which contains former members of cluster 1 (natives) and cluster 2 (non-natives). This new cluster (3) groups together those native speakers who behave in a "non-native way" and those non-native speakers who behave in a near-native way.

Table 4.16 Cluster membership (four clusters).

Case number	Cluster	Distance	Case number	Cluster	Distance	Case number	Cluster	Distance
1	1	2.37	20	2	1.75	39	4	0.69
2	1	1.06	21	2	0.74	40	4	2.04
3	1	1.77	22	2	1.55	41	4	0.85
4	1	1.27	23	2	2.66	42	4	0.47
5	1	1.77	24	2	3.35	43	4	1.26
6	1	1.25	25	3	3.42	44	4	0.29
7	1	2.26	26	3	1.84	45	4	1.76
8	1	0.90	27	3	0.36	46	4	0.27
9	1	0.56	28	3	1.97	47	4	0.76
10	2	1.17	29	3	3.09	48	4	1.25
11	1	1.03	30	4	2.94	49	4	2.28
12	2	0.91	31	4	1.87	50	4	0.96
13	2	2.79	32	4	2.60	51	4	1.85
14	2	1.01	33	4	2.53	52	4	1.67
15	2	0.48	34	4	2.19	53	4	2.63
16	2	0.88	35	4	1.17	54	4	3.32
17	2	2.22	36	4	2.62	55	4	3.79
18	2	2.22	37	4	1.87	56	4	4.49
19	2	1.29	38	4	1.87			

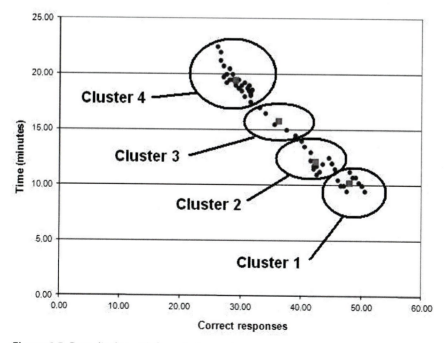

Figure 4.5 Data display with four cluster centres.

Non-hierarchical cluster analysis is the most useful approach to finding clusters due to its simplicity and the fact that it can be rapidly carried out by means of standard statistical packages. Non-hierarchical cluster analysis is also a valuable exploratory analysis when the number of observations is too large to make dendrograms practical.

4.3 Discriminant function analysis

Discriminant function analysis (DFA, hereafter) is concerned with the problem of assigning individuals, for whom several variables have been measured, to certain groups that have already been identified in the sample. It is used to determine those variables that discriminate between two or more naturally occurring groups. This problem is quite different from cluster analysis (see section 4.2), the main purpose of which is to search for that structure in the data which enables clusters of individuals such as subjects, variables, and so on to be identified. Cluster analysis can be applied to any kind of data, numerical or categorical, providing that a measure of dissimilarity can be defined and calculated for each pair of individuals. By contrast, DFA is a technique used for verifying that apparent clusters are real and for deciding to which cluster a new individual should be assigned. For example, someone may want to investigate which variables discriminate between university graduates who decide (1) to continue with postgraduate studies, (2) to start their own business, or (3) to apply for a job. For that purpose the researcher could collect data on numerous variables prior to students' graduation. After graduation, most students will naturally fall into one of the three categories. DFA could then be used to determine which variable(s) are the best predictors of students' subsequent choice.

DFA involves the prediction of a categorical dependent variable by one or more independent variables. It uses the set of independent variables to separate cases based on groups one defines; the grouping variable is the dependent variable and it is categorical. DFA creates new variables based on linear combinations of the independent set that one provides. These new variables are defined so that they separate the groups as far apart as possible. How well the model performs is usually reported in terms of classification efficiency, that is, how many cases would be correctly assigned to their groups using the new variables from DFA. The new variables can also be used to classify a new set of cases. If DFA is effective for one set of data, the classification table of correct and incorrect estimates will yield a high percentage of correct ones.

DFA is statistically the opposite of the multivariate analysis of variance (MANOVA). In MANOVA, the independent variables are the groups and the dependent variables are the predictors. In DFA, the independent variables are the predictors and the dependent variables are the groups. As previously mentioned, DFA is normally used to predict membership in naturally occurring groups. It answers the question: can a combination of variables be used to predict group membership?

Usually, several variables are included in a study to see which ones contribute to the discrimination between groups.

DFA shares all the usual assumptions of correlation, requiring linear and homoscedastic[6] relationships, and interval or continuous data. It also assumes the dependent variable is categorical. It is broken into a two-step process:

1. Significance testing: a test is used to check whether the discriminant model as a whole is significant.
2. Classification: if the test reveals significance, then the individual independent variables are assessed to see which differ significantly in mean by group and these are used to classify the dependent variable.

Again we shall present the technique via an example; Internet expansion has facilitated the existence of a great amount of information and many documents which are within the user's reach. Nevertheless, the major problem continues to be the difficulty of accessing relevant information on a particular topic. Our first research question concerns whether a number of variables selected can differentiate among the text categories. A secondary aim addresses the question of whether automatic text classification is plausible with a limited and easily computable group of linguistic variables.

Samples were taken from free online academic journals and scientific magazines related to three domains: economics, medicine and linguistics. For each of the three domains, three written texts (1,000 words long) were collected. The variables used were selected on the basis of previous research, using the criteria that these should be linguistic and quantitative and should require minimal computational costs. The variables used for the present study were:

- number of types (different word forms)
- type–token ratio (mean distribution of different word forms throughout the text)
- number of sentences
- average sentence length (in words)
- number of one-letter words
- number of two-letter words
- number of long words (words > fifteen letters)
- average word length (in letters).

The next step was to compute the texts by means of a standard concordance program[7] to obtain the values for each of the variables with respect to each individual text. The values are given in Table 4.17.

---

6. Those that have equal statistical variances.
7. A computer program that lets you create wordlists and search natural language text files for words, phrases and patterns.

Table 4.17 Discrimination variables and values.

Domain	Types	Type–token ratio	Sentences	Average sentence length	1-letter words	2-letter words	>15-letter words	Average word-length
Economics	434	43.10	35	28.14	25	166	2	5.46
Economics	448	44.23	44	23.00	35	168	0	4.75
Economics	456	44.44	43	23.70	25	166	3	5.09
Linguistics	346	38.84	27	36.44	30	176	4	5.47
Linguistics	454	40.91	39	22.13	50	177	2	5.40
Linguistics	402	39.30	33	30.94	55	184	7	5.15
Medicine	364	35.97	31	31.81	32	150	2	5.46
Medicine	375	35.48	28	36.36	52	151	1	5.17
Medicine	392	37.73	40	25.73	59	149	1	5.09

Our aim is twofold:

1. to predict the categorical dependent variable (*domain*), to *a priori* defined groups, for eight independent variables (*types, type–token ratio, number of sentences, average sentence length, number of one-letter words, number of two-letter words, number of words with more than fifteen letters* and *average word length*), and to check if the discriminant model as a whole is significant; and
2. if the model shows significance, then to assess the individual independent variables, selecting those variables with a greater discriminant capacity, and to generate a predictive discriminant model to classify new cases.

With more than one independent variable, it is very time-consuming to do all the calculations manually, so we shall present the results of the DFA using SPSS, commenting only on those data tables which are relevant to our analysis.

Table 4.18 shows the means and standard deviation scores on each variable for domains (economics, linguistics and medicine), and also the overall mean standard deviations on each variable.

Next, a tolerance test is undertaken to assess the viability of all independent variables prior to analysis. SPSS produces two variables which fail the tolerance test (Table 4.19). Consequently, these variables are excluded as predictors in the DFA:

- number of long words (words > fifteen letters)
- average word length.

The tolerance is an indication of the percentage of variance in the predictor that cannot be accounted for by the other predictors; hence, very small values indicate that a predictor contains redundant information. The minimum required tolerance level is 0.001.

Table 4.18 Means and standard deviations for all independent variables.

Domain		Mean	Standard deviation	Valid N (listwise)	
				Unweighted	Weighted
Economics	Types	446.0000	11.13553	3	3.000
	TT_ratio	43.9233	0.72072	3	3.000
	Sentence	40.6667	4.93288	3	3.000
	A_sentence	24.9467	2.78757	3	3.000
	Word_1	28.3333	5.77350	3	3.000
	Word_2	166.6667	1.15470	3	3.000
	Word_15	1.6667	1.52753	3	3.000
	A_word_l	5.1000	0.35511	3	3.000
Linguistics	Types	400.6667	54.01234	3	3.000
	TT_ratio	39.6833	1.08694	3	3.000
	Sentence	33.0000	6.00000	3	3.000
	A_sentence	29.8367	7.21852	3	3.000
	Word_1	45.0000	13.22876	3	3.000
	Word_2	179.0000	4.35890	3	3.000
	Word_15	4.3333	2.51661	3	3.000
	A_word_l	5.3400	0.16823	3	3.000
Medicine	Types	377.0000	14.10674	3	3.000
	TT_ratio	36.3933	1.18323	3	3.000
	Sentence	33.0000	6.24500	3	3.000
	A_sentence	31.3000	5.33332	3	3.000
	Word_1	47.6667	14.01190	3	3.000
	Word_2	150.0000	1.00000	3	3.000
	Word_15	1.3333	0.57735	3	3.000
	A_word_l	5.2400	0.19468	3	3.000
Total	Types	407.8889	41.61864	9	9.000
	TT_ratio	40.0000	3.38571	9	9.000
	Sentence	35.5556	6.28711	9	9.000
	A_sentence	28.6944	5.51206	9	9.000
	Word_1	40.3333	13.54622	9	9.000
	Word_2	165.2222	12.81384	9	9.000
	Word_15	2.4444	2.06828	9	9.000
	A_word_l	5.2267	0.24285	9	9.000

Table 4.19 Variables that do not pass the tolerance test.

	Intra-group variance	Tolerance	Minimum tolerance
Word_15	3.000	0.000	0.000
A_word_length	0.064	0.000	0.000

Table 4.20 gives information on the ratio of importance of the dimensions (functions) which classify cases of the dependent variable. There is one *eigenvalue* for each discriminant function. For two-group DFA, there is one discriminant function and one eigenvalue, which account for 100 per cent of the explained variance; for three-group DFA there will be two discriminant functions and two eigenvalues, and so on. Note that the number of discriminant functions is equal to the number of groups we want to classify minus one. If there is more than one discriminant function, the first will be the largest and most important one, the second the next most important in explanatory power, and so on.

The *canonical correlation* is a measure of the association between the groups formed by the dependent variable and the given discriminant function. When the canonical correlation is zero, there is no relation between the groups and the function. However, when the canonical correlation is large, then there is a high correlation between the discriminant functions and the groups; that is, it tells you how useful each function is in determining group differences.

The data relative to our model reveals that the first function explains 99.3 per cent of the variance, whereas the second one only explains 0.7 per cent. Consequently, most of the discriminating power for the model is associated with the first discriminant function. The canonical correlation indexes show a high correlation between the discriminant functions and the groups (1.000 and 0.979). That is, each function contributes significantly to determining group differences.

Table 4.20 Eigenvalues.

Function	Eigenvalue	% of variance	Cumulative %	Canonical correlation
1	3,086.505	99.3	99.3	1.000
2	23.217	0.7	100.0	0.979

Now we shall look at the significance testing, in order to know whether our discriminant model as a whole is significant or not. SPSS performs the *Wilks's lambda* test (Table 4.21). This multivariate test is a statistic that tells us about the "fit" of the data. Because all *p*-values are less than 0.05, we can say that the model is a good fit for the data; that is, the predicting variables[8] used discriminate positively.

Table 4.21 Wilks's lambda.

Test of function(s)	Wilks's lambda	Chi-square	*df*	Sig.
1–2	0.000	39.278	12	0.000
2	0.041	11.155	5	0.048

---

8. Except for those variables that did not pass the tolerance test (*number of long words* and *average word length*) and were excluded from the model.

Table 4.22 gives the classification table that we get by selecting that option in the SPSS dialogue box. It gives information about actual group membership versus predicted group membership. The overall percentage correctly classified is 100; that is, all original grouped cases were correctly classified by means of the two discriminant functions inferred from the data provided. This speaks very much in favour of our model and its predictive power.

Table 4.22 Classification results.

Domain			Predicted group membership			Total
			Economics	Linguistics	Economics	
Original	Count	Economics	3	0	0	3
		Linguistics	0	3	0	3
		Medicine	0	0	3	3
	%	Economics	100.0	0.0	0.0	100.0
		Linguistics	0.0	100.0	0.0	100.0
		Medicine	0.0	0.0	100.0	100.0

Once the DFA has turned out to be positive, we can try a stepwise procedure instead. This will allow us to assess each individual independent variable in order to select the best predictor or set of predictors. SPSS now optimizes and simplifies the model and outputs a new model with similar predictive power, using just the three best predictors (Table 4.23):

- type–token ratio
- number of sentences
- number of two-letter words.

Table 4.23 Best predictors and coefficients.

	Function	
	1	2
TT_ratio	10.845	−1.054
Sentence	−10.536	0.856
Word_2	2.494	0.749

We can also get a graph (Figure 4.6) of the different groups, based on the three best predictors (*type–token ratio, number of sentences* and *number of two-letter words*). This gives us a visual representation that shows how the three groups separate out from one another using these three predictors. The lack of overlapping reveals that the linguistic domains are clearly distinct from each other and that the model seems precise as no misclassifications are found. Not all discriminant

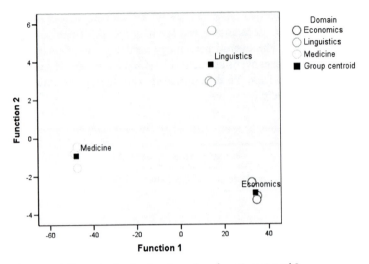

Figure 4.6 Domain distribution based on functions 1 and 2.

functions will separate groups so perfectly. Sometimes you can find predictors that differentiate between the groups statistically, while the graph still shows the groups as fairly jumbled.

A further use of DFA is that, once those variables with a greater discriminant capacity have been selected, it is possible to generate a predictive discriminant model to classify new cases. Selecting the SPSS option *Fisher function coefficients* gives us Table 4.24, with a constant value and a number of coefficients for each of the best predictors (*type-token ratio, number of sentences* and *number of two– letter words*) with reference to each linguistic domain (*economics, linguistics* and *medicine*).

Table 4.24 Discriminant function coefficients.

	Domain		
	Economics	Linguistics	Medicine
TT_ratio	5,858.542	5,641.913	4,983.110
Sentence	−1,005.599	−968.610	−855.386
Word_2	516.530	500.034	440.505
(Constant)	−151,261.400	−140,717.047	−109,601.071

This gives three equations, one for each linguistic domain:

Economics = −151,261.400 + 5,858.542 × *tt-ratio* − 1,005.599 × *sentence*
+516,530 × *word-2*

Linguistics = −140,717.047 + 5,641.913 × *tt-ratio* − 968.610 × *sentence* + 500.034 × *word-2*

Medicine = −109,601.071 + 4,983.110 ×*tt-ratio* − 855.386 × *sentence* + 440.505 × *word-2*

To illustrate the applicability in prediction of the equations above, we can take, for example, a 1,000-token text randomly chosen from economic, linguistic and/ or medicine journals/magazines. Imagine that when we compute it, we get the following values on the variables *type–token ratio, number of sentences* and *number of two-letter words*:

- type–token ratio = 45.61
- number of sentences = 41
- number of two-letter words = 170.

Using the above discriminant equations and instantiating the values for *type–token ratio, number of sentences* and *number of two-letter words*, we can calculate the scores of the three discriminant functions:

Economics = −151,261.400 + 5,858.542 × 45.61 − 1,005.599 × 41 + 516.530 × 170
= 162,527.241

Linguistics = −140,717.047 + 5,641.913 × 45.61 − 968.610 × 41 + 500.034 × 170
= 161,903.374

Medicine = −109,601.071 + 4,983.110 × 45.61 − 855.386 × 41 + 440.505 × 170
= 157,493.600

The randomly chosen text with *type–token ratio = 45.61; number of sentences = 41*; and *number of two-letter words = 170* will be assigned to the domain, related to one of the three functions above, that has the largest resulting value. So maximizing the three coefficients we find that this text is most likely to be an economics text, as *Economics* is the highest resulting coefficient (162,527.241); and in second place, it would be classified under *Linguistics* (161,903.374). Similarly, the least likely group membership would be *Medicine* (157,493.600), as the coefficient obtained in the medicine equation is the lowest one.

In order to explore the real predictive power of our DFA model a little further, we have compiled a test data set from the Internet of nine randomly chosen texts from the fields of economics, linguistics and medicine. Note that we also kept a record of the linguistic domain of each text in order to compare it with the domain assigned by our DFA.

Table 4.25 Test texts.

Text	Domain	Type–token ratio	Number of sentences	2-letter words
1	Economics	45.61	41	170
2	Economics	44.23	44	168
3	Economics	44.44	43	166
4	Linguistics	38.84	27	176
5	Linguistics	40.91	39	177
6	Linguistics	39.30	33	184
7	Medicine	35.97	31	150
8	Medicine	35.48	28	151
9	Medicine	37.73	40	149

Once the values for the predicting variables *type–token ratio, number of sentences* and *number of two-letter words* were computed, we instantiated them in the three discriminant functions (DFs), maximized the values and verified that our DFA model assigned all nine texts correctly (Table 4.26; maximized values are in italics). Interestingly, the values for economics and linguistics are very close in some instances, whereas differences between economics/linguistics and medicine are greater. Consequently, economics and linguistics texts are more difficult to tell apart than economics/linguistics and medicine ones. Furthermore, these minor divergences between economics and linguistics coefficients might be a potential indicator of wrong assignments in some texts, when our model failed in assigning a text either to the economics domain or the linguistics domain.

Table 4.26 Domain assignment of test texts.

Text	Domain	DF: Economics	DF: Linguistics	DF: Medicine	Domain assigned
1	Economics	*151,789.78*	151,553.70	148,356.29	Economics
2	Economics	*150,392.60*	150,211.64	147,169.74	Economics
3	Economics	*151,595.43*	151,364.98	148,190.57	Economics
4	Linguistics	140,042.48	*140,268.37*	138,376.38	Linguistics
5	Linguistics	140,619.00	*140,823.84*	138,867.29	Linguistics
6	Linguistics	140,836.05	*141,052.26*	139,060.33	Linguistics
7	Medicine	105,776.29	107,200.75	*109,200.18*	Medicine
8	Medicine	106,438.93	107,842.08	*109,765.12*	Medicine
9	Medicine	106,520.40	107,913.00	*109,831.47*	Medicine

Recall that the major purpose of DFA is to predict membership of two or more mutually exclusive groups from a set of predictors, when there is no natural ordering of the groups. So we may ask whether we can predict whether people vote *A* or *B* from knowledge of their age, their social status, attitudes, values and so on. The commonest use of discriminant analysis is in situations where there are just two categories in the dependent variable; but as we have seen, it can be used for multi-way categories. This is an advantage over other statistical techniques, such as logistic regression.

A further contribution of DFA is the possibility of creating new models for classifying new cases, using not all predicting variables, but just a limited number of them: the best predictors, with similar or identical discriminatory power. This reduces the dimensionality of the data and produces *low-cost* models, not only computationally speaking, but also with regard to the time and effort spent on the data collection process.

4.4 Factor analysis

Factor analysis is a statistical procedure used to reveal the latent structure of a set of variables, that is, to discover simple patterns in the relationships among the variables. In particular, it seeks to discover if the observed variables can be explained largely or entirely in terms of a much smaller number of variables, called factors. This statistical approach involves finding a way of condensing the information contained in a number of original variables into a smaller set of dimensions (factors) with the minimum loss of information. The new factors are used as explanatory variables during choice modelling. The main applications of factor analytic techniques are:

- to reduce the number of variables, and
- to detect structure in the relationships between variables, that is to classify variables.

Therefore, factor analysis is applied as a data reduction or structure detection method. It makes the building of connections between facts going on continuously in the human mind explicit and more precise.

Let us look at a specific example. Imagine we would like to analyse a number of easily computable linguistic variables to examine their variation in six different language domains: *cooking recipes, ecology, music, oncology, physics* and *religion*. After a thorough literature review, we come up with seventeen linguistic variables (Table 4.27), grouped into three categories:

1. Variables of punctuation (8): *periods/1,000 words; commas/1,000 words; semi-colons/1,000 words; colons/1,000 words; dashes/1,000 words; pairs of parentheses/1,000 words; exclamation marks/1,000 words;* and *question marks/1,000 words.*
2. Lexical distribution variables (7): *words/sentence; characters/sentence; standardized type–token ratio; word length in orthographic letters; words>6 characters; hapax legomena*[9] and *hapax dislegomena*[10].

---

9. Words occurring a single time in the corpus.
10. Words that occur twice in the corpus.

3. Variables of readability grades[11] (2): *Automated Readability Index* and *Coleman–Liau Index*.

Table 4.27[12] shows the values of the seventeen variables for twelve randomly chosen sample texts belonging to the six domains under investigation (*cooking recipes, ecology, music, oncology, physics* and *religion*).

Table 4.27 Data relative to the twelve text samples.

Text	P1	P2	P3	P4	P5	P6	P7	P8	LD1
1	64.89	54.70	4.00	11.58	12.93	9.11	0.44	0.00	17.87
2	49.03	48.51	5.13	1.78	11.58	18.28	0.00	0.22	26.23
3	39.59	58.27	6.45	4.89	15.80	7.34	0.00	1.33	27.41
4	58.30	48.49	7.56	2.22	21.81	29.60	0.00	0.00	22.53
5	53.10	32.44	1.77	21.33	34.88	12.88	0.00	0.00	22.13
6	45.31	55.12	3.12	3.56	11.16	4.46	0.00	0.67	22.01
7	70.52	36.62	9.99	7.32	11.98	7.99	0.00	0.00	15.06
8	60.48	47.72	9.41	2.69	23.52	40.99	0.00	0.00	22.21
9	38.15	68.94	2.01	6.02	4.02	14.06	0.00	1.34	27.65
10	50.00	51.33	0.00	0.00	10.00	10.67	0.00	0.00	23.98
11	59.49	40.11	1.34	2.01	41.44	20.05	0.00	0.00	25.85
12	43.97	50.63	12.66	6.00	7.33	14.66	0.00	0.00	24.24

Text	LD2	LD3	LD4	LD5	LD6	LD7	RG1	RG2
1	79.16	35.27	4.43	276.00	265.00	92.33	8.36	8.62
2	133.77	34.27	5.10	442.66	304.66	74.66	15.70	13.10
3	143.08	42.07	5.22	471.00	391.33	84.00	16.85	13.85
4	118.50	38.30	5.26	505.00	307.66	82.00	14.60	13.86
5	107.99	34.37	4.88	416.66	264.33	70.66	12.61	11.59
6	112.25	45.17	5.10	442.00	437.00	84.33	13.59	12.88
7	67.48	38.30	4.48	267.00	277.00	101.00	7.20	8.59
8	118.60	43.00	5.34	548.00	378.00	105.00	14.82	14.30
9	129.95	40.20	4.70	346.00	325.00	90.00	14.53	11.80
10	135.01	45.60	5.63	590.00	398.00	95.00	17.08	16.11
11	122.27	36.70	4.73	385.00	312.00	63.00	13.77	10.90
12	111.50	38.60	4.60	348.00	363.00	66.00	12.36	10.05

We shall perform the analysis by means of SPSS, with the following selections and options:

---

11. The *Automated Readability Index* and *Coleman-Liau Index* are readability tests designed to gauge the understandability of a text. Their output is an approximate representation of the US grade level needed to comprehend the text.
12. *P1* stands for *Punctuation Variable 1* (= *periods/1,000 words*), *P2 for Punctuation Variable 2*, and so on; similarly, *LD1* for *Lexical Distribution Variable 1* (= *words/sentence*), etc. and *RG1* for *Readability Grade Variable 1* (*Automated Readability Index*), etc.

- Select *P1* through to *RG2* as analysis variables.
- Specify *Principal Component* as the extraction method (with eigenvalues over 1)
- Select *Varimax* factor rotation.[13]
- Select *Display factor score coefficient matrix*. This shows the coefficients by which variables are multiplied to obtain factor scores. It also shows the correlations between factor scores.

These selections produce a solution using principal components extraction, which is then rotated for ease of interpretation. Components with eigenvalues greater than 1 are saved to the working file. We get the following results:

- *Communalities* (Table 4.28): these indicate the amount of variance in each variable that is accounted for. *Initial communalities* are estimates of the variance in each variable accounted for by all components or factors. For principal components extraction, this is always equal to 1.0 for correlation analyses. Extraction communalities are estimates of the variance in each variable accounted for by the factors (or components) in the factor solution. The communalities in this table are all high, which indicates that the extracted components represent the variables well. Small values would indicate variables that do not fit well with the factor solution, and should possibly be dropped from the analysis.

Table 4.28 Communalities.

	Initial	Extraction
Periods/1,000 words	1.000	0.940
Commas/1,000 words	1.000	0.974
Semi-colons/1,000 words	1.000	0.876
Colons/1,000 words	1.000	0.613
Hyphens/1,000 words	1.000	0.791
Parentheses/1,000 words	1.000	0.891
Excl. marks/1,000 words	1.000	0.811
Quest. marks/1,000 words	1.000	0.762
Words/sentence	1.000	0.981
Characters/sentence	1.000	0.988
Standardized type–token ratio	1.000	0.916
Word length	1.000	0.949
Long word count > 6/text	1.000	0.966
Hapax legomena/text	1.000	0.853
Hapax dislegomena/text	1.000	0.837
Automated Readability Index	1.000	0.991
Coleman–Liau Index	1.000	0.968

- *Initial eigenvalues* (Table 4.29): this table gives the variance explained by the initial solution, extracted components and rotated components. The *Total* column

---

13. Rotation is used to simplify interpretation of a factor analysis. It does not change the total variance, but does alter the distribution of the variance across the factors.

gives the amount of variance in the original variables accounted for by each component. The *% of Variance* column gives the ratio, expressed as a percentage, of the variance accounted for by each component to the total variance in all of the variables. The *Cumulative %* column gives the percentage of variance accounted for by the first *n* components. For example, the cumulative percentage for the second component is the sum of the percentage of variance for the first and second components. Note how the first eleven components account for 100 per cent of the variance. This means that the contribution of components 12 to 17 is virtually irrelevant.

Table 4.29 Initial eigenvalues.

Component	Initial eigenvalues		
	Total	% of variance	Cumulative %
1	7.258	42.696	42.696
2	3.006	17.683	60.378
3	2.512	14.776	75.154
4	1.316	7.741	82.895
5	1.013	5.960	88.855
6	0.658	3.869	92.724
7	0.522	3.071	95.796
8	0.434	2.555	98.351
9	0.190	1.118	99.470
10	0.061	0.358	99.828
11	0.029	0.172	100.000
12	8.44×10^{-16}	4.97×10^{-15}	100.000
13	2.35×10^{-16}	1.38×10^{-15}	100.000
14	-1.59×10^{-18}	-9.33×10^{-18}	100.000
15	-1.33×10^{-16}	-7.81×10^{-16}	100.000
16	-2.38×10^{-16}	-1.40×10^{-15}	100.000
17	-1.64×10^{-15}	-9.63×10^{-15}	100.000

- *Extraction sums of squared loadings* (Table 4.30): this shows the extracted components. They explain nearly 89 per cent of the variability in the original seventeen variables, so we can considerably reduce the complexity of the data set by using these five components, with only 11 per cent loss of information.

Table 4.30 Extraction sums of squared loadings.

Total	% of variance	Cumulative %
7.258	42.696	42.696
3.006	17.683	60.378
2.512	14.776	75.154
1.316	7.741	82.895
1.013	5.960	88.855

- *Rotation sums of squared loadings* (Table 4.31): the rotation maintains the cumulative percentage of variation explained by the extracted components, but that variation is now spread more evenly over the components. The large changes in the individual totals suggest that the rotated component matrix will be easier to interpret than the unrotated matrix. Note that we are left with just five components.

Table 4.31 Rotation sums of squared loadings.

Total	% of variance	Cumulative %
5.702	33.543	33.543
3.420	20.119	53.662
3.167	18.632	72.294
1.413	8.310	80.604
1.403	8.251	88.855

- *Rotated solution graph* (Figure 4.7): this screen plot helps us to determine the optimal number of components. The eigenvalue of each component in the initial solution is plotted. Generally, we want to extract the components on the steep slope (Figure 4.8); the components on the shallow slope contribute little to the solution.
- *Rotated component matrix* (Table 4.32): this helps us to determine what each component represents. The first component is most highly correlated with *word length, long word count > 6/text* and *Coleman–Liau Index. Word length* is the best representative, however, because it is less correlated with the other four

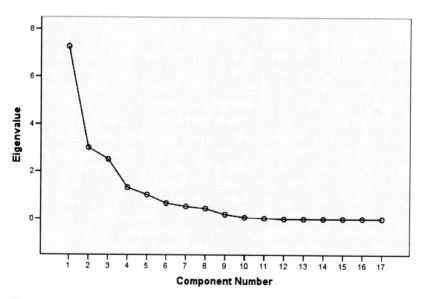

Figure 4.7 Rotated solution graph.

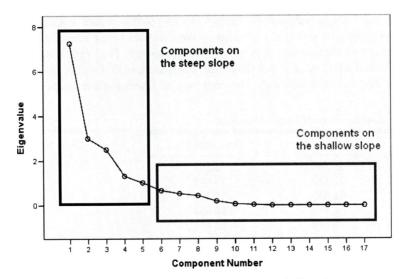

Figure 4.8 Rotated solution graph: steep slope versus shallow slope components.

components. The second component is most highly correlated with *words/sentence*; the third component is most highly correlated with *commas/1,000 words*; the fourth component is most highly negatively correlated with *semi-colons/1,000 words*; and the fifth component is most highly negatively correlated with *parentheses/1,000 words*. This suggests that we can focus on *word length, words/sentence, commas/1,000 words, semi-colons/1,000 words* and *parentheses/1,000 words* in further analyses.

There is also an option to suppress absolute values less than a specified value (by default 0.1). This option ensures that factor loadings within ± 0.1 are not displayed in the output. This option is useful for assisting in interpretation. For our research we set the value at 0.4 (Table 4.33) and present the loadings in order of size. Now we have a much neater display of the data, facilitating its interpretation. The items that load highly on Factor 1 are related to: *word length, long word count > 6/text, Coleman–Liau Index, standardized type–token ratio, hapax legomena/text, Automated Readability Index, colons/1,000 words* and *exclamation marks/1,000 words*. The items highly loading on Factor 2 are: *words/sentence, hapax dislegomena/text, periods/1,000 words* and *characters/sentence*. The three items that load highly on Factor 3 are: *commas/1,000 words, hyphens/1,000 words* and *question marks/1,000 words*. Finally, Factors 4 and 5 each have a single high-loading item: *semi-colons/1,000 words* and *parentheses/1,000 words*, respectively.

Additionally, we can save the factor scores for each subject (texts in our case). These scores can be used for further analysis, or simply to identify groups of texts that score highly on particular factors (Table 4.34).

Table 4.32 Rotated component matrix.

	Component				
	1	2	3	4	5
Periods/1,000 words	−0.254	−0.725	−0.525	−0.030	0.272
Commas/1,000 words	0.124	0.168	**0.953**	0.121	0.082
Semi-colons/1,000 words	−0.181	−0.174	0.044	**−0.875**	0.210
Colons/1,000 words	−0.558	−0.055	−0.324	0.321	−0.300
Hyphens/1,000 words	−0.001	0.188	−0.815	0.243	0.181
Parentheses/1,000 words	0.283	−0.001	−0.263	−0.234	**0.829**
Exclamation marks/1,000 words	−0.513	−0.490	0.240	0.461	0.193
Question marks/1,000 words	0.082	0.416	0.704	0.122	−0.267
Words/sentence	0.310	**0.878**	0.269	0.125	0.158
Characters/sentence	0.606	0.724	0.210	0.152	0.173
Standardized type–token ratio	0.784	−0.187	0.394	−0.146	−0.298
Word length	**0.950**	0.096	−0.033	0.122	0.143
Long word count > 6/text	0.934	0.142	−0.118	0.105	0.219
Hapax legomena/text	0.748	0.126	0.380	−0.233	−0.282
Hapax dislegomena/text	0.306	−0.776	0.365	0.001	0.090
Automated Readability Index	0.747	0.598	0.147	0.148	0.181
Coleman–Liau Index	0.929	0.222	0.064	0.156	0.163

Table 4.33 Rotated component matrix with suppressed loadings < 0.4 and sorted by size.

	Component				
	1	2	3	4	5
Word length	0.950				
Long word count > 6/text	0.934				
Coleman–Liau Index	0.929				
Standardized type–token ratio	0.784				
Hapax legomena/text	0.748				
Automated Readability Index	0.747	0.598			
Colons/1,000 words	−0.558				
Exclamation marks/1,000 words	−0.513	−0.490		0.461	
Words/sentence		0.878			
Hapax dislegomena/text		−0.776			
Periods/1,000 words		−0.725	−0.525		
Characters/sentence	0.606	0.724			
Commas/1,000 words			0.953		
Hyphens/1,000 words			−0.815		
Question marks/1,000 words		0.416	0.704		
Semi-colons/1,000 words				−0.875	
Parentheses/1,000 words					0.829

Table 4.34 Factor scoring.

Text	Factor 1	Factor 2	Factor 3	Factor 4	Factor 5
1	−1.62889	−1.55568	0.76312	1.46418	0.61303
2	−0.16316	0.93422	0.02658	0.00548	0.9369
3	0.5369	0.9358	0.92255	0.05696	−0.56164
4	0.43085	−0.05933	−0.44144	−0.31796	1.33898
5	−0.51338	0.56883	−1.90167	1.12784	−0.88693
6	0.79378	−0.26758	0.50277	−0.10233	−1.71076
7	−0.85848	−1.6802	−0.50758	−1.33776	−0.98187
8	1.22559	−0.93289	−0.2229	−0.74038	1.57135
9	−0.54945	0.83698	1.85057	0.51551	0.11472
10	1.90428	−0.60402	0.06764	0.92164	−0.52787
11	−0.37517	0.98501	−1.30568	0.37544	0.35953
12	−0.80286	0.83887	0.24603	−1.96862	−0.26544

We note that Text 10, for example, scored highest in Factor 1 (*word length, long word count > 6/text, Coleman–Liau Index, standardized type–token ratio, hapax legomena/text, Automated Readability Index, colons/1,000 words* and *exclamation marks/1,000 words*) and Text 1 has its highest score in Factor 4 (*semi-colons/1,000 words*).

But we can do even better by saving the component scores in the *Factor score coefficient matrix* (Table 4.35). This allows us to estimate the actual values of individual cases (observations) for the factors; for each case and each component, the component score is computed by multiplying the case's original variable values by the component's score coefficients. For example, for Factor 1, we get:

$$
\begin{aligned}
Factor\ 1\ =\ &0.033(\text{periods}/1,000\ \text{words}) - 0.085(\text{commas}/1,000\ \text{words}) \\
&- 0.071(\text{semi-colons}/1,000\ \text{words}) - 0.056(\text{colons}/1,000\ \text{words}) \\
&+ 0.034(\text{hyphens}/1,000\ \text{words}) - 0.018(\text{parentheses}/1,000\ \text{words}) \\
&- 0.109(\text{excl. marks}/1,000\ \text{words}) - 0.055(\text{quest. marks}/1,000\ \text{words}) \\
&- 0.067(\text{words}/\text{sentence}) + 0.027(\text{characters}/\text{sentence}) \\
&+ 0.213(\text{stand. type–token ratio}) + 0.208(\text{word length}) \\
&+ 0.196(\text{long word count} > 6/\text{text}) + 0.166(\text{hapax legomena/text}) \\
&+ 0.118(\text{hapax dislegomena/text}) + 0.080(\text{Autom. Readability Index}) \\
&+ 0.178(\text{Coleman–Liau Index})
\end{aligned}
$$

The resulting five component score variables are representative of, and can be used in place of, the seventeen original variables with only an 11 per cent loss of information.

In this example, we have reduced the size of the data file from seventeen variables to just five components by using factor analysis with a principal components extraction.

In factor analysis, the experimenter has a choice of methods of factoring which will produce different solutions. A preliminary solution from any of the methods

Table 4.35 Factor score coefficient matrix.

	Component				
	1	2	3	4	5
Periods/1,000 words	0.033	−0.216	−0.101	0.054	0.149
Commas/1,000 words	−0.085	−0.003	0.381	0.115	0.257
Semi-colons/1,000 words	−0.071	0.050	0.052	−0.620	0.143
Colons/1,000 words	−0.056	0.018	−0.124	0.202	−0.225
Hyphens/1,000 words	0.034	0.080	−0.286	0.145	0.010
Parentheses/1,000 words	−0.018	0.012	0.028	−0.116	0.599
Exclamation marks/1,000 words	−0.109	−0.184	0.218	0.412	0.309
Question marks/1,000 words	−0.055	0.102	0.206	0.052	−0.082
Words/sentence	−0.067	0.272	0.078	0.026	0.168
Characters/sentence	0.027	0.180	0.038	0.066	0.131
Standardized type–token ratio	0.213	−0.163	0.027	−0.084	−0.288
Word length	0.208	−0.082	−0.071	0.107	0.003
Long word count > 6/text	0.196	−0.057	−0.091	0.091	0.052
Hapax legomena/text	0.166	−0.031	0.012	−0.182	−0.277
Hapax dislegomena/text	0.118	−0.341	0.168	0.110	0.103
Automated Readability Index	0.080	0.120	0.007	0.078	0.105
Coleman–Liau Index	0.178	−0.040	−0.030	0.124	0.046

might allow a decision about the number of factors and will give an estimate of the communalities. Without changing the number of factors or the communalities it is possible to alter the factor loadings by rotating the factors to search for loading patterns that offer simple interpretation.

The step of interpreting the data complicates things slightly. It is not always easy to identify common themes among the various variables that load on a factor and we should not always expect the mathematical factors produced by our analysis to represent some real-world construct. Recall, for instance, Factor 1 above with high loadings on *word length, long word count > 6/text, Coleman–Liau Index, standardized type–token ratio, hapax legomena/text, Automated Readability Index, colons/1,000 words* and *exclamation marks/1,000 words*. Under what heading would we group these variables? Note that Factor 1 is made up of variables belonging to punctuation (*exclamation marks/1,000 words*), lexical distribution (*standardized type–token ratio, word length, words> 6/text, hapax legomena*) and a variable of readability grade (*Coleman–Liau Index*).

However, we believe that the benefits of reducing the data file and using uncorrelated predictors outweigh this cost. This data reduction technique tries to reduce a list of variables or other measures to their essence: that is, a smaller set of factors that capture the patterns seen in the data. The main benefits of factor analysis are that investigators can focus their attention on the unique core elements instead of the redundant attributes, and that it can function as a data "pre-processor" for other multivariate techniques, such as regression models or cluster analysis.

4.5 Multiple regression

Multiple regression is an extension of simple regression (see section 3.2.5). Simple regression has only one independent variable. Multiple regression fits a model for one dependent variable based on more than one independent variable. The general purpose of multiple regression is to learn more about the relationship between several independent variables and a dependent variable.

Multiple regression can establish that a set of independent variables explains a proportion of the variance in a dependent variable at a significant level, and it can also establish the relative predictive importance of the independent variables. It allows us to predict someone's score on a particular variable on the basis of her scores on several other variables.

In the humanities and social sciences multiple regression procedures are widely used in research. In general, multiple regression allows the researcher to ask the general question "What is the best predictor of...?" An example might help here. Suppose we were interested in predicting how much a student enjoys an academic module. Variables such as perception of usefulness, previous qualifications, age, number of semesters studied at university and parents' socioeconomic status might all contribute. If we collected data on all of these variables, perhaps by surveying, say, a hundred university students, we would be able to see how many and which of these variables give rise to the most accurate prediction of academic-module satisfaction. We might find that academic-module satisfaction is most accurately predicted by type of perception of usefulness, previous qualifications and age, whereas the other variables do not help us to predict academic-module satisfaction.

To perform multiple regression, the variables used should either be interval or continuous and they should be related linearly. At least thirty data points are required for an accurate analysis. Although all multiple regression calculations are relatively easy to calculate, they are time-consuming to do by hand, so this type of analysis is generally performed using statistical packages.

Whereas in simple regression, the algebraic relation for the regression line was expressed by:

$$y = \alpha + \beta x$$

where y stands for the dependent variable, α is a constant (where the regression line intercepts the y-axis), β the slope or regression coefficient and x the independent variable. For multiple regression, we predict y using two or more independent variables $(x_1, x_2, ... x_n)$ and the equation takes the following form:

$$y = \alpha + \beta_1 x_1 + \beta_2 x_2 + ...\beta_n x_n$$

The βs are the regression coefficients, representing the amount the dependent variable y changes when the corresponding independent variable changes one unit. The α is the constant, where the regression line intercepts the y-axis, representing the amount the dependent y will be when all the independent variables are *zero*.

Consider the following hypothetical situation. A researcher is interested in detecting which variables best predict students' motivation in the foreign language context. She chooses thirty-two students and persuades them to take a standardized questionnaire to determine their motivation and additionally collects data on:

- students' (i) age, (ii) previous year's score in the foreign language subject (Score) and (iii) years of extra-curricular study in foreign languages (ECS)
- students' perception of various aspects of foreign languages: (i) fun, (ii) interest in learning (Int.), (iii) autonomous learning (AL), (iv) attention paid to lessons (Att.), (v) effort devoted, (vi) importance and usefulness (I&U), (vii) challenge in learning a foreign language (Chall.) and (viii) materials and aids used in the foreign language classroom (M&A).

The researcher has some knowledge drawn from previous studies that some of the variables in students' perception regarding various aspects in foreign languages might be positive predictors for students' motivation. The data for the thirty-two students are given in Table 4.36.

To check on the predictive power of these variables, the researcher can start by using the simple linear regression technique. Figures 4.9 to 4.13 show the scattergrams which can be constructed from data relating motivation to (i) students' age, (ii) previous year's score in the foreign language class and (iii) years of extra-curricular study in foreign languages, (iv) students' perception of fun, (v) interest, (vi) autonomous learning, (vi) attention paid to foreign language lessons, (vii) effort devoted, (viii) importance and usefulness of studying foreign languages, (ix) challenge in learning a foreign language and (x) materials and aids used in the foreign language classroom.

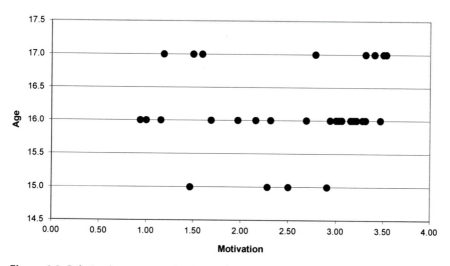

Figure 4.9 Relation between motivation and age.

Table 4.36 Hypothetical students' data.

Student	Motiv.	Age	Score	ECS	Fun	Int.	AL	Att.	Effort	I&U	Chall.	M&A
1	1.47	15	50	1	2	1.75	1.5	1	1	1.5	1	2
2	2.28	15	51	2	3	2.75	1	2	2.5	3	2	2
3	1.97	16	63	0	2.5	1.75	1.5	2	2	2	3	1
4	2.69	16	53	0	3	2.5	2	2.5	3	3.5	2	3
5	3.00	16	71	0	3	3	3	3	3	3	3	3
6	2.16	16	51	0	2	2.75	1.5	2.5	2.5	2	2	2
7	2.50	15	68	2	2.5	3	2.5	3	3	3	2	1
8	3.41	17	69	3	3.5	3.75	3.5	3.5	3.5	3.5	4	2
9	3.50	17	72	3	3.5	3.5	4	3.5	3.5	3	3	4
10	0.94	16	51	0	1	0.5	1	1.5	1.5	0.5	0.5	1
11	1.50	17	50	0	2	2	1	1	1	2	1	2
12	3.03	16	66	2	3	3.75	3	3.5	3	3	3	2
13	1.00	16	51	0	1	1	1	1.5	1.5	0.5	0.5	1
14	3.19	16	64	1	3.5	3.5	2.5	3	3.5	3.5	3	3
15	3.53	17	71	3	4	4	3.75	3	3.5	3	3	4
16	3.47	16	73	3	4	3.75	4	4	3.5	3.5	3	2
17	3.16	16	73	0	4	3.75	3.5	3	3	3	3	2
18	2.78	17	61	0	3	2.75	3	3	3	3.5	3	1
19	3.06	16	72	3	3.5	3	3.5	3	3	3.5	4	1
20	1.16	16	52	0	1	1.25	1.5	1.5	1	1	1	1
21	1.19	17	50	0	1.5	1.5	1	1	1.5	1.5	0.5	1
22	3.03	16	67	2	2.5	3.25	2.5	3	3	3	3	4
23	3.00	16	73	0	3	2.5	2.5	3	3	4	3	3
24	3.22	16	70	3	4	3.75	3	3	3.5	3.5	3	2
25	1.59	17	60	0	2.5	1.75	1	1	2	1.5	1	2
26	1.69	16	50	0	2.5	2	1	1	2	2	1	2
27	2.31	16	50	0	2.5	2.5	1	3	2	2.5	2	3
28	2.91	15	61	0	3	2.25	2	2.5	3	3.5	3	4
29	2.94	16	62	1	3	3	2.5	3	3	3	3	3
30	3.31	17	72	0	4	3.5	3.5	3	3.5	3.5	3	3
31	3.28	16	70	2	3	3.75	3.5	3.5	3.5	3	3	3
32	3.31	16	68	2	3.5	3.5	3.5	3.5	3	3.5	3	3

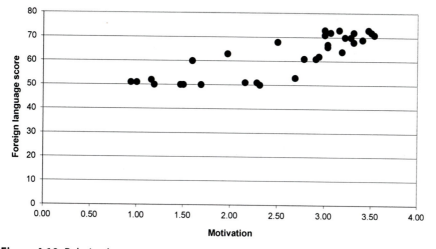

Figure 4.10 Relation between motivation and foreign language scores.

From the scattergrams it is clear that some variables seem to correlate with motivation: (i) foreign language score, (ii) fun, (iii) interest, (iv) autonomous learning, (v) attention, (vi) effort, (vii) importance and usefulness and (viii) challenge. However, (i) age, (ii) extra-curricular learning and (iii) materials and aids used in the foreign language classroom do not seem to correlate very strongly with motivation; the complete correlation matrix and significance values are given in Tables 4.37 and 4.38 respectively.

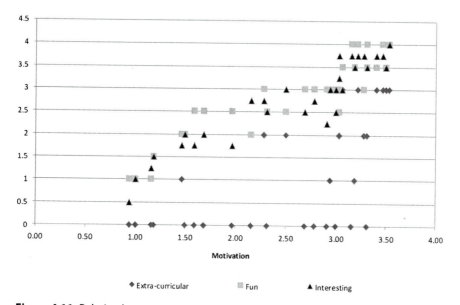

Figure 4.11 Relation between motivation and extra-curricular learning/fun/interest.

Table 4.37 Correlation matrix.

	Motiv.	Age	Score	ECS	Fun	Int.	AL	Att.	Effort	I&U	Chall.	M&A
Motiv.	1.00											
Age	0.09	1.00										
Score	0.84	0.16	1.00									
ECS	0.60	-0.01	0.55	1.00								
Fun	0.91	0.14	0.78	0.54	1.00							
Int.	0.94	0.12	0.76	0.66	0.88	1.00						
AL	0.89	0.22	0.90	0.65	0.80	0.85	1.00					
Att.	0.91	0.02	0.79	0.58	0.74	0.85	0.86	1.00				
Effort	0.95	0.09	0.82	0.57	0.86	0.88	0.84	0.88	1.00			
I&U	0.91	-0.04	0.69	0.47	0.85	0.81	0.71	0.79	0.85	1.00		
Chall.	0.92	0.05	0.82	0.54	0.82	0.82	0.82	0.86	0.85	0.86	1.00	
M&A	0.61	0.05	0.36	0.20	0.49	0.51	0.38	0.44	0.52	0.50	0.42	1.00

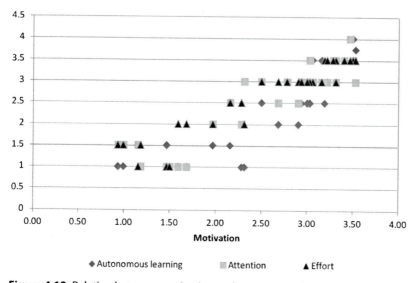

Figure 4.12 Relation between motivation and autonomous learning/attention/effort.

The best predictor for motivation seems to be students' perception of the effort they devote to learning a foreign language within a classroom context. Now, let us begin by fitting the simple regression model:

$$y = \alpha + \beta x$$

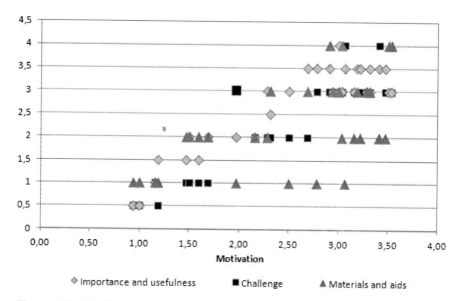

Figure 4.13 Relation between motivation and importance and usefulness/challenge/ materials and means.

Table 4.38 Significance values.

	Motiv.	Age	Score	ECS	Fun	Int.	AL	Att.	Effort	I&U	Chall.	M&A
Motiv.												
Age	0.306											
Score	0.000	0.194										
ECS	0.000	0.488	0.001									
Fun	0.000	0.229	0.000	0.001								
Int.	0.000	0.258	0.000	0.000	0.000							
AL	0.000	0.116	0.000	0.000	0.000	0.000						
Att.	0.000	0.460	0.000	0.000	0.000	0.000	0.000					
Effort	0.000	0.308	0.000	0.000	0.000	0.000	0.000	0.000				
I&U	0.000	0.417	0.000	0.003	0.000	0.000	0.000	0.000	0.000			
Chall.	0.000	0.383	0.000	0.001	0.000	0.000	0.000	0.000	0.000	0.000		
M&A	0.000	0.400	0.022	0.131	0.002	0.002	0.016	0.006	0.001	0.002	0.008	

Using the predictor *effort* and by means of the least squares criterion (see section 3.2.5), we find that the regression that fits best is:

$y = 0.44 + 0.949x$

To estimate the prediction error of our simple regression model, we calculate the differences between the observed motivation value and the predicted motivation value. The error, the squared error for each prediction and the sum of squared errors are given in Table 4.39.

Table 4.39 Prediction error of simple regression model.

Student	Motivation	Effort	Prediction	Error	Error²
1	1.47	1	1.39	0.080	0.0064
2	2.28	2.5	2.81	−0.531	0.2822
3	1.97	2	2.34	−0.369	0.1363
4	2.69	3	3.29	−0.600	0.3594
5	3	3	3.29	−0.287	0.0824
6	2.16	2.5	2.81	−0.656	0.4307
7	2.5	3	3.29	−0.787	0.6194
8	3.41	3.5	3.76	−0.355	0.1262
9	3.5	3.5	3.76	−0.262	0.0684
10	0.94	1.5	1.86	−0.926	0.8575
11	1.5	1	1.39	0.111	0.0123
12	3.03	3	3.29	−0.256	0.0654
13	1	1.5	1.86	−0.864	0.7456
14	3.19	3.5	3.76	−0.574	0.3295
15	3.53	3.5	3.76	−0.230	0.0530
16	3.47	3.5	3.76	−0.293	0.0857
17	3.16	3	3.29	−0.131	0.0171
18	2.78	3	3.29	−0.506	0.2558
19	3.06	3	3.29	−0.225	0.0504
20	1.16	1	1.39	−0.233	0.0542
21	1.19	1.5	1.86	−0.676	0.4570
22	3.03	3	3.29	−0.256	0.0654
23	3	3	3.29	−0.287	0.0824
24	3.22	3.5	3.76	−0.543	0.2946
25	1.59	2	2.34	−0.744	0.5539
26	1.69	2	2.34	−0.651	0.4232
27	2.31	2	2.34	−0.026	0.0007
28	2.91	3	3.29	−0.381	0.1450
29	2.94	3	3.29	−0.350	0.1222
30	3.31	3.5	3.76	−0.449	0.2016
31	3.28	3.5	3.76	−0.480	0.2306
Total					7.2149

It is important to be clear what we are going to predict or estimate, using a regression model. Going back to our previous example, there are two possibilities: (1) we might wish to estimate the sample mean of motivation for all students attending foreign language lessons for a given effort rate, x, or (2) we might wish to predict the motivation of an individual student attending foreign language lessons with an effort rate of, say, 3.5. In both cases, we should not expect an exact prediction, but we can obtain a confidence interval for motivation of a population/individual with effort x.

To estimate the confidence interval, we would first need to calculate the error standard deviation of our sample data. This can be done using the formula:

$$error\_sd = \sqrt{\frac{\sum error^2}{n-2}}$$

which gives:

$$error\_sd = \sqrt{\frac{7.2149}{30}} = 0.49$$

For a confidence interval with a 5 per cent critical value (i.e. 95% certainty), we now need to check the t-score for $df = n - 2$ at $p = 0.05$ (Appendix 3); in our case, the t-score for $df = 30$ ($32 - 2 = 30$), with $p = 0.05$ is 2.042. We need this t-score to make sure that if 100 samples were repeatedly chosen at random from a population with $p = 0.05$, then for 95 per cent of the chosen samples the confidence interval will be true. Finally, the interval is a result of applying the formula:

confidence interval $\pm$ *t-score* $\times$ *error-sd*

For our example, this gives:

confidence interval $\pm 2.042 \times 0.49 = 1$

So the confidence interval for our simple regression model is:

$y + 1$

To estimate the sample mean of motivation for all students attending foreign language lessons given their effort rate x, we calculate the mean of predictions (2.94) and estimate:

2.94 ± 1

Hence, with 95 per cent confidence, we can say that the predicted mean motivation for students attending foreign language lessons with a given effort rate lies between 1.94 and 3.94.

Similarly, we can also predict the motivation of an individual student attending foreign language lessons with an effort rate of, say, 3.5:

$$y = 0.44 + 0.949 \times 3.5 = 3.76$$

And we can calculate the confidence interval:

$$3.76 \pm 1$$

We can conclude that as a result of our regression model, we are 95 per cent confident that a randomly chosen student with an effort rate of 3.5 will have a motivation of between 2.76 and 4.76.

However, we might consider that this interval is too wide to be useful. In order to fit a better prediction model, we could try taking into account not just the variable of effort but also other highly correlating variables, such as interest or challenge, among others. To do this, we need to extend our regression model and include more than one independent variable. The most obvious way to do this is to add extra variables to our previous model:

$$y = \alpha + \beta_1 x_1 + \beta_2 x_2 + \dots \beta_n x_n$$

With more than one independent variable, it is rather tedious and time-consuming to carry out the calculations by hand and we shall present the results obtained using a statistical package.[14]

For the computation of the multiple regression model, we have additionally chosen to include new independent variables stepwise and to exclude those variables that do not contribute to the model. Overall, we get seven possible models (see Table 4.40).

The error standard deviations clearly improve along the models, which should be compared with our initial simple regression model of 0.49 when the model containing only the variable effort was fitted. We also find that the least squares regression estimates of the seven models give the following results:

Model 1: $y = -0.04 + 0.549x_1 + 0.403x_2$

Model 2: $y = 0.117 + 0.363x_1 + 0.321x_2 + 0.253x_3$

Model 3: $y = 0.053 + 0.301x_1 + 0.288x_2 + 0.271x_3 + 0.121x_4$

Model 4: $y = 0.096 + 0.258x_1 + 0.229x_2 + 0.235x_3 + 0.133x_4 + 0.124x_5$

Model 5: $y = 0.073 + 0.186x_1 + 0.188x_2 + 0.158x_3 + 0.125x_4 + 0.163x_5 + 0.162x_6$

---

14. SPSS (www.spss.com).

Table 4.40 Multiple regression models.

Model	R^2	Error standard deviation
(1)	0.946	0.198
(2)	0.971	0.148
(3)	0.986	0.106
(4)	0.991	0.085
(5)	0.997	0.046
(6)	0.998	0.041
(7)	1.000	0.002

(1) Effort, Interest
(2) Effort, Interest, Challenge
(3) Effort, Interest, Challenge, Materials & Aims
(4) Effort, Interest, Challenge, Materials & Aims, Auton. Learning
(5) Effort, Interest, Challenge, Materials & Aims, Auton. Learning, Import. & Usefulness
(6) Effort, Interest, Challenge, Materials & Aims, Auton. Learning, Import, & Usefulness, Attention
(7) Effort, Interest, Challenge, Materials & Aims, Auton, Learning, Import. & Usefulness. Attention. Perception of Fun

Model 6: $y = 0.061 + 0.164x_1 + 0.180x_2 + 0.143x_3 + 0.126x_4 + 0.151x_5 + 0.163x_6 + 0.06x_7$

Model 7: $y = 0.002 + 0.126x_1 + 0.125x_2 + 0.125x_3 + 0.125x_4 + 0.125x_5 + 0.125x_6 + 0.124x_7 + 0.124x_8$

where x_1 stands for effort, x_2 for interest, x_3 for challenge, x_4 for materials and aids, x_5 for autonomous learning, x_6 for importance and usefulness, x_7 for attention, and x_8 for fun.

As expected, the inclusion of additional variables has improved the modelling, explaining more of the variability in the motivation scores, thus reducing the level of error standard deviation. In fact, the percentage reduction (R^2) in the variance of the motivation scores has increased from 90 per cent (using the variable of effort only[15]) to 94 per cent (using effort and interest) and up to 100 per cent using effort, interest, challenge, materials and aids, autonomous learning, importance and usefulness, attention, and fun.

Table 4.41 shows the 95 per cent confidence intervals for each of the seven models. It can be seen that the intervals in models that use more variables become more precise than those obtained with fewer scores, ranging from 0.408 (with two independent variables) down to 0.002 (using eight independent variables). This contrasts with our initial simple regression model obtained from a single independent variable, with a confidence interval of 1.

---

15. See the correlation matrix (Table 4.37), where R(*motivation and effort*) = 0.95. The percentage can be calculated by just squaring the R.

Table 4.41 95 per cent confidence intervals of the various models.

Model	(1)	(2)	(3)	(4)	(5)	(6)	(7)
Confidence interval	0.408	0.293	0.206	0.162	0.088	0.076	0.002

(1) Effort, Interest
(2) Effort, Interest, Challenge
(3) Effort, Interest, Challenge, Materials & Means
(4) Effort, Interest, Challenge, Materials & Means, Auton, Learning
(5) Effort, Interest, Challenge, Materials & Means, Auton. Learning, Import. & Usefulness
(6) Effort, Interest, Challenge, Materials & Means, Auton. Learning, Import. & Usefulness, Attention
(7) Effort, Interest, Challenge, Materials & Means, Auton. Learning. Import. & Usefulness, Attention, Perception of Fun

To evaluate the precision of our multiple regression models, let us compare the simple regression model (using the variable of effort) with models 1 and 7 (Table 4.42).

Table 4.42 Intervals for simple regression model and multiple regression models 1 and 7.

	Independent variables used		
	1 (simple regression)	2 (model 1)	8 (model 7)
Intervals	1.94 – 3.94	2.16 – 2.97	2.49 – 2.51

Clearly, the multiple regression models constrain the intervals and gain in precision, particularly model 7: the interval of model 1 has a range of 0.81 units, from 2.16 to 2.97; whereas the range of model 7 is only 0.02, from 2.49 to 2.51. On the opposite side, we find the simple regression model, whose interval is probably too wide to be useful for our purposes, ranging from 1.94 to 3.94, that is, 2 units.

It is also interesting to see how the statistical package, using the option for stepwise regression, chose the best models by first including all the possible independent variables one at a time and then excluding those variables that did not contribute to the modelling of the data: (i) age, (ii) previous year's score in the foreign language subject and (iii) extra-curricular learning.

5 Word frequency lists

5.1 Typology and usefulness

In the preceding chapters we looked at a number of techniques for quantitative analysis that are commonly used in applied linguistic research. Although most readers will have encountered some of these previously in their readings, we have tried to cover these statistical techniques in greater depth and, additionally:

- examine the assumptions that underlie the use of the various techniques, and
- look at examples of research studies that use the various analyses described.

Increasingly, applied linguists handle quantitative data in their research, but so do phoneticians, sociolinguists, psycholinguists, computational linguists and particularly corpus linguists. In corpus linguistics, the most frequently used statistic is the frequency list of occurrence of some linguistic item or the frequency of co-occurrence of two or more linguistic variables. To put it succinctly, a frequency list is a sorted list of words (word types) together with their frequency, where frequency usually means the number of occurrences of (a) repeating item(s) in a given text or corpus. A frequency list can be understood as a preliminary survey of the content of a text or corpus. Despite its apparent simplicity it is a powerful tool.

Frequency lists are produced by identifying first each word form (type) in the text or corpus, counting identical types and listing them with their number of occurrences. As an example, consider the following extract:[1]

> The day begins early. On November 4, in villages, towns and cities across the United States, thousands of volunteers will rise before dawn to lend a hand for the U.S. elections. Some will line up outside campaign headquarters, eager to pick up the flyers, pamphlets and signs they will distribute at polling places in the hope of still influencing voters' decisions.
>
> Others will go directly to the school cafeterias, gymnasiums and community centers that serve as polling places to assist in checking

---

1. U.S. Election Day a Celebration of Political Activism: www.america.gov/st/elections08-english/2008/October/20061103131535abretnuh0.6453821.html?CP.rss=true

voter rolls, setting up voting machines and ensuring the elections are conducted in accordance with all applicable laws and regulations.

For these dedicated volunteers, Election Day is the culmination of months of hard work – a day when volunteers of all ages and backgrounds enjoy the excitement and occasional chaos of democracy in action.

A simple word frequency program[2] produces various sequences; the simplest one would be to show the word forms in order of appearance in the text, like the characters in a movie cast list. This gives the following list (Table 5.1):

Table 5.1 Frequency list: order of appearance in the text.

Word	Frequency	Word	Frequency	Word	Frequency
THE	9	OUTSIDE	1	VOTER	1
DAY	3	CAMPAIGN	1	ROLLS	1
BEGINS	1	HEADQUARTERS	1	SETTING	1
EARLY	1	EAGER	1	VOTING	1
ON	1	PICK	1	MACHINES	1
NOVEMBER	1	FLYERS	1	ENSURING	1
IN	5	PAMPHLETS	1	ARE	1
VILLAGES	1	SIGNS	1	CONDUCTED	1
TOWNS	1	THEY	1	ACCORDANCE	1
AND	7	DISTRIBUTE	1	WITH	1
CITIES	1	AT	1	ALL	2
ACROSS	1	POLLING	2	APPLICABLE	1
UNITED	1	PLACES	2	LAWS	1
STATES	1	HOPE	1	REGULATIONS	1
THOUSANDS	1	STILL	1	THESE	1
OF	6	INFLUENCING	1	DEDICATED	1
VOLUNTEERS	3	VOTERS'	1	ELECTION	1
WILL	4	DECISIONS	1	IS	1
RISE	1	OTHERS	1	CULMINATION	1
BEFORE	1	GO	1	MONTHS	1
DAWN	1	DIRECTLY	1	HARD	1
TO	4	SCHOOL	1	WORK	1
LEND	1	CAFETERIAS	1	WHEN	1
A	2	GYMNASIUMS	1	AGES	1
HAND	1	COMMUNITY	1	BACKGROUNDS	1
FOR	2	CENTERS	1	ENJOY	1
U.S.	1	THAT	1	EXCITEMENT	1
ELECTIONS	2	SERVE	1	OCCASIONAL	1
SOME	1	AS	1	CHAOS	1
LINE	1	ASSIST	1	DEMOCRACY	1
UP	3	CHECKING	1	ACTION	1

---

2. For example, the demo version of MonoConc at www.athel.com/README.html

Note that once word forms have appeared and been accounted for, they are no longer displayed, just counted. This list might be interesting for examining the appearance of specific content words in a text and exploring its reading difficulty, language specificity, and so on. It is also possible to identify changes in the nature of the text(s). Word types that appear for the first time some way into the text might be an indication that at that text position there could be a change in topic.

Alternatively, the list can be displayed alphabetically for easier consultation (Table 5.2).

Table 5.2 Frequency list: alphabetical order.

Word	Frequency	Word	Frequency	Word	Frequency
A	2	EAGER	1	PLACES	2
ACCORDANCE	1	EARLY	1	POLLING	2
ACROSS	1	ELECTION	1	REGULATIONS	1
ACTION	1	ELECTIONS	2	RISE	1
AGES	1	ENJOY	1	ROLLS	1
ALL	2	ENSURING	1	SCHOOL	1
AND	7	EXCITEMENT	1	SERVE	1
APPLICABLE	1	FLYERS	1	SETTING	1
ARE	1	FOR	2	SIGNS	1
AS	1	GO	1	SOME	1
ASSIST	1	GYMNASIUMS	1	STATES	1
AT	1	HAND	1	STILL	1
BACKGROUNDS	1	HARD	1	THAT	1
BEFORE	1	HEADQUARTERS	1	THE	9
BEGINS	1	HOPE	1	THESE	1
CAFETERIAS	1	IN	5	THEY	1
CAMPAIGN	1	INFLUENCING	1	THOUSANDS	1
CENTERS	1	IS	1	TO	4
CHAOS	1	LAWS	1	TOWNS	1
CHECKING	1	LEND	1	U.S.	1
CITIES	1	LINE	1	UNITED	1
COMMUNITY	1	MACHINES	1	UP	3
CONDUCTED	1	MONTHS	1	VILLAGES	1
CULMINATION	1	NOVEMBER	1	VOLUNTEERS	3
DAWN	1	OCCASIONAL	1	VOTER	1
DAY	3	OF	6	VOTERS'	1
DECISIONS	1	ON	1	VOTING	1
DEDICATED	1	OTHERS	1	WHEN	1
DEMOCRACY	1	OUTSIDE	1	WILL	4
DIRECTLY	1	PAMPHLETS	1	WITH	1
DISTRIBUTE	1	PICK	1	WORK	1

However, some researchers might be more interested in studying word formations, with special interest in word endings, that is, inflections. In that case, a reversed alphabetically ordered frequency list might be most interesting (Table 5.3).

Table 5.3 Frequency list: alphabetically reversed order.

Word	Frequency	Word	Frequency	Word	Frequency
A	2	OCCASIONAL	1	IS	1
DEDICATED	1	ALL	2	ROLLS	1
CONDUCTED	1	STILL	1	GYMNASIUMS	1
UNITED	1	WILL	4	SIGNS	1
AND	7	SCHOOL	1	BEGINS	1
HAND	1	WHEN	1	DECISIONS	1
LEND	1	CAMPAIGN	1	REGULATIONS	1
HARD	1	IN	5	ELECTIONS	2
ACCORDANCE	1	ON	1	TOWNS	1
OUTSIDE	1	CULMINATION	1	CHAOS	1
THE	9	ACTION	1	VOLUNTEERS	3
APPLICABLE	1	ELECTION	1	OTHERS	1
SOME	1	DAWN	1	CENTERS	1
LINE	1	GO	1	VOTERS	1
HOPE	1	TO	4	HEADQUARTERS	1
ARE	1	UP	3	FLYERS	1
BEFORE	1	NOVEMBER	1	ACROSS	1
THESE	1	EAGER	1	U.S.	1
RISE	1	VOTER	1	PAMPHLETS	1
DISTRIBUTE	1	FOR	2	LAWS	1
SERVE	1	AS	1	AT	1
OF	6	CAFETERIAS	1	THAT	1
INFLUENCING	1	THOUSANDS	1	EXCITEMENT	1
CHECKING	1	BACKGROUNDS	1	ASSIST	1
POLLING	2	PLACES	2	DAY	3
ENSURING	1	AGES	1	DEMOCRACY	1
VOTING	1	VILLAGES	1	THEY	1
SETTING	1	CITIES	1	EARLY	1
WITH	1	MACHINES	1	DIRECTLY	1
PICK	1	STATES	1	ENJOY	1
WORK	1	MONTHS	1	COMMUNITY	1

The usefulness of this wordlist is that the influence of prefixes is reduced and words such as *influencing, checking, polling, ensuring, voting* and *setting* are grouped together, just like *early* and *directly.* This sorting provides useful information on word endings and suffixation, not provided by other frequency listings.

Although these wordlists are convenient for some purposes, it is often more useful to produce frequency ordered lists, in order to explore which word types are most frequent in a text or corpus and compare them with other texts or corpora (Table 5.4).

Descending frequency order lists are probably among the most useful ones for exploring texts and corpora, examining their component features and comparing them with other texts and corpora. However, when producing long lists, it may become difficult to find a specific word type, so along with a frequency ordered

Table 5.4 Frequency list: frequency order.

Word	Frequency	Word	Frequency	Word	Frequency
THE	9	CHECKING	1	NOVEMBER	1
AND	7	CITIES	1	OCCASIONAL	1
OF	6	COMMUNITY	1	ON	1
IN	5	CONDUCTED	1	OTHERS	1
TO	4	CULMINATION	1	OUTSIDE	1
WILL	4	DAWN	1	PAMPHLETS	1
DAY	3	DECISIONS	1	PICK	1
UP	3	DEDICATED	1	REGULATIONS	1
VOLUNTEERS	3	DEMOCRACY	1	RISE	1
A	2	DIRECTLY	1	ROLLS	1
ALL	2	DISTRIBUTE	1	SCHOOL	1
ELECTIONS	2	EAGER	1	SERVE	1
FOR	2	EARLY	1	SETTING	1
PLACES	2	ELECTION	1	SIGNS	1
POLLING	2	ENJOY	1	SOME	1
ACCORDANCE	1	ENSURING	1	STATES	1
ACROSS	1	EXCITEMENT	1	STILL	1
ACTION	1	FLYERS	1	THAT	1
AGES	1	GO	1	THESE	1
APPLICABLE	1	GYMNASIUMS	1	THEY	1
ARE	1	HAND	1	THOUSANDS	1
AS	1	HARD	1	TOWNS	1
ASSIST	1	HEADQUARTERS	1	U.S.	1
AT	1	HOPE	1	UNITED	1
BACKGROUNDS	1	INFLUENCING	1	VILLAGES	1
BEFORE	1	IS	1	VOTER	1
BEGINS	1	LAWS	1	VOTERS'	1
CAFETERIAS	1	LEND	1	VOTING	1
CAMPAIGN	1	LINE	1	WHEN	1
CENTERS	1	MACHINES	1	WITH	1
CHAOS	1	MONTHS	1	WORK	1

wordlist it might be practical to produce an alphabetically ordered one, which would make it easier to search and reference individual words.

To illustrate the potential of frequency lists, consider the following data from the British National Corpus[3] (BNC, hereafter), showing the sixty most used word forms in English (Table 5.5).

To facilitate interpretation, frequencies are given per million words. For example, the definite article *the* occurs on average 61,873 times in million-word-long English language extracts. The complete corpus is made up of samples of written and spoken language from a wide range of sources, designed to represent a wide cross-section

3. www.natcorp.ox.ac.uk/

Table 5.5 The sixty most frequent word forms in the British National Corpus (averaged per million words).

Word	Frequency	Word	Frequency	Word	Frequency
THE	61,873	NOT	4,625	WILL	2,448
OF	29,414	THIS	4,619	THERE	2,395
AND	26,829	BUT	4,541	IF	2,371
TO	25,384	THEY	4,334	CAN	2,344
A	21,264	HIS	4,269	ALL	2,277
IN	18,126	FROM	4,135	HER	2,183
IT	10,892	HAD	4,090	AS	2,086
IS	9,984	SHE	3,803	WHO	2,054
WAS	9,239	WHICH	3,720	HAVE	2,052
I	8,846	OR	3,708	DO	1,966
FOR	8,334	WE	3,580	THAT	1,948
YOU	6,955	AN	3,431	ONE	1,905
HE	6,813	WERE	3,228	SAID	1,853
BE	6,625	THAT	2,869	THEM	1,734
WITH	6,520	BEEN	2,687	SOME	1,712
ON	6,473	HAVE	2,685	COULD	1,684
THAT	6,290	THEIR	2,609	HIM	1,650
BY	5,073	HAS	2,594	INTO	1,635
AT	4,782	WOULD	2,552	ITS	1,631
ARE	4,709	WHAT	2,495	THEN	1,607

of current British English, both spoken and written. It has a hundred million words altogether, containing 939,028 different word types. Consequently, the data and analysis obtained from the BNC can be extrapolated to general English. Therefore, we can say that the average number of occurrences of each word form in English is 106.49 (100,000,000/939,028). What is more, the sixty most used words in English occur altogether 394,534 times per one million words, that is, 39.45 per cent of the English language. Within the sixty most frequent English words, only closed-class items are found: articles, prepositions, conjunctions, auxiliary verbs, pronouns and modal verbs. No content word (noun, lexical verb, adjective or adverb) is found among them. Furthermore, we can also calculate the weight or "importance" of a word form. Table 5.6 shows the prominence of the twenty most frequent English words.

The definite article *the* accounts for 6.19 per cent of all English language outcomes (written and oral), followed by the preposition *of* with nearly 3 per cent. It is also interesting that the twenty most frequent types in English account for nearly 30 per cent of the language. That is to say that with just these twenty word forms we are able, on average, to construct 30 per cent of all English written and oral productions. In addition, we can use our BNC frequency list and compare it with other frequency lists obtained from, say, novels. This could give us interesting information on the overuse or underuse of specific word forms. The data in Table 5.7 compares the top ten general English word forms with Chapter 1 of Herman Melville's *Moby Dick*.

Table 5.6 Word form weight of the twenty most frequent types in the British National Corpus, averaged per million words.

Word	Frequency	Cumulative frequency	% weight	Cumulative %
THE	61,873	61,873	6.19	6.19
OF	29,414	91,287	2.94	9.13
AND	26,829	118,116	2.68	11.81
TO	25,384	143,500	2.54	14.35
A	21,264	164,764	2.13	16.48
IN	18,126	182,890	1.81	18.29
IT	10,892	193,782	1.09	19.38
IS	9,984	203,766	1.00	20.38
WAS	9,239	213,005	0.92	21.30
I	8,846	221,851	0.88	22.19
FOR	8,334	230,185	0.83	23.02
YOU	6,955	237,140	0.70	23.71
HE	6,813	243,953	0.68	24.40
BE	6,625	250,578	0.66	25.06
WITH	6,520	257,098	0.65	25.71
ON	6,473	263,571	0.65	26.36
THAT	6,290	269,861	0.63	26.99
BY	5,073	274,934	0.51	27.49
AT	4,782	279,716	0.48	27.97
ARE	4,709	284,425	0.47	28.44

Table 5.7 Top ten types: general English versus *Moby Dick*.

English		*Moby Dick*	
Word	% weight	Word	% weight
THE	6.19	THE	5.51
OF	2.94	OF	3.59
AND	2.68	AND	3.27
TO	2.54	A	3.00
A	2.13	TO	2.38
IN	1.81	IN	2.15
IT	1.09	I	1.93
IS	1.00	IS	1.52
WAS	0.92	IT	1.48
I	0.88	THAT	1.39

It is interesting to note the coincidence between the most used words in general English and Melville's novel, particularly among the top six types: *the, of, and, to, a* and *in*. Another revealing finding is Melville's underuse of the definite article *the* and the preposition *to* compared to general English and his overuse of the indefinite article *a*, prepositions *of* and *in*, and the conjunction *and*. A striking contrast aris-ing from this comparison is perhaps that found between the use of the first person singular pronoun *I* in general English and in *Moby Dick*. Melville clearly overuses *I* compared to general English; the relative frequency or percentage weight is roughly twice that of general English (0.88 versus 1.93). This difference begins to look sig-nificant, although further statistical analyses would be needed to establish the level of significance involved. Furthermore, this overuse of *I* would suggest that Melville might be resorting to some type of first person narration, which is indeed true.

Other appealing comparisons can be made between different languages to exam-ine whether there is any correlation between the most used word types or not. Table 5.8 shows the top ten word forms in English and Spanish.

Table 5.8 Top ten types: English versus Spanish.

English			Spanish		
Word	Frequency	% weight	Word	Frequency	% weight
THE	61,873	6.19	DE	61,194	6.12
OF	29,414	2.94	LA	38,739	3.87
AND	26,829	2.68	QUE	33,755	3.38
TO	25,384	2.54	Y	28,289	2.83
A	21,264	2.13	EL	27,990	2.80
IN	18,126	1.81	EN	26,296	2.63
IT	10,892	1.09	A	21,567	2.16
IS	9,984	1.00	LOS	16,433	1.64
WAS	9,239	0.92	SE	13,332	1.33
I	8,846	0.88	NO	11,718	1.17

We can see that the most frequent Spanish type is the preposition *de* (*of* in English). The second ranked word is the feminine definitive article *la*, and so on. There seems to be some correlation between both languages. A further finding is that both languages only have closed-class items among their most frequent words; content words are missing in both. However, we can do even better. Notice that the English definite article *the* actually stands for masculine, feminine and neuter nouns in singular and plural. This would correspond to Spanish *la* (singular feminine), *el* (singular masculine), *las* (plural feminine) and *los* (plural masculine). This informa-tion is missing from the frequency lists above. To get this information we would need to lemmatize the word form: that is, join all derived and inflected forms into a single canonical form. This canonical form is also known as dictionary form or simple lemma. It is precisely that word form we use when looking up a word in a dictionary. Lemmatized frequency lists are more elaborate and sophisticated as the texts need to have been processed using a lemmatizer.[4] Table 5.9 compares the two languages using the top ten lemmatized words.

---

4.   A lemmatizer reduces all words in a list or text to their base form. That is, it groups together the different inflected forms of a word so they can be analysed as a single item. For example *am, are, is, was, were* and *been* are grouped into *be*.

Table 5.9 Top ten lemmas: English versus Spanish.

English			Spanish		
Word	Frequency	% weight	Word	Frequency	% weight
THE	61,873	6.19	EL/LA	85,370	8.54
BE	42,277	4.23	DE	61,194	6.12
OF	29,414	2.94	QUE	33,755	3.38
AND	26,829	2.68	Y	28,289	2.83
A	21,264	2.13	EN	26,296	2.63
IN	18,126	1.81	A	21,567	2.16
TO	16,209	1.62	SER	15,981	1.60
HAVE	13,655	1.37	UN	15,841	1.58
IT	10,892	1.09	LO	15,053	1.51
TO	9,175	0.92	NO	11,718	1.17

Now we have a more realistic comparison of the most used lemmas in both languages. Note that we now have two *tos* in English. Actually the first *to* is the infinitive marker while the second one is the preposition. In addition, if we pair and rank the lemmas of English with their Spanish counterparts, we can obtain a neat comparison (Table 5.10) with a *Spearman* $\rho = 0.571$ and *Sig* $= 0.139$, which is not statistically significant but which hints that there may be some sort of parallel behaviour across both languages.

Table 5.10 Paired and ranked top ten lemmas: English versus Spanish.

English		Spanish	
Word	Rank	Word	Rank
THE	1	EL/LA	1
BE	2	SER	7
OF	3	DE	2
AND	4	Y	4
A	5	UN	8
IN	6	EN	5
IT	9	LO	9
TO	10	A	6

When studying a word, it is often useful to consider the different forms of the word collectively. That is, although the computer identifies *am, is, are, was, were, been, being* and *be* as different words, we may want to discuss them altogether or investigate their frequency as a group, lemma *be*. We can make even more use of the lemmatized lists, if we group the word forms under the same lemma with their individual frequencies. Table 5.11 gives a lemmatized list extract (ranging from *be* to *beach*). The frequency shown opposite the lemma is the total while the indented lines show the frequencies for the individual word forms. For example, in the BNC the most frequent word form of the lemma *be* is the simple present third person singular *is* with 9,982 occurrences per million words.

Table 5.11 Lemmatized list extract.

BE		42,277
	'M	658
	'RE	835
	'S	3,190
	AM	250
	ARE	4,707
	BE	6,644
	BEEN	2,686
	BEING	862
	IS	9,982
	WAS	9,236
	WERE	3,227
BEACH		**48**
	BEACH	38
	BEACHES	10

Without any comparison, it is difficult to know what is meant when we say that all inflected forms of *be* occur 42,277 times altogether in the BNC. Is this particularly common or rare? A quick comparison regarding the use of the various word forms of the verb lemma *be* in general English versus *Moby Dick* produces the following results (Table 5.12): overall the verb *be* is used less by Melville than in general English. However, it is interesting to note (1) the absence of contracted forms in *Moby Dick*, and (2) Melville's overuse of *is*, *being* and *am* and his underuse of *are*, *be*, *been* and *was*.

Table 5.12 Use of *be*: general English versus *Moby Dick*.

English			Moby Dick		
Lemma	Word form	% weight	Lemma	Word form	% weight
BE		4.23	**BE**		3.27
	'M	0.07		'M	0.00
	'RE	0.08		'RE	0.00
	'S	0.32		'S	0.00
	AM	0.03		AM	0.18
	ARE	0.47		ARE	0.22
	BE	0.66		BE	0.40
	BEEN	0.27		BEEN	0.09
	BEING	0.09		BEING	0.18
	IS	1.00		IS	1.52
	WAS	0.92		WAS	0.36
	WERE	0.32		WERE	0.31

The possible list sequences we have seen so far are likely to be appropriate for a wide range of research, although some will be more useful for one type of study than another.

More specific or more project-oriented frequency lists might demand more elaborate wordlists; for example, specific frequency ranges and/or words with similar occurrence frequencies. If we take our sample text above, therefore, we can examine, for example, those words that occurred once only in the text (Table 5.13).

Table 5.13 Word forms with frequency = 1.

ACCORDANCE	1	EAGER	1	REGULATIONS	1
ACROSS	1	EARLY	1	RISE	1
ACTION	1	ELECTION	1	ROLLS	1
AGES	1	ENJOY	1	SCHOOL	1
APPLICABLE	1	ENSURING	1	SERVE	1
ARE	1	EXCITEMENT	1	SETTING	1
AS	1	FLYERS	1	SIGNS	1
ASSIST	1	GO	1	SOME	1
AT	1	GYMNASIUMS	1	STATES	1
BACKGROUNDS	1	HAND	1	STILL	1
BEFORE	1	HARD	1	THAT	1
BEGINS	1	HEADQUARTERS	1	THESE	1
CAFETERIAS	1	HOPE	1	THEY	1
CAMPAIGN	1	INFLUENCING	1	THOUSANDS	1
CENTERS	1	IS	1	TOWNS	1
CHAOS	1	LAWS	1	U.S.	1
CITIES	1	LEND	1	UNITED	1
COMMUNITY	1	LINE	1	VILLAGES	1
CONDUCTED	1	MACHINES	1	VOTER	1
CULMINATION	1	MONTHS	1	VOTERS'	1
DAWN	1	OCCASIONAL	1	VOTING	1
DECISIONS	1	ON	1	WHEN	1
DEDICATED	1	OTHERS	1	WITH	1
DEMOCRACY	1	OUTSIDE	1	WORK	1
DIRECTLY	1	PAMPHLETS	1		
DISTRIBUTE	1	PICK	1		

Taking more extensive samples or corpora might allow us to examine low frequency words or rare words across registers or between oral and written language, British English and American English, and so on.

Other possibilities can include word length sequences. These lists may be useful for examining word form complexity, especially when combined with alphabetic or frequency order within word length. Table 5.14 shows the first sixty word forms of Shakespeare's *Hamlet*, sorted by their length (one letter, two letters, etc).

This can also be used as a basis for the calculation of statistics relating to word length, such as the mean word length in letters, or relative frequency of words regarding their word length. Table 5.15 displays the statistics on word length for *Hamlet*.

Table 5.14 The sixty shortest word forms in *Hamlet*.

Word	Frequency	Word	Frequency	Word	Frequency
A	517	NO	142	BEG	7
I	562	OF	660	BID	6
AM	54	ON	131	BUT	268
AN	57	OR	111	CAN	36
AS	225	SO	198	CRY	5
AT	85	TO	747	DAY	24
AY	39	UP	35	DID	65
BE	229	US	70	DIE	7
BY	119	WE	145	EAR	17
DO	157	ACT	14	EAT	5
GO	70	AGE	10	END	17
HA	10	AIR	13	ERE	14
HE	216	ALL	112	EYE	15
HO	15	AND	901	FAR	11
IF	115	ANY	14	FAT	6
IN	426	ARE	131	FIE	6
IS	348	ARM	6	FIT	12
IT	417	ART	17	FLY	6
ME	235	BAD	6	FOR	249
MY	516	BED	14	GET	9

Table 5.15 Statistics on word length in *Hamlet*.

Mean word length (in characters)		4.05
Word length standard deviation		2.01
	FREQ	**%**
1-letter words	1,263	4.23
2-letter words	5,600	18.77
3-letter words	6,562	22.00
4-letter words	6,973	23.38
5-letter words	3,404	11.41
6-letter words	2,313	7.75
7-letter words	1,668	5.59
8-letter words	946	3.17
9-letter words	564	1.89
10-letter words	324	1.09
11-letter words	138	0.46
12-letter words	55	0.18
13-letter words	17	0.06
14-letter words	2	0.01
Total	29,829	100.00

We realize that Shakespeare resorts most frequently to two-, three-, four- and five-letter words in *Hamlet*, with an average word length of 4.05 letters per word. Note that, on the whole, shorter words are easier and faster to articulate and are, on average, more frequent and more common than longer words. This might give us a hint as to one of the goals Shakespeare was probably aiming at with *Hamlet*: a vivid and dynamic play with a lot of action and, probably, one that was also easy to understand and accessible to most readers.

Not only researchers but also language teachers can benefit from frequency lists. Suppose a teacher of English is interested in presenting not only lists of words but also word clusters, that is, words which are repeatedly found together in each others' company. They represent a tight relationship, like multi-word units or groups or phrases. Language is phrasal and textual. Words keep company: the extreme example is an idiom, where they are bound tightly to each other, but all words have a tendency to cluster together with certain others. This teacher, then, produces a frequency list of two-word clusters, extracted from real English texts for his teaching purposes. He chooses Lewis Carroll's *Alice's Adventures in Wonderland*.[5] Table 5.16 displays the thirty most common two-word clusters.

Many of the two-word clusters are mere repetitions of very common syntagmatic clusters: *of the, in a, in the, and the, at the*, and so on. However, some clusters introduce new vocabulary: *Mock Turtle, the Gryphon, the Hatter, the Duchess*, and so on. Others introduce collocation patterns: *went on, to herself, said to, out of*, and so on.

From this data it becomes apparent that the most frequent clusters are probably less interesting as very common syntagmatic clusters and many frequent proper names occur in them. More interesting word patterning can be found among less frequent clusters. Look at Table 5.17; it displays three-word clusters within the frequency range 9–7.

Here we find some very useful collocations that could be presented in the foreign language classroom: *as well as, join the dance, seemed to be, the end of, at any rate, a good deal, and looked at, back to the, in the distance* and *out of sight*. Additionally, four-word clusters can also contribute very positively to finding real collocations for pedagogical purposes (Table 5.18): *a minute or two, in a tone of, (the) moral of that (is), I beg your pardon* and *in a great hurry*.

5.1.1 Stoplist

Frequency lists show the number of times that each word appears in a text or corpus so that the lexical content of different texts or corpora can be compared. In short, frequency lists show the contents of texts or corpora. However, the main problem with these plain lists is that despite the comparatively high occurrence frequencies of very common words such as *a, the, of, in*, and so on, within most texts or corpora, these are unlikely to provide conclusive evidence on the vocabulary or lexis of texts

---

5.　http://fiction.eserver.org/novels/alice_in_wonderland.html

Table 5.16 Two-word clusters in *Alice's Adventures in Wonderland*.

Two-word cluster	Frequency	%
SAID THE	207	0.78
OF THE	129	0.48
SAID ALICE	115	0.43
IN A	96	0.36
AND THE	83	0.31
IN THE	77	0.29
IT WAS	75	0.28
TO THE	69	0.26
THE QUEEN	65	0.24
AS SHE	61	0.23
THE KING	60	0.23
A LITTLE	59	0.22
SHE HAD	59	0.22
AT THE	58	0.22
SHE WAS	55	0.21
AND SHE	53	0.2
MOCK TURTLE	53	0.2
THE GRYPHON	52	0.2
THE MOCK	52	0.2
TO BE	52	0.2
THE HATTER	51	0.19
WENT ON	48	0.18
TO HERSELF	45	0.17
YOU KNOW	45	0.17
SAID TO	39	0.15
OUT OF	37	0.14
THE DUCHESS	37	0.14
THERE WAS	35	0.13
ON THE	34	0.13
SHE SAID	34	0.13

or corpora. These are words which, on the basis of their high frequency alone, would be found in most texts or corpora.

Suppose we want to examine the content words of our sample text above. Simple frequency lists would just generate lists of the sort displayed in Tables 5.1 to 5.4. The first five most common words – *the, and, of, in* and *to* – contribute little to our knowledge about the content of the text.

One solution is to use a *stoplist*. Simply, a stoplist is a filter module that takes out certain commonly occurring words based on the hypothesis that they appear frequently in all texts or corpora and that their appearance contributes nothing, or very little, to explaining the content or topic of a text or corpora.

The words usually contained in a stoplist are the so-called closed-class items. The set of items is *closed* in the sense that they cannot normally be extended by the

Table 5.17 Three-word clusters in *Alice's Adventures in Wonderland.*

Three-word cluster	Frequency	%
AS WELL AS	9	0.03
IN A LOW	9	0.03
JOIN THE DANCE	9	0.03
SEEMED TO BE	9	0.03
THE END OF	9	0.03
AT ANY RATE	8	0.03
IN A VERY	8	0.03
SAID THE DORMOUSE	8	0.03
SAID THE MOUSE	8	0.03
SHE COULD NOT	8	0.03
THAT IT WAS	8	0.03
THAT SHE WAS	8	0.03
THE KING SAID	8	0.03
A GOOD DEAL	7	0.03
AND LOOKED AT	7	0.03
BACK TO THE	7	0.03
I DON'T KNOW	7	0.03
IN THE DISTANCE	7	0.03
IT WOULD BE	7	0.03
OUT OF SIGHT	7	0.03

Table 5.18 Four-word clusters in *Alice's Adventures in Wonderland.*

Four-word cluster	Frequency	%
SAID THE MOCK TURTLE	19	0.07
SHE SAID TO HERSELF	16	0.06
A MINUTE OR TWO	11	0.04
SAID THE MARCH HARE	7	0.03
AS WELL AS SHE	6	0.02
IN A TONE OF	6	0.02
MORAL OF THAT IS	6	0.02
THE MORAL OF THAT	6	0.02
WELL AS SHE COULD	6	0.02
AND THE MORAL OF	5	0.02
AS SHE SAID THIS	5	0.02
I BEG YOUR PARDON	5	0.02
IN A GREAT HURRY	5	0.02
THE LITTLE GOLDEN KEY	5	0.02
THE POOR LITTLE THING	5	0.02

creation of additional members, that is, the inventory of subject personal pronouns is fixed (*I, you, he, she, it, we, you* and *they*) and cannot be extended by adding new items. These items are said to constitute a system in that they are both reciprocally exclusive and reciprocally defining.[6]

Consequently, items included in a stoplist (examples in brackets) are:

- pronouns (*he*)
- determiners (*a, the*)
- prepositions (*in, for*)
- conjunctions (*and, or*)
- auxiliary and modal verbs (*be, will*)
- demonstratives (*this, those*).

In addition, some stoplists also include:

- contractions (*aren't*)
- abbreviations (*etc.*)
- high frequency nouns (*people*)
- high frequency verbs (*go*)
- high frequency adjectives (*good*)
- high frequency adverbs (*again*)
- high frequency predeterminers (*all*)
- high frequency numerals (*one, two*).

The aim of the stoplist is to display only those words that determine the content or topic of a text or corpus, that is, content words – nouns, verbs, adjectives and adverbs. This clearly optimizes the lists for examining only open-class items. Table 5.19 displays a fragment of a stoplist, showing the first hundred stoplist items.

To show its usefulness, if we filter out the stoplist items of our sample text, we obtain the following frequency list (Table 5.20), containing only content words that are very much oriented towards the real topic of the text: *Election Day*.

A more ambitious example using stoplists might be to compare the content words used in two different texts or corpora, for example, in two plays by Shakespeare: *Hamlet* and *Julius Caesar*. Table 5.21 displays and compares the thirty most frequent content words extracted from *Hamlet* and *Julius Caesar*.

A quick glance at the content words reveals some coincidences in the topic of both plays:

- love: *heart* and *love*
- death: *dead* (Hamlet); *fear* and *blood* (J. Caesar)
- religion: *god(s)* and *lord*; *pray* (Hamlet).

---

6. See Quirk and Greenbaum (1985: 19).

Table 5.19 Extract of a stoplist.

A	ALREADY	APPRECIATE	BECOMING	C'S
A'S	ALSO	APPROPRIATE	BEEN	CAME
ABLE	ALTHOUGH	ARE	BEFORE	CAN
ABOUT	ALWAYS	AREN'T	BEFOREHAND	CAN'T
ABOVE	AM	AROUND	BEHIND	CANNOT
ACCORDING	AMONG	AS	BEING	CANT
ACCORDINGLY	AMONGST	ASIDE	BELIEVE	CAUSE
ACROSS	AN	ASK	BELOW	CAUSES
ACTUALLY	AND	ASKING	BESIDE	CERTAIN
AFTER	ANOTHER	ASSOCIATED	BESIDES	CERTAINLY
AFTERWARDS	ANY	AT	BEST	CHANGES
AGAIN	ANYBODY	AVAILABLE	BETTER	CLEARLY
AGAINST	ANYHOW	AWAY	BETWEEN	CO
AIN'T	ANYONE	AWFULLY	BEYOND	COM
ALL	ANYTHING	B	BOTH	COME
ALLOW	ANYWAY	BE	BRIEF	COMES
ALLOWS	ANYWAYS	BECAME	BUT	CONCERNING
ALMOST	ANYWHERE	BECAUSE	BY	CONSEQUENTLY
ALONE	APART	BECOME	C	CONSIDER
ALONG	APPEAR	BECOMES	C'MON	CONSIDERING

Table 5.20 Frequency list of content words.

Word	Frequency	Word	Frequency	Word	Frequency
ACCORDANCE	1	DISTRIBUTE	1	OCCASIONAL	1
ACTION	1	EAGER	1	PAMPHLETS	1
AGES	1	EARLY	1	PICK	1
APPLICABLE	1	ELECTION	1	PLACES	2
ASSIST	1	ELECTIONS	2	POLLING	2
BACKGROUNDS	1	ENJOY	1	REGULATIONS	1
BEGINS	1	ENSURING	1	RISE	1
CAFETERIAS	1	EXCITEMENT	1	ROLLS	1
CAMPAIGN	1	FLYERS	1	SCHOOL	1
CENTERS	1	GYMNASIUMS	1	SERVE	1
CHAOS	1	HAND	1	SETTING	1
CHECKING	1	HARD	1	SIGNS	1
CITIES	1	HEADQUARTERS	1	STATES	1
COMMUNITY	1	HOPE	1	TOWNS	1
CONDUCTED	1	INFLUENCING	1	UNITED	1
CULMINATION	1	LAWS	1	VILLAGES	1
DAWN	1	LEND	1	VOLUNTEERS	3
DAY	3	LINE	1	VOTER	1
DECISIONS	1	MACHINES	1	VOTERS'	1
DEDICATED	1	MONTHS	1	VOTING	1
DEMOCRACY	1	NOVEMBER	1	WORK	1

Table 5.21 Frequency list of content words: *Hamlet* versus *Julius Caesar*.

Hamlet		Julius Caesar	
Content word	Frequency	Content word	Frequency
LORD	225	CÆSAR	182
HAMLET	78	BRUTUS	144
SIR	75	CASSIUS	75
LOVE	68	MEN	65
KING	67	ANTONY	64
SPEAK	63	MAN	56
GIVE	59	LORD	47
MAKE	55	DAY	46
FATHER	53	NIGHT	41
MAN	52	SPEAK	41
NIGHT	46	NOBLE	39
TIME	46	ROME	38
HEAVEN	45	CÆSAR'S	37
MINE	40	HEAR	37
MOTHER	39	GIVE	35
DEATH	38	LOVE	34
PLAY	35	STAND	34
GOD	34	MARK	32
SOUL	34	DEATH	29
HEAR	33	FEAR	29
LAERTES	33	HAND	29
LIFE	33	HEART	27
HORATIO	31	GREAT	26
HEART	30	MAKE	26
MADE	30	CASCA	25
DEAD	29	GODS	25
PRAY	29	TIME	25
HOLD	28	BLOOD	24
LEAVE	28	FRIENDS	24
DEAR	27	ART	23

But also differences:

• in Hamlet, family plays an important role: *father* and *mother*
• the word *love* is more prominent in Hamlet than in Julius Caesar.

Of course, these extracts are merely used to exemplify the issue and no conclusions can be arrived at without the use and contrast of more exhaustive lists and the use of descriptive and inferential statistics.

5.2 Keywords

Excluding closed-class items from frequency lists significantly improves the output of text-specific vocabulary. However, we can do even better. When comparing texts, such as the example above on *Hamlet* and *Julius Caesar*, it is easy to find similarities, when the same instances are found in both texts, or differences, when some instances only occur in one of the texts. The problem is sometimes found when examining similarities. Think of the co-occurrence of the word *love* in *Hamlet* and *Julius Caesar*. Although it seems obvious from the data that *love* is more prominent in *Hamlet* compared to *Julius Caesar*, we cannot draw any supported conclusion. We would necessarily have to resort to statistics to analyse the keywords present in the texts.

To put it succinctly, keywords are word forms that occur unusually frequently in a text of interest. This frequency is compared to the keyword's frequency in some kind of reference corpus. The reference-corpus wordlist should be big enough to be able to work out significant differences. The identification of such keywords will help to characterize the subject matter or genre of the text. For example, a text concerned with legal issues would contain significantly more legal terms, such as *act, article, penalty, delinquency*, and so on than a general corpus.

Some concordancing tools, such as WordSmith[7], are able to identify keywords, comparing the frequency wordlist of the text, play or corpus being analysed with a reference corpus, such as the BNC. Table 5.22 displays the top twenty-five keywords of one of Barack Obama's speeches on economy[8] contrasted with the BNC. Note that we have also filtered out all closed-class items.

A glance at Table 5.22 reveals many economy terms: *tax, economy, debt, foreclosure, homeowners, giveaways, trillion, jobs, millions, CEOS, bills, invert, workers.* Note that each keyword has a:

- frequency index: number of occurrences in the text (i.e. Obama's speech)
- percentage: relative frequency within the text
- frequency index in the reference corpus (RC; i.e. BNC)
- percentage: relative frequency within the reference corpus
- keyness: this measure compares the relative frequencies of a word in a text versus a reference corpus. A word that is frequent in one text and rare in the reference corpus gets a high keyness value.

The keyness calculation can be performed either by using the classic chi-square test of significance with Yates's correction for a 2×2 table (see section 3.3.3), or Ted Dunning's *log-likelihood* test[9], which gives a better estimate of keyness, especially when contrasting long texts or a whole genre against a reference corpus.

---

7. A demo version is available at www.lexically.net/wordsmith
8. www.nytimes.com/2008/06/09/us/politics/09transcript-obama.html
9. See Dunning (1993).

Table 5.22 Top twenty-five economy keywords used by Barack Obama.

Key word	Frequency	%	RC frequency	RC %	Keyness	p
MCCAIN	18	0.39	22		304.68	0.0000
AMERICANS	18	0.39	2,745		142.88	0.0000
BUSH	15	0.33	3,367		107.59	0.0000
TAX	22	0.48	16,339	0.02	106.30	0.0000
ECONOMY	19	0.42	10,365	0.01	103.16	0.0000
DEBT	15	0.33	5,400		93.63	0.0000
FORECLOSURE	6	0.13	34		86.08	0.0000
FAMILIES	14	0.31	8,222		73.99	0.0000
HOMEOWNERS	5	0.11	97		60.01	0.0000
GIVEAWAYS	4	0.09	19		58.68	0.0000
PRESIDENT	14	0.31	15,747	0.02	56.49	0.0000
COUNTRY	16	0.35	27,959	0.03	51.39	0.0000
AMERICA	11	0.24	8,934		51.23	0.0000
AFFORD	9	0.20	4,392		50.80	0.0000
STRUGGLING	7	0.15	1,811		48.24	0.0000
FACING	8	0.18	3,834		45.44	0.0000
TRILLION	4	0.09	122		44.47	0.0000
JOHN	15	0.33	30,968	0.03	43.61	0.0000
JOBS	10	0.22	9,596		43.37	0.0000
FISCAL	6	0.13	1,320		43.26	0.0000
MILLIONS	7	0.15	2,638		43.05	0.0000
CEOS	3	0.07	20		42.14	0.0000
BILLS	7	0.15	3,015		41.22	0.0000
INVEST	6	0.13	1,575		41.17	0.0000
WORKERS	11	0.24	14,614	0.01	40.93	0.0000

- probability value: the *p*-value is that used in standard chi-square and other statistical tests. This value ranges from 0 to 1. A value of 0.01 suggests a 1 per cent danger of being wrong in claiming a relationship: 0.05 would give a 5 per cent danger of error. In the social sciences a 5 per cent risk is usually considered acceptable.

Let us now focus on one keyword from Obama's speech. The word *tax* occurs twenty-two times, comprising 0.48 per cent of all word occurrences. Its frequency in the reference corpus is 16,339, comprising just 0.02 of all word occurrences. The keyness value is 106.30, which is significant at the 0.05 per cent level.

To calculate the *log-likelihood*, we first need to construct a contingency table as shown in Table 5.23, where a = observed occurrences of word w in the text, b = observed occurrences of word w in the reference corpus, c = number of words in the text, and d = number of words in reference corpus.

Table 5.23 Contingency table.

	Text	Corpus	Total
Frequency of word	a	b	a + b
Frequency of other words	c − a	d − b	c + d − a − b
Total	c	d	c + b

Table 5.24 gives the observed values.

Table 5.24 Contingency table with observed values.

	Text	Corpus	Total
Frequency of word	22	16,339	16,361
Frequency of other words	4,507	99,983,661	99,988,168
Total	4,529	100,000,000	100,004,529

Values *a* and *b* are the observed values, and we need to calculate the expected values, just as we did for the chi-square, using the following formula:

$$E = \frac{\sum row \times \sum column}{\sum cells}$$

Thus, we get the expected values shown in Table 5.25.

Table 5.25 Contingency table with expected values.

	Text	Corpus	Total
Frequency of word	0.74	16,360.26	16,361
Frequency of other words	4,528.26	99,983,639.74	99,988,168
Total	4,529	100,000,000	100,004,529

We can then calculate the log-likelihood (*LL*) value according to this formula:

$$LL = 2\left\{\left[a \times \ln\left(\frac{a}{E_1}\right)\right] + \left[b \times \ln\left(\frac{b}{E_2}\right)\right]\right\}$$

Which when applied to our *tax* example gives:

$$LL = 2\left\{\left[22 \times \ln\left(\frac{22}{0.74}\right)\right] + \left[16,339 \times \ln\left(\frac{16,339}{16,360.26}\right)\right]\right\} = 106.74$$

The higher the *LL*-value, the more significant the difference is between two frequency scores. An *LL*-value of 3.8 or higher is significant at the level of $p < 0.05$ and an *LL*-value of 6.6 or higher is significant at $p < 0.01$. Consequently, we conclude that the word *tax* is a keyword in Barack Obama's economy speech and, therefore, a text-specific vocabulary item.

Keyness values can be positive or negative: positive keyness means that a specific keyword occurs more often in the text or corpus under investigation than would be expected by chance in comparison with the reference corpus. Negative keyness indicates that a keyword occurs less often in the text or corpus under investigation than would be expected by chance in comparison with the reference corpus.

5.3 Text annotation

The analysis of word meaning is complicated by the fact that many word forms and lemmas in English have multiple grammatical functions. For example, the word *to* can be used either as an infinitive marker or a preposition. When the words in a corpus have not been annotated for their grammatical categories or other type of linguistic information, the corpus is referred to as untagged or unannotated. Obviously, the utility of the corpus increases when it has been tagged or annotated, making it no longer a body of text where linguistic information is implicitly present, but one which may be considered a repository of linguistic information. This implicit information can be made explicit through the process of adding information. For example, the form *is* contains the implicit part-of-speech information: third person singular present tense verb, but it is not made explicit in the text or corpus. However, in a tagged or annotated corpus the form *is* might appear as *is_VAuxZ*, with the code *VAuxZ* indicating that it is a third person singular present tense (*Z*) form of an auxiliary verb (*VAux*). Such types of annotation allow researchers to obtain more sophisticated information about the language data contained in the corpus.

Frequency lists based on untagged corpora are limited in usefulness, because they do not tell us which grammatical uses are common or rare. In fact, we might consider *to* as a preposition to be a different word from *to* as an infinitive marker; from this perspective, a list from an untagged corpus cannot even tell us the frequencies of words. To determine which occurrences of *to* are prepositions, we must look at the forms in context, determine their grammatical category and keep count. While such a solution is not overwhelming for small texts, it would be too time-consuming or impossible with large corpora, such as the BNC. A more efficient solution is to use tagged corpora, that is a corpus in which each word has been coded or tagged for its grammatical category. Using a tagged corpus, we can do automatic frequency counts for each grammatical word separately. Table 5.26 shows a section of a frequency list of the twenty most frequent English lemmas with their parts-of-speech and frequencies. With this information from the tagged BNC, we can go on exploring the occurrences of *to* in more detail, looking at the distribution of its preposition and infinitive-marker forms and comparing them.

Table 5.26 Top twenty English lemmas with POS-tags.

Lemma	POS	Frequency	Lemma	POS	Frequency
THE	det	61,873	I	pron	8,875
BE	v	42,277	FOR	prep	8,412
OF	prep	29,414	THAT	conj	7,308
AND	conj	26,829	YOU	pron	6,954
A	det	21,264	HE	pron	6,810
IN	prep	18,126	WITH	prep	6,575
TO	inf.-marker	16,209	ON	prep	6,475
HAVE	v	13,655	DO	v	5,596
IT	pron	10,892	BY	prep	5,096
TO	prep	9,175	AT	prep	4,790

So *to* is used altogether 16,209 + 9,175 = 25,384 times, with the following distribution (Table 5.27):

Table 5.27 Frequency distributions of *to*.

	Frequency	%
Infinitive marker	16,209	63.86
Preposition	9,175	36.14
Total	25,384	100.00

Clearly, the probability of finding *to* functioning as an infinitive marker is nearly twice that of finding it as a preposition. This simple analysis would have been extremely tedious and time-consuming if we had not had a part-of-speech tagged corpus at our disposal. These types of annotation make it faster and easier to retrieve and analyse information about the language contained in the corpus.

5.3.1 Types of annotation

Apart from part-of-speech annotation, there are also other very useful kinds of linguistic annotation. Most of these annotations or taggings involve the attachment of special codes or tags to words in order to indicate particular features. In the section that follows, we shall briefly review some of the main types of annotation.

We have already introduced two types of annotation: part-of-speech annotation (Table 5.26) and lemmatization (Tables 5.9 and 5.10). Part-of-speech tagging is probably the most basic type of linguistic corpus annotation. It is particularly useful because it increases the specificity of data retrieval from corpora, and is essential for more in-depth analysis.

It is very common to combine various types of information within the same frequency lists. Table 5.28 displays the first sixty alphabetically ordered lemmas of the BNC. Note that the frequency ranking and word class have been added.

Table 5.28 Lemmas in the BNC: alphabetically ordered frequency list.

Frequency order	Frequency within BNC	Lemma	POS	Frequency order	Frequency within BNC	Lemma	POS
5	2,186,369	A	det	3,707	1,842	ACCENT	n
2,107	4,249	ABANDON	v	507	20,373	ACCEPT	v
5,204	1,110	ABBEY	n	2,351	3,647	ACCEPTABLE	a
966	10,468	ABILITY	n	2,895	2,702	ACCEPTANCE	n
321	30,454	ABLE	a	997	10,099	ACCESS	n
6,277	809	ABNORMAL	a	4,516	1,389	ACCESS	v
3,862	1,744	ABOLISH	v	4,024	1,637	ACCESSIBLE	a
5,085	1,154	ABOLITION	n	1,207	8,374	ACCIDENT	n
4,341	1,471	ABORTION	n	3,418	2,065	ACCOMMODATE	v
179	52,561	ABOUT	adv	2,085	4,305	ACCOMMODATION	n
69	144,554	ABOUT	prep	1,892	4,885	ACCOMPANY	v
3,341	2,139	ABOVE	a	5,648	968	ACCOMPLISH	v
942	10,719	ABOVE	adv	5,723	947	ACCORD	n
786	12,889	ABOVE	prep	5,613	976	ACCORD	v
2,236	3,941	ABROAD	adv	3,443	2,042	ACCORDANCE	n
5,106	1,146	ABRUPTLY	adv	646	15,722	ACCORDING	prep
1,602	5,949	ABSENCE	n	3,214	2,288	ACCORDINGLY	adv
4,266	1,504	ABSENT	a	536	19,260	ACCOUNT	n
2,435	3,489	ABSOLUTE	a	1,562	6,130	ACCOUNT	v
1,651	5,782	ABSOLUTELY	adv	5,011	1,184	ACCOUNTABILITY	n
2,907	2,684	ABSORB	v	3,289	2,199	ACCOUNTANT	n
5,769	932	ABSORPTION	n	4,018	1,640	ACCOUNTING	a
4,083	1,605	ABSTRACT	a	5,279	1,084	ACCUMULATE	v
5,655	966	ABSURD	a	5,570	987	ACCUMULATION	n
2,461	3,428	ABUSE	n	3,934	1,692	ACCURACY	n
4,570	1,364	ABUSE	v	2,743	2,928	ACCURATE	a
1,974	4,594	ACADEMIC	a	4,436	1,423	ACCURATELY	adv
5,342	1,059	ACADEMIC	n	5,088	1,153	ACCUSATION	n
5,453	1,025	ACADEMY	n	2,190	4,047	ACCUSE	v
5,188	1,114	ACCELERATE	v	4,521	1,387	ACCUSED	a

Other sorting possibilities can include all derived or inflected word forms of a lemma (Table 5.29).

Metalinguistic data, such as part-of-speech tags, can also be used to extract information on the composition of texts or corpora regarding grammatical categories, for example extracting only prepositions (Table 5.30), or the forty most frequently used nouns (lemmas) in English (Table 5.31).

Sometimes part-of-speech tags or morphological information is not enough and researchers want to explore syntactic structures and/or syntactic functions. Texts or corpora with syntactic labels are known as *treebank* or *parsed* corpora. Succinctly, a treebank is a text corpus in which each sentence has been parsed, that is, annotated with syntactic structure and/or functions, and where the syntactic structure is commonly represented as a tree structure. Treebanks are often created on top of a corpus that has already been annotated with part-of-speech tags.

Treebanks can be created completely manually, where linguists tag each sentence with syntactic labels, or semi-automatically, by means of a computational tool: a parser. The parser assigns some syntactic labels, which are then checked by linguists. For example, the following is the parsing for the first sentence of our sample text: *The day begins early*:

```
(S  (NP  (DT The)
         (NN day))
    (VP  (VBZ begins)
         (ADVP (ADV early)))
    (. .))
```

Using a treebank, we can search for specific syntactic structures. Figure 5.1 displays some subject-noun phrases found in the Penn Treebank.[10]

```
(NP-SBJ  (DT  The)
         (NN  company))
(NP-SBJ  (DT  The)
         (NN  woman))
(NP-SBJ  (DT  The)
         (NNP Senate))
(NP-SBJ  (NNP Gates))
(NP-SBJ  (NNP President)
         (NNP Reagan))
(NP-SBJ  (PRP She))
(NP-SBJ  (PRP They))
(NP-SBJ  (PRP We))
```

Figure 5.1 Noun phrase samples from the Penn Treebank.

---

10. The Penn Treebank Project: www.cis.upenn.edu/~treebank/home.html

Table 5.29 Lemmas with associated word forms in the BNC.

Lemma	POS	Word form	Frequency per million words	Lemma	POS	Word form	Frequency per million words
A	Det		25,056	ABSENT	Adj	absent	15
		a	21,626	ABSOLUTE	Adj	absolute	35
		an	3,430	ABSOLUTELY	Adv	absolutely	58
ABANDON	Verb		44	ABSORB	Verb		27
		abandon	12			absorb	8
		abandoned	26			absorbed	15
		abandoning	5			absorbing	2
		abandons	1			absorbs	2
ABBEY	NoC		20	ABSTRACT	Adj	abstract	19
		abbey	19	ABUSE	NoC		37
		abbeys	1			abuse	34
ABERDEEN	NoP		14			abuses	3
ABILITY	NoC	Aberdeen	105	ABUSE	Verb		12
		abilities	13			abuse	2
		ability	91			abused	7
ABLE	Adj	able	304			abuses	1
ABOLISH	Verb		20			abusing	2
		abolish	6	AC	NoC		15
		abolished	11			a.c.	8
		abolishes	1			ac	7
		abolishing	2	ACADEMIC	Adj	academic	47

Headword	POS	Form	Frequency
ABOLITION	NoC	abolition	12
ABORTION	NoC		15
		abortion	12
		abortions	3
ABOUT	Adv	about	447
ABOUT	Prep	about	1524
ABOVE	Adj	above	27
ABOVE	Adv	above	94
ABOVE	Prep	above	137
ABROAD	Adv	abroad	39
ABRUPTLY	Adv	abruptly	12
ABSENCE	NoC		60
		absence	58
		absences	2
ACADEMY	NoC		15
		academies	1
		academy	14
ACCELERATE	Verb		10
		accelerate	4
		accelerated	4
		accelerates	1
		accelerating	1
ACCENT	NoC		18
		accent	14
		accents	4

Table 5.30 List of prepositions.

Lemma	POS	Frequency
OF	prep	30,934
IN	prep	19,243
TO	prep	10,393
FOR	prep	8,879
ON	prep	6,807
WITH	prep	6,750
AT	prep	5,342
BY	prep	5,172
FROM	prep	4,345
AS	prep	2,020

Table 5.31 The forty most used English nouns.

Lemma	POS	Frequency	Lemma	POS	Frequency
TIME	n	1,834	COMPANY	n	578
YEAR	n	1,639	PROBLEM	n	565
PEOPLE	n	1,254	SERVICE	n	545
WAY	n	1,126	HAND	n	533
MAN	n	980	PARTY	n	530
DAY	n	927	SCHOOL	n	522
THING	n	776	PLACE	n	515
CHILD	n	710	POINT	n	492
GOVERNMENT	n	669	HOUSE	n	490
PART	n	658	COUNTRY	n	482
LIFE	n	644	WEEK	n	475
CASE	n	636	MEMBER	n	471
WOMAN	n	631	END	n	452
WORK	n	622	WORD	n	438
SYSTEM	n	619	EXAMPLE	n	434
GROUP	n	607	FAMILY	n	428
NUMBER	n	606	FACT	n	422
WORLD	n	591	STATE	n	414
AREA	n	584	PERCENT	n	412
COURSE	n	578	HOME	n	399

There are enormous possibilities for exploiting this resource more fruitfully and exploring the structure of the language. In turn, treebanks and corpora are sometimes enhanced with semantic or other linguistic information.

Regarding semantic annotated corpora, there are two types of semantic annotation: the marking of semantic relationships between items in the text, for example the agents or patients of particular actions; and the marking of semantic features of words in the text, essentially the annotation of word senses in one form or another.

The	00000000
soldiers	23241000
platted	21072000
a	00000000
crown	21110400
of	00000000
thorns	13010000
and	00000000
put	21072000
it	00000000
on	00000000
his	00000000
head	21030000
and	00000000
they	00000000
put	21072000
on	00000000
him	00000000
a	00000000
purple	31241100
robe	21110321

Figure 5.2 Semantic tagged example.

Source: Example extracted from McEnery and Wilson (1996: 51).

There is no general agreement about which semantic features ought to be anno-tated for sense disambiguation or semantic networks. The example above (Figure 5.2) is intended to give the reader an idea of the types of categories used in semantic tagging.

The numerical codes stand for:

00000000	Low content word (and, the, a, of, on, his, etc.)
13010000	Plant life in general
21030000	Body and body parts
21072000	Object-oriented physical activity (e.g. put)
21110321	Men's clothing: outer clothing
21110400	Headgear
23231000	War and conflict: general
31241100	Colour

Aspects of language at the levels of text and discourse are one of the least frequently encountered annotations in corpora. Stenström[11] annotated the London-Lund spoken corpus with sixteen discourse tags. They included categories such as (examples in brackets):

- apologies (sorry, excuse me)
- greetings (hello)
- hedges (kind of, sort of thing)
- politeness (please)
- responses (really, that's right).

Another type of discourse and text linguistic annotation refers to anaphoric annotation, that is, pronoun reference. This annotation scheme co-indexes pronouns and noun phrases (see Figure 5.3).

```
S.1   (0) The state Supreme Court has refused to release
{1 [2 Rahway State Prison 2] inmate 1}} (1 James Scott 1) on
bail .
S.2 (1 The fighter 1) is serving 30-40 years for a 1975 armed
robbery conviction .
S.3 (1 Scott 1) had asked for freedom while <1 he waits for an
appeal decision .
S.4 Meanwhile , [3 <1 his promoter 3] , {{3 Murad Muhammed 3} ,
said Wednesday <3 he netted only $15,250 for (4 [1 Scott 1] 's
nationally televised light heavyweight fight against {5 ranking
contender 5}} (5 Yaqui Lopez 5) last Saturday 4) .
S.5 (4 The fight , in which [1 Scott 1] won a unanimous
decision over (5 Lopez 5) 4) , grossed $135,000 for [6
[3 Muhammed 3] 's firm 6], {{6 Triangle Productions of
Newark 6} , <3 he said .
```

Figure 5.3 Example of anaphoric annotation.

Source: Example extracted from http://ucrel.lancs.ac.uk/annotation.html

The use of the same index 1, 2, ... *n* binds one syntactic constituent to another to which it is coreferential or semantically equivalent. In the following list, *i* represents an arbitrary index:

(i i) OR	
[i...]	enclose a constituent (normally a noun phrase) entering into an equivalence 'chain'
<i	indicates a pronoun with a preceding antecedent

11. See Stenström (1984).

>i   indicates a pronoun with a following antecedent

{{i i}   enclose a noun phrase entering into a copular relationship with a preceding noun phrase

{i i}}   enclose a noun phrase entering into a copular relationship with a following noun phrase

(0)   represents an anaphoric barrier, in effect, the beginning of a new text.

Spoken language corpora can also be transcribed using a form of phonetic transcription. Figure 5.4 shows a sample of the ten-million-word Spoken Dutch Corpus. The corpus can be manipulated by means of a sophisticated software tool COREX, equipped with a browser, a viewer for orthography and annotations, plus a waveform display and audio player, and a search module. The text corpus sequences are aligned with their phonetic transcription and recording.

Prosodic annotation aims to indicate patterns of intonation, stress and pauses in speech. It is a much more difficult type of annotation to achieve than the types discussed above: it cannot be done automatically and requires careful listening by a trained ear. A set of special characters is used to represent prosodic features: stressed syllables, unstressed syllables, and so on. Prosody is considerably more impressionistic than other linguistic levels in corpus annotation. There are sometimes considerable differences among these transcriptions.

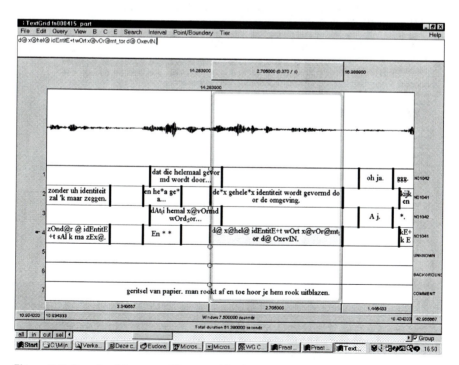

Figure 5.4 Sample of the ten-million-word Spoken Dutch Corpus.

```
9 1a 1  10 1 1 B   11 1((I`ve been)) ^waiting to c\ontact#        /
9 1a 1  20 1 1 B   11 1[dhi:] ^s\/ecretary#                       /
9 1a 1  30 1 2 B   11 1^of _[dhi:] !British . [@:m] 'Society for  /
9 1a 1  30 1 1 B   11 1'Nineteenth 'Century :St\udies#            /
9 1a 1  40 1 1 B   11 1^there`s [ei] com"!m\/ittee 'meeting#      /
9 1a 1  50 1 2 B   11 1in the ^\/English de'partment . [@:m] {this /
9 1a 1  50 1 1 B   11 1^morning at _ten o`cl/ock#}# .             /
9 1a 1  60 1 1 B   11 1and I`m a ^member of the comm/ittee#       /
```

Figure 5.5 Example of prosodic annotation from the London-Lund Corpus.

Note: For more details see www.helsinki.fi/varieng/CoRD/corpora/LLC/index.html

Clearly, corpus annotation enriches a corpus in order to aid the process of exploitation, as it makes explicit what is implicit; it does not introduce new information. For any level of linguistic information (lemmas, parts-of-speech, semantic annotation, discourse tags, phonetic and/or prosodic annotations) encoded explicitly in a corpus, the range of information that a linguist can extract from the corpus, and speed at which he can do so, increases exponentially. Figure 5.6 gives an example of a

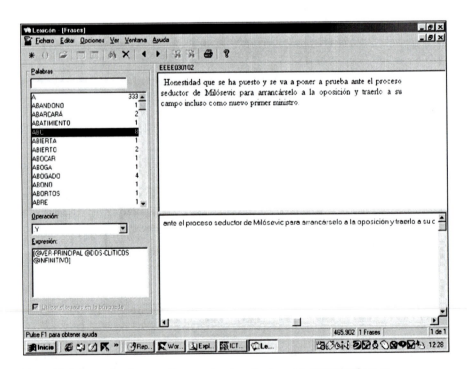

Figure 5.6 Example of a complex search using the Spanish CUMBRE Corpus.

complex search using a sub-corpus of the Spanish CUMBRE Corpus,[12] according to the following search criteria: (1) main verb, (2) in infinitive form and (3) two clitics. The result is that just a single item meets all these conditions in the 465,902-token sub-corpus, namely: *arrancárselo*.

5.4 Comparing wordlists

The comparison of two or more wordlists can be of special interest for researchers wanting to deepen their analyses in studying which words are used across different linguistic domains and which of these words are domain specific. Similarly, investigators in diachronic approaches to the study of language might wish to know which words were most prominently used in different periods of time. Of course, the usefulness of wordlist comparison extends also to other areas, such as stylistic comparisons. For example, we may be studying several versions of a news item, a novel, or different translations of a novel in which one version uses *kill* and another version uses *murder*, *slaughter*, *assassinate* and *execute*.

Some concordance software, for example WordSmith, offers the possibility of wordlist comparison. These applications compare all the words in two or more lists and report on their total occurrence (in all texts) and partial occurrences (in each text), including the number of texts each of these words occurs in.

Table 5.32 shows a fragment of the list of content words occurring in *Hamlet* over the five acts. Additionally, information is supplied on the total occurrences and the number of acts each word occurs in. For example, *abominably* occurs a single time in Act 1, and *aboard* occurs three times in two acts (Act 1 and 4), twice in Act 1 and once in Act 4.

If the information is ordered by *Acts* and *Total*, we can discover which high frequency words are more evenly distributed throughout the acts (for more information on dispersion see section 5.5.3). Table 5.33 displays the fact that the word *lord* is the most frequent word present in all five acts: it is particularly frequent in Acts 1, 2 and 3, but less so in Acts 4 and 5.

Alternatively, if we do not have such sophisticated applications at our disposal, we can still perform wordlist comparisons. For practical reasons and to illustrate the issue, first, let us take two fictitious play-texts: This is the first text:

A B C D E A F B G F H

And this is the second one:

A B C I J A K B L K L M

---

12. A twenty-million-word corpus of contemporary Spanish.

Table 5.32 Comparing content words across *Hamlet.*

Word	Total	Acts	Act 1	Act 2	Act 3	Act 4	Act 5
ABATE	1	1	0	0	0	1	0
ABATEMENTS	1	1	0	0	0	1	0
ABHORRED	1	1	0	0	0	0	1
ABILITY	1	1	0	0	0	0	1
ABOARD	3	2	2	0	0	1	0
ABOMINABLY	1	1	0	0	1	0	0
ABRIDGMENT	1	1	0	1	0	0	0
ABROAD	1	1	1	0	0	0	0
ABSENT	1	1	0	0	0	0	1
ABSOLUTE	2	1	0	0	0	0	2
ABSTINENCE	1	1	0	0	1	0	0
ABSTRACTS	1	1	0	1	0	0	0
ABSURD	2	2	1	0	1	0	0
ABUS'D	1	1	1	0	0	0	0
ABUSE	1	1	0	0	0	1	0
ABUSES	1	1	0	1	0	0	0
ACCENT	2	2	0	1	1	0	0
ACCESS	1	1	0	1	0	0	0
ACCIDENT	3	2	0	0	2	1	0
ACCIDENTAL	1	1	0	0	0	0	1

Table 5.33 Comparing content words across *Hamlet*: ordered by distribution across acts.

Word	Total	Acts	Act 1	Act 2	Act 3	Act 4	Act 5
LORD	225	5	56	61	51	26	31
GOOD	110	5	20	29	22	21	18
HAMLET	78	5	19	7	11	18	23
SIR	75	5	3	13	13	13	33
LOVE	68	5	8	13	28	11	8
KING	67	5	14	10	13	18	12
SPEAK	63	5	27	8	14	7	7
GIVE	59	5	13	8	15	12	11
MAKE	55	5	8	11	19	7	10
MAN	52	5	10	14	9	9	10
NIGHT	46	5	22	7	9	6	2
TIME	46	5	10	11	10	6	9
HEAVEN	45	5	22	6	11	3	3
MOTHER	39	5	4	1	24	8	2
DEATH	38	5	6	4	5	16	7
PLAY	35	5	2	7	19	1	6
GOD	34	5	7	11	4	9	3
SOUL	34	5	8	4	14	5	3
HEAR	33	5	9	5	10	3	6
LIFE	33	5	7	4	9	7	6

We start by producing the frequency lists for both corpora, giving for text 1:

A	2
B	2
C	1
D	1
E	1
F	2
G	1
H	1

And for text 2:

A	2
B	2
C	1
I	1
J	1
K	2
L	2
M	1

Now if we merge both lists into a single list[13] and produce a meta-frequency list from the merged one, we get the results shown in Table 5.34.

Table 5.34 Merging two frequency lists and obtaining a meta-frequency list.

List 1 + List 2			Meta list	
	A	2	A	2
	B	2	B	2
	C	1	C	2
List 1	D	1	D	1
	E	1	E	1
	F	2	F	1
	G	1	G	1
	H	1	H	1
	A	2	I	1
	B	2	J	1
	C	1	K	1
List 2	I	1	L	1
	J	1	M	1
	K	2		
	L	2		
	M	1		

---

13. The actual frequencies within each individual list are normally not considered when producing frequency lists.

Looking at the meta-list we can observe that words have only two possible frequencies: 1 or 2. This is exactly what happened above (Tables 5.32 and 5.33) using more sophisticated concordance software: frequency 1 means that the word occurs in a single text and frequency 2 that the word occurs in both texts. However, this has a drawback as we cannot distinguish to which text words with a frequency of 1 belong. Even sophisticated concordancers are unable to do this. To know in which text the word occurs, we would need to go through the data and check. This information is not shown explicitly.

Let us explore this issue a little further. Obviously, when we have two different wordlists, produced from two different sources (texts or corpora), there are three possibilities: a word may occur either (1) in text 1, (2) in text 2 or (3) in both (Figure 5.7).

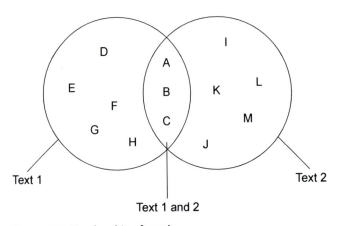

Figure 5.7 Membership of words.

One possibility for expanding and improving our meta-frequency list would be not just to merge frequency lists 1 and 2, but to merge frequency list 1, taken once, with frequency list 2, taken twice. The rationale for this will become clear below. For the moment, note that this produces the following meta-frequency list (Table 5.35).

The resulting meta-frequency list ranges now from 1 to 3:

- Frequency 1 indicates that the word belongs to just text 1; remember that this list has just been counted once: *D*, *E*, *F*, *G* and *H*.
- Frequency 2 means that the word belongs to just text 2, as we counted the frequency list of text 2 twice: *I*, *J*, *K*, *L* and *M*.
- Frequency 3 means that the word is used in both text 1 and text 2: *A*, *B* and *C*.

Of course we can also compare three or more texts. With three texts (1, 2 and 3), there would be three frequency lists produced; one for each text. However, the possible membership would be:

Table 5.35 Merging two frequency lists and obtaining a meta-frequency list.

List 1 + List 2 + List 2			Meta List	
List 1	A	2	A	3
	B	2	B	3
	C	1	C	3
	D	1	D	1
	E	1	E	1
	F	2	F	1
	G	1	G	1
	H	1	H	1
	A	2	I	2
	B	2	J	2
	C	1	K	2
	I	1	L	2
	J	1	M	2
	K	2		
	L	2		
List 2	M	1		
	A	2		
	B	2		
	C	1		
	I	1		
	J	1		
	K	2		
	L	2		
	M	1		

- text 1
- text 2
- text 3
- text 1 and 2
- text 1 and 3
- text 2 and 3
- text 1, 2 and 3.

This gives seven possible memberships altogether and, consequently, the frequency range in our meta-frequency list would need to range from 1 to 7. So if 1 stands for membership in text 1, and 2 for membership in text 2, we would need to duplicate the frequency list of text 2. Frequency 3 would indicate membership in 1 and 2, as the frequency list of text 1 is just counted once and the frequency list of text 2 twice. Frequency 4 would stand for membership in text 3, which in turn would mean that the frequency list of text 3 needs to be copied four times, not three times. Next, frequency 5 shows membership in text 1 and text 3. Frequency 6 indicates membership in text 2 and 3 and finally, frequency 7 membership in all three texts. This is more easily visualized on a *Venn Diagram* (Figure 5.8).

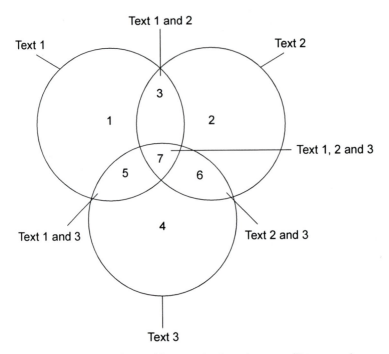

Figure 5.8 Membership and frequencies for a three wordlist comparison.

Let us illustrate this with three play-texts: text 1: *A A C E E G*; text 2: *B C C F G G*; and text 3: *D D E E F G*. We shall produce the frequency lists for each text. For text 1 we obtain:

A	2
C	1
E	2
G	1

Text 2:

B	1
C	2
F	1
G	2

And text 3:

D	2
E	2
F	1
G	1

We now count the frequency list of text 1 once, of text 2 twice and of text 3 four times. The resulting merged list and meta-list are presented in Table 5.36.

Table 5.36 Merging three frequency lists and obtaining a meta-frequency list.

List 1 + (2 × List 2) + (4 × List 3)			Meta List	
List 1	A	2	A	1
	C	1	B	2
	E	2	C	3
	G	1	D	4
	B	1	E	5
	C	2	F	6
	F	1	G	7
List 2	G	2		
	B	1		
	C	2		
	F	1		
	G	2		
List 3	D	2		
	E	2		
	F	1		
	G	1		
	D	2		
	E	2		
	F	1		
	G	1		
	D	2		
	E	2		
	F	1		
	G	1		
	D	2		
	E	2		
	F	1		
	G	1		

Looking at the meta-frequency list, we see that the frequencies range from 1 to 7, which stand for the following memberships:

- frequency 1 = occurrence in text 1: *A*
- frequency 2 = occurrence in text 2: *B*
- frequency 3 = occurrence in texts 1 and 2: *C*
- frequency 4 = occurrence in text 3: *D*
- frequency 5 = occurrence in texts 1 and 3: *E*
- frequency 6 = occurrence in texts 2 and 3: *F*
- frequency 7 = occurrence in texts 1, 2 and 3: *G*

More generally, we can compare as many frequency lists as we want to. The number of times each list needs to be taken is calculated in the base of 2. That is, for two texts, we need to take the frequency list of one of the texts once ($2^0 = 1$) and the other frequency list twice ($2^1 = 2$). For three texts, we would need to take list 1 once ($2^0 = 1$), list 2 twice ($2^1 = 2$) and list 3 four times ($2^2 = 4$). Table 5.37 gives the number of times each frequency list needs to be counted, depending on the number of lists in the comparison.

Table 5.37 Comparing up to six different wordlists.

Lists compared	List 6 2^5	List 5 2^4	List 4 2^3	List 3 2^2	List 2 2^1	List 1 2^0	Frequency range
2					2	1	1–3
3				4	2	1	1–7
4			8	4	2	1	1–15
5		16	8	4	2	1	1–31
6	32	16	8	4	2	1	1–63

For example, imagine that we need to compare four different frequency wordlists, each one corresponding to four different linguistic domains, for example text 1: medicine; text 2: religion; text 3: technology; and text 4: linguistics. We would need to take text 1 once, text 2 twice, text 3 four times and text 4 eight times. The frequencies of the meta-frequency list would range from 1 to 15, indicating the memberships shown in Table 5.38.

Table 5.38 Membership for a four frequency wordlist comparison.

Frequency	Membership			
	Medicine	Religion	Technology	Linguistics
1	X			
2		X		
3	X	X		
4			X	
5	X		X	
6		X	X	
7	X	X	X	
8				X
9	X			X
10		X		X
11	X	X		X
12			X	X
13	X		X	X
14		X	X	X
15	X	X	X	X

5.5 Frequency distributions

The more a linguistic corpus grows, the fewer new items are encountered and the fewer unexpected cases are to be found. That is, while any linguistic corpus increases linearly in tokens in a completely regular or stable shape, its increase in types, although close to that of tokens at the beginning, starts declining the more the corpus grows, as it contributes fewer new types. The cumulative words (tokens) are distributed linearly, while the cumulative word forms (types) are distributed curvilinearly. Similarly, this fall or gradual decline, as regards types, would be more dramatic with respect to lemmas. Words (tokens), word forms (types) and lemmas follow graphically the slopes shown below, where the tokens represent a linear function and the types and lemmas a kind of parabolic function (Figure 5.9).

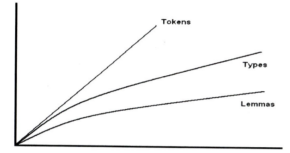

Figure 5.9 Tokens, types and lemmas.

5.5.1 Relationship between tokens and types

To analyse the relationship between tokens, types and lemmas, let us start by taking nine random extracts of 10,000 tokens each from Herman Melville's novel, *Moby Dick*. The basic statistics are given in Table 5.39.

Table 5.39 Basic statistics on *Moby Dick* extracts.

	Tokens	Types	Standardized type–token ratio
Moby Dick (total)	212,538	17,089	46.94
Extract 1	10,000	2,701	47.39
Extract 2	10,000	2,657	48.50
Extract 3	10,000	2,798	45.00
Extract 4	10,000	2,687	47.00
Extract 5	10,000	2,734	47.76
Extract 6	10,000	2,743	46.63
Extract 7	10,000	2,765	46.98
Extract 8	10,000	2,745	47.14
Extract 9	10,000	2,654	47.34

The *type–token ratio* (TTR) is calculated in the following way:

$$TTR = \left(\frac{types}{tokens}\right) \times 100$$

The TTR expresses the ratio between types and tokens in percentages, that is, the percentage of different word forms per 100 words. But TTR varies very widely in accordance with the length of the text which is being studied. A 1,000 word article might have a TTR of 50 per cent; a shorter one might reach 75 per cent; ten million words will probably give a TTR of about 1.75 per cent, and so on. Thus TTR is rather meaningless in most cases, unless we are dealing with a corpus comprising many equal-sized text segments, as TTR is heavily dependent on text length: shorter texts exhibit higher TTRs while longer texts have lower TTRs. However, we are normally dealing with texts of different lengths and the conventional TTR will not help much. Instead, some concordance software, for example WordSmith, computes an alternative TTR, that is, the standardized TTR (STTR), where a new TTR is calculated every *n* words[14] until it reaches the end of the text or corpus, and the average TTR is computed out of all partial TTRs.

Now, with the data of the ten 10,000-token extracts (in this example we can use STTR or TTR, irrespectively), we can examine how the types grow in Melville's novel. Again, we then randomly take one of the ten extracts and start adding a new extract to it, and calculate its STTR again. This will produce a first chunk of 10,000 tokens, a second one of 20,000 tokens, a third one of 30,000 tokens and so on, until we get the final chunk of 100,000 words. For each chunk we compute the number of types (Table 5.40).

Table 5.40 Type-growing in *Moby Dick.*

Tokens	Types	STTR
10,000	2,743	46.63
20,000	4,232	46.94
30,000	5,287	47.04
40,000	6,301	46.88
50,000	7,205	46.71
60,000	8,009	47.07
70,000	8,809	47,66
80,000	9,532	46.52
90,000	10,329	46.82
100,000	11,013	47.06

A visual display of the data reveals how the number of types evolves when increasing gradually by 10,000 words each time, until it reaches its full 100,000-word

---

14. By default n = 1,000 tokens.

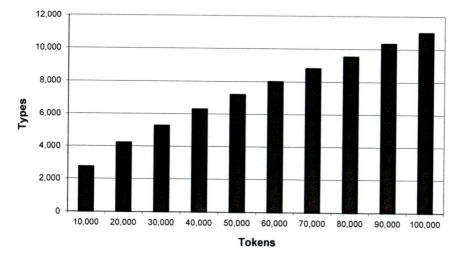

Figure 5.10 Type-token relationship in *Moby Dick*.

extent. Figure 5.10 and Table 5.41 show how *Moby Dick* grows from 2,743 types, with 10,000 tokens, up to 11,013 types with 100,000 tokens. That is, while the number of tokens in the novel increased ten times, types only increased 4.01 times.

Table 5.41 Percentage of type growth in *Moby Dick*.

Tokens	Types	Type increase	% increase
10,000	2,743	2743	100.00
20,000	4,232	1,489	35.18
30,000	5,287	1,055	19.95
40,000	6,301	1,014	16.09
50,000	7,205	904	12.55
60,000	8,009	804	10.04
70,000	8,809	800	9.08
80,000	9,532	723	7.58
90,000	10,329	797	7.72
100,000	11,013	684	6.21

Next we shall attempt to model the type growth of Melville's novel. Figure 5.10 and Table 5.41 indicate that the increase in types is not linear, but curvilinear. To know whether there is any relationship between tokens and types, we shall perform a non-linear regression analysis by means of SPPS, running all possible non-linear regression analyses[15] and seeing which best fits the data.

---

15. Among the non-linear regression models tested are: *logarithmic, inverse, quadratic, cubic, power, compound, S, logistic, grown* and *exponential*.

The best result is obtained with the non-linear power regression model. Figure 5.11 shows the regression model against the real observed data. We can observe how the observed data nearly always falls on the estimation curve of the model. This is a typical SPSS output; what matters are the estimation parameters (constant and b1); they allow us to see the relationship between types and tokens:

types = constant × tokens^{b1}

Additionally, using the estimated values of the estimation parameters (see Table 5.42), we obtain the equation that describes the model:

$$y = 11.041 \times x^{0.599}$$

Or, as *y* stands for the dependent variable (types) and *x* for the independent (tokens), we can transcribe the equation into:

types = 11.041 × *tokens*$^{0.599}$

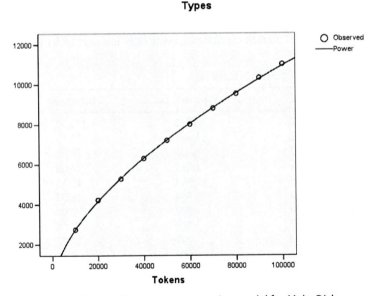

Figure 5.11 Observed data versus regression model for *Moby Dick*.

Table 5.42 Data on the model fit and beta coefficients for *Moby Dick*.

Equation	Summary of the model					Estimation parameters	
	R sq	F	df1	df2	Sig.	Constant	b1
Power	1.000	34,073.774	1	8	0.000	11.041	0.599

Using this equation we can estimate the expected types for Melville's novel and compare them with the real observed data, and evaluate the error margin(s) (Table 5.43).

Table 5.43 Observed data versus modelled data for *Moby Dick*.

Tokens	Observed Types	Modelled Types	Error
10,000	2,743	2,771	−28
20,000	4,232	4,199	33
30,000	5,287	5,356	−69
40,000	6,301	6,365	−64
50,000	7,205	7,276	−71
60,000	8,009	8,117	−108
70,000	8,809	8,904	−95
80,000	9,532	9,647	−115
90,000	10,329	10,353	−24
100,000	11,013	11,028	−15

The total error margin ranges from −115 to 33, that is, 148 types altogether, which is very positive indeed. However, the most important conclusion is that there seems to be a relationship between types and tokens, and, furthermore, this relationship can be statistically modelled. In our analysis of *Moby Dick*, the equation to predict the number of different types, once we know the number of tokens, is as follows:

$$types = 11.041 \times tokens^{0.599}$$

A final test could be to predict the total number of types in Herman Melville's novel. We know that the total number of tokens is 212,538 and the total number of observed types is 17,089. Inserting the value for total tokens in our model equation, we get the following:

$$types = 11.041 \times 212,538^{0.599} = 17,336$$

Eliminating the decimal part, we can see that the model only overpredicts 247 types (17,336 − 17,089 = 247).

Of course, this equation varies depending on the text or corpus. Different novels, plays, texts, authors, corpora, languages, and so on of necessity exhibit a different relationship between types and tokens. So researchers would need to obtain the individual coefficients for each model.

5.5.2 Zipf's Law

A long time ago Zipf[16] observed the distribution of word frequencies in English and found that given some corpus of natural language utterances, the frequency of any word is inversely proportional to its rank in the frequency table. That is:

$$frequency = \frac{C}{rank}$$

where C is a constant.

Thus, the most frequent word will occur approximately twice as often as the second most frequent word, which occurs twice as often as the fourth most frequent word, and so on. For example, in the BNC *the* is the most frequently occurring word, and by itself accounts for 6.19 per cent of all word occurrences (61,873 over one million). True to Zipf's Law, the second-place word *of* accounts for nearly 3 per cent of words (29,418 occurrences).

There are many ways to state Zipf's Law but the simplest is procedural: take, for example, the twenty most frequent English words (Table 5.44); count the number of

Table 5.44 Zipf's Law on the twenty most frequent English words.

Word form	Frequency	Rank	Constant = freq × rank
THE	61,873	1	61,873
OF	29,414	2	58,828
AND	26,829	3	80,487
TO	25,384	4	101,536
A	21,264	5	106,320
IN	18,126	6	108,756
IT	10,892	7	76,244
IS	9,984	8	79,872
WAS	9,239	9	83,151
I	8,846	10	88,460
FOR	8,334	11	91,674
YOU	6,955	12	83,460
HE	6,813	13	88,569
BE	6,625	14	92,750
WITH	6,520	15	97,800
ON	6,473	16	103,568
THAT	6,290	17	106,930
BY	5,073	18	91,314
AT	4,782	19	90,858
ARE	4,709	20	94,180

---

16. See Zipf (1935).

times each word appears and rank them according to their frequency. If we multiply the frequency of each word with its rank position, we get a value which is more or less constant throughout the sample.

constant ≈ frequency × rank

Another example: let us take all the words in the body of the text of Herman Melville's novel, *Moby Dick*, rank the words and get the constant for each word. However, instead of showing the data numerically, we shall plot the data on a graph sorted by rank, with the most frequently appearing word first, and so on (Figure 5.12).

The shape of the curve for the text, and all Zipf curves in general, has a tendency to hug the axes of the diagram when plotted on linear scales. If the Zipf curve is plotted on a double-logarithmic diagram, then it appears as a straight line with a slope of −1 (Figure 5.13).

A brief description of the data on *Moby Dick* is that it follows a Zipf distribution, exhibiting:

- a few elements that score *very* high (the left tail in the diagrams), for example *the, of, and, a, to, in,*
- a medium number of elements with middle-of-the-road scores (the middle part of the diagram): for example *finest, fisherman, fled, flies,* and
- a huge number of elements that score very low (the right tail in the diagram), for example *worldly, worming, wring, youngish.*

Zipf's Law has been shown to characterize the use of words in a natural language (like English), so a language typically has a few words (*the, and,* etc.) that are used

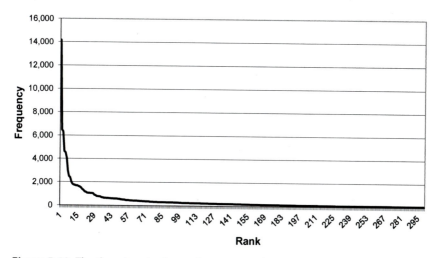

Figure 5.12 The three hundred most frequent words in *Moby Dick* ordered by rank.

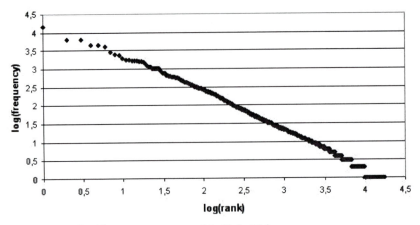

Figure 5.13 Word frequency versus rank in *Moby Dick*.

Note: In a double-logarithmic plane for $N = 17.088$.

very often, quite a lot of words (*dog*, *house*, etc.) that are used relatively frequently, and an abundance of words (*double-logarithmic*, etc.) that are very rarely or almost never used.

5.5.3 Measuring dispersion

There is no doubt that the statistic most used when analysing texts and corpora is the frequency of occurrence of a linguistic item (word form, lemma, part-of-speech tag, etc.). However, apart from its apparent objectivity, frequency of occurrences can be misleading if not used and/or compared with other parameters or measures. To illustrate this issue, consider the following case: we have just noticed that two word forms, *daughter* and *eye*, both occur fifteen times in *Hamlet*. Consequently, we shall interpret this finding as an indication of their overall similar importance within *Hamlet*. However, a look at how these words are distributed in the play suggests a very different result. While *daughter* occurs in three of the five acts, *eyes* occurs in all five acts. Furthermore, *daughter* occurs eleven out of the fifteen times in Act 2, while *eye* exhibits a less biased distribution (Table 5.45).

Table 5.45 Distribution of *daughter* and *eye* throughout *Hamlet*.

	Act 1	Act 2	Act 3	Act 4	Act 5	Total
Daughter	2	11	0	2	0	15
Eye	6	1	1	6	1	15

This indicates that *daughter* is particularly related to the topic dealt with in Act 2, in contrast to *eye*, which seems less topic-dependent. This assessment is supported by further evidence: if we analyse which characters utter *daughter* and *eye*, we obtain the findings shown in Table 5.46.

Table 5.46 Distribution of *daughter* and *eye* by characters.

	Fortinbras	Hamlet	Horatio	King	Laertes	Ophelia	Polonius	Queen	Total
Daughter	0	3	0	0	0	2	10	0	15
Eye	1	4	1	5	1	1	0	2	15

This indicates that these two words are far from being equally distributed across the play and that, more generally, frequency data should be supplemented with information on the dispersion of the items in question.

Among the many dispersion measures,[17] we shall present here Gries's *Deviation of Proportions*[18] (*DP*, hereafter), and apply it to the data given above.

To calculate the *DP* of a word in a text or corpus, we need to:

1. Determine the sizes of each text/corpus part. Going to our example, we would need to know the size (in tokens) of each of the five acts in *Hamlet*, and normalize the parts against the overall text size.
2. Determine the frequencies of the word(s) under investigation in each text/corpus part where the word(s) occur(s), and, again, normalize the data against the overall number of occurrences.
3. Calculate all pairwise absolute differences between the normalized observed and expected occurrences, add them up, and divide the result by two. This gives the *DP* value, ranging from 0 to 1, where values close to 0 indicate that the word under investigation is distributed quite regularly across the text/corpus parts. In contrast, values close to 1 indicate that the word under investigation is distributed completely irregularly or is biased.

Let us exemplify this by means of our previous example from *Hamlet*. First, let us determine the sizes of the five acts (Table 5.47) and normalize the data against the overall size (29,765 tokens). The normalized data will serve as the expected distribution to be contrasted with the real observed data.

Table 5.47 Sizes of the five acts in *Hamlet*: normalized expected data.

	Act 1	Act 2	Act 3	Act 4	Act 5	Total
Tokens	6,600	5,639	6,999	5,089	5,438	29,765
%	22.17	18.95	23.51	17.10	18.27	100.00
Normalized data	0.22	0.19	0.24	0.17	0.18	1.00

17. See Carroll (1970), Juilland *et al.* (1970), Rosengren (1971), Lyne (1985).
18. See Gries (2008).

Now, we tabulate the observed data of the two words under investigation, *daughter* and *eye*, across the five acts, and normalize their frequencies against the overall occurrences (fifteen in both cases). This will be our observed data (Table 5.48).

Table 5.48 Word distribution throughout acts: normalized observed data.

		Act 1	Act 2	Act 3	Act 4	Act 5	Total
Daughter	Tokens	2	11	0	2	0	15
	%	13.33	73.33	0.00	13.33	0.00	100.00
	Normalized data	0.13	0.73	0.00	0.13	0.00	1.00
Eye	Tokens	6	1	1	6	1	15
	%	40.00	6.67	6.67	40.00	6.67	100.00
	Normalized data	0.40	0.07	0.07	0.40	0.07	1.00

Finally, we proceed to the last step: calculating the absolute differences between the normalized observed and expected values (Table 5.49).

Table 5.49 Differences between the observed and expected values.

		Act 1	Act 2	Act 3	Act 4	Act 5	Total
Daughter	Observed	0.13	0.73	0.00	0.13	0.00	1.00
	Expected	0.22	0.19	0.24	0.17	0.18	1.00
	Difference	0.09	0.54	0.24	0.04	0.18	1.09
Eye	Observed	0.40	0.07	0.07	0.40	0.07	1.00
	Expected	0.22	0.19	0.24	0.17	0.18	1.00
	Difference	0.18	0.12	0.17	0.23	0.11	0.81

The different sums for *daughter* and *eye* are 1.09 and 0.81, respectively, and their definite *DP* values are 0.545 (1.09/2) and 0.405 (0.81/2). Clearly the higher *DP* value for *daughter* indicates that its distribution is less regular, more biased and more concentrated in specific parts of the play. In contrast, *eye* exhibits a more regular distribution throughout the play and is probably also less linked to any particular topic or subtopic in *Hamlet*.

There is no doubt about the usefulness of frequency lists for linguistic research; however, it seems wise to follow up this information with additional data or analyses about the distribution of the linguistic items under investigation.

6 Words in context

6.1 Concordances

Frequency lists allow researchers to consider the general profile of the words that make up a text. However, by doing this we lose the contextual information, that is, the surrounding words that go with the specific word(s) under investigation.

Concordance programs can display the occurrences of a chosen word with its surrounding context. Such displays are called concordance listings. In one common type of display, each occurrence of the chosen word is presented on a single line, with the word in the middle and context on each side. Figure 6.1 shows this kind of display for twenty occurrences of *crisis*. These displays are referred to as *KWIC* – Key Word In Context.[1]

A concordance was originally a reference work designed to assist in the exegesis of biblical and other socially valued texts. In it, all occurrences of terms, names, and so on that were felt to be significant were collected and presented in a way that would help the researcher. The effort involved in such a task, when undertaken manually, was very great; in fact, it was virtually impossible, unless researchers had an army of collaborators at their command.

Concordance lists are arranged in the order of occurrence within the original text. They are probably the oldest and most common application of computers in the humanities and are at the centre of corpus linguistics, because they give access to many important language patterns in texts. Definite patterns emerge from a detailed examination of concordance lines. Concordances of major works such as the Bible and Shakespeare have been available for many years. Even from short lists, it is possible to see how concordance lines can reveal, for example, the different meanings of a word. Consider the concordance lines for *bank* given in Figure 6.2. We have numbered the instances for easy referencing. Note that instances 1, 2, 7 and 8 relate to an establishment for keeping money; the clues for grouping these meanings are given by some co-occurring words, such as *benefits, Reserve, lift, Deutsche, National Australia* and *lower exposure*. Instances 3, 4 and 10 convey a sense of land along the sides of a river (*walk, river, south, Thames, northern, narrow muddy shore*). Instances 5 and 9 use *bank* with the meaning of store of *blood*. Finally, instance 6 conveys the meaning of mass of *clouds*.

---

1. The concept of *keyword* in the context of concordances or concordance listings is different from the notion of *keyword* discussed in section 5.2.

```
     planning recognises that people in [[CRISIS]] often interact better on the edges
            met in the earlier financial [[CRISIS]]," said Chairman of Wing Tai Limited
       Bishops Speak Out On Middle East [[CRISIS]].
                    I think there's a huge [[CRISIS]] of belonging in postmodern culture.
         immediately, the scale of the [[CRISIS]] means the human and socio
           strong, but until the WorldCom [[CRISIS]] bottoms, the currency will be
          ramifications of the OPEC fuel [[CRISIS]].
                    the midst of an injury [[CRISIS]] they will always be there
               Germany out of their worst [[CRISIS]] to the World Cup.
               was called to discuss the [[CRISIS]].
          are especially hard-hit by the [[CRISIS]] and yet they are rarely
              busy trying to survive my [[CRISIS]], but the web site eventually
          "War cannot resolve the gulf [[CRISIS]]," and urging him to avoid a
                                      The [[CRISIS]] has also spawned a network
                    in this country is in [[CRISIS]].
                    their way out of the [[CRISIS]].
             the other hand, the Asian [[CRISIS]] has already provoked a resurgence
                    There is an emissions [[CRISIS]].
               And there is a political [[CRISIS]].
      has largely escaped the California [[CRISIS]] because it owns its own
```

Figure 6.1 Sample of concordance listings for *crisis*.

```
 1    part that really benefits your [[BANK]] account," says Kirstie.
 2                      The Reserve [[BANK]] has decided against a lift
 3              like to walk the river [[BANK]], of the Murray River, at
 4      at Rotherhithe on the south [[BANK]] of the River Thames in
 5          at the Red Cross Blood [[BANK]] hooked up to a machine that
 6            As though they were a [[BANK]] of clouds, and reads a
 7    Tellingly, a recent Deutsche [[BANK]] report on ResMed is headed
 8              National Australia [[BANK]] has the lowest exposure to
 9            down to the blood [[BANK]] in the Student Union and
10      he noticed that the northern [[BANK]] had a narrow muddy shore.
```

Figure 6.2 Concordances for *bank*.

The *KWIC* concordance is not the only possible form, but it is the one most commonly used. The computer has made concordances easy to compile and it is relatively easy to get a list of all the occurrences of a particular word in context and, through the context, we can see all the meanings associated with the word.

Concordance packages are equipped with sophisticated built-in sorts of facilities which allow the lines to be rearranged into alternative sequences. These computer-generated concordances can be very flexible; the context of a word can be selected according to various criteria. In section 6.1.2, we shall describe other possible outputs.

Although the use of concordances generated from texts or corpora provides a more solid empirical basis than other traditional approaches, concordances can actually provide too much data. For example, a *KWIC* concordance for *time* in the LACELL Corpus[2] generated 35,753 entries. Simply determining the number of different senses in a database of this size is a daunting task. Grouping different uses

2. A twenty-million-word corpus of contemporary English: www.um.es/grupos/grupo-lacell/quees.php

accurately or ranking them in order of importance and/or similarity is not feasible without the use of additional techniques and sorting tools.

6.1.1 Determining the context

As already mentioned, the *KWIC* concordance format is the one most commonly used, where the word under investigation is highlighted at the centre with its context (co-occurring words) on each side. This format has the advantage of allowing quick and easy scanning of the lines and showing context patterns.

However, despite this advantage, some researchers might want more than the mere context exhibited in *KWIC* concordance listings. For instance, lexicographers need to view and examine larger contexts to determine the different meanings of a word. This means that the context of the basic *KWIC* concordance should be variable in length and form. Many concordance packages allow various display options.

By default, *KWIC* concordance listings display a limited context of five words on each side (Figure 6.3), which can be augmented or adjusted to the size of the stretch of text that best meets our research goals. Figure 6.4 shows the same concordance lines but with an augmented context of eight words on each side.

Other display options include the possibility of determining the context in characters. Figure 6.5 shows a context limitation of fifty characters on both sides.

Line, sentence and even paragraph contexts are possible. Figure 6.6 gives a sentence context display. Optionally, this concordance software splits the window into two sub-windows: the lower gives the concordances, and by just clicking on the desired concordance line, the upper window shows the full sentence.

Other concordance software not only displays the full sentence but also refers back to the original text and shows the text with the embedded concordance sentence and the keyword highlighted (Figure 6.7).

```
   ... infrastructure on the altar of [[tax]] breaks for big corporations and  ...
             ... the road and riddle our [[tax]] code with special interest favors  ...
            ... of billions of dollars on [[tax]] breaks for big corporations and  ...
   ... homeowners relief by offering a [[tax]] credit to low- and middle-income  ...
               ... also have to reform a [[tax]] code that rewards wealth over  ...
   ... of special interest loopholes and [[tax]] shelters; a tax code that  ...
          ... loopholes and tax shelters; a [[tax]] code that continues George Bush's  ...
   ... corporations and wealthy CEOs; a [[tax]] code that has plunged this  ...
            ... couldn't vote for the Bush [[tax]] breaks in good conscience because  ...
   ... McCain, because these same Bush [[tax]] cuts are now his central  ...
                  ... for a new round of [[tax]] giveaways that are twice as  ...
          ... spend nearly $2 trillion on [[tax]] breaks for corporations, including $1. ...
                  ... 1.2 billion on a [[tax]] break for Exxon Mobil. That  ...
           ... approach. I will reform our [[tax]] code so that it's simple,  ...
   ... down the corporate loopholes and [[tax]] havens, and I'll use the  ...
          ... help pay for a middle-class [[tax]] cut that will provide $1,  ...
           ... companies like Exxon pay a [[tax]] on their windfall profits, and  ...
            ... make up for his enormous [[tax]] giveaway indicates that John McCain  ...
   ... Bush economic policies - more [[tax]] cuts to the wealthy, more  ...
         ... to the wealthy, more corporate [[tax]] breaks, more mountains of debt,  ...
           ... They don't like seeing their [[tax]] dollars wasted. But we also  ...
```

Figure 6.3 *KWIC* concordance listings with a standard context: five words on each side.

```
   ...and energy, and infrastructure on the altar of [[tax]] breaks for big corporations and wealthy CEOs -  ...
        ... the rules of the road and riddle our [[tax]] code with special interest favors and corporate loopholes. ...
   ... problem spending hundreds of billions of dollars on [[tax]] breaks for big corporations and a permanent occupation  ...
   ... I'll provide struggling homeowners relief by offering a [[tax]] credit to low- and middle-income Americans that would  ...
           ... care system, we also have to reform a [[tax]] code that rewards wealth over work - a  ...
   ... page after page of special interest loopholes and [[tax]] shelters; a tax code that continues George Bush's  ...
   ... of special interest loopholes and tax shelters; a [[tax]] code that continues George Bush's billion-dollar giveaways to  ...
   ... giveaways to big corporations and wealthy CEOs; a [[tax]] code that has plunged this country deeper and  ...
             ... said that he couldn't vote for the Bush [[tax]] breaks in good conscience because they were too  ...
   ... changed about John McCain, because these same Bush [[tax]] cuts are now his central economic policy. Not  ...
               ... is now calling for a new round of [[tax]] giveaways that are twice as expensive as the  ...
           ... His policy will spend nearly $2 trillion on [[tax]] breaks for corporations, including $1.2 billion for  ...
               ... wants to spend $1.2 billion on a [[tax]] break for Exxon Mobil. That isn't just irresponsible. ...
   ... company. I'll take a different approach. I will reform our [[tax]] code so that it's simple, fair, and advances  ...
   ... the money to help pay for a middle-class [[tax]] havens, and I'll use the money to help  ...
             ... I'll make oil companies like Exxon pay a [[tax]] on their windfall profits, and we'll use the  ...
   ... implementing will somehow make up for his enormous [[tax]] giveaway indicates that John McCain was right when  ...
       ... a continuation of Bush economic policies - more [[tax]] cuts to the wealthy, more corporate tax breaks,  ...
               ... more tax cuts to the wealthy, more corporate [[tax]] breaks, more mountains of debt, and little to  ...
   ... work, and self-reliance. They don't like seeing their [[tax]] dollars wasted. But we also believe in an  ...
```

Figure 6.4 *KWIC* concordance listings with an augmented context: eight words on each side.

```
   ... n, and energy, and infrastructure on the altar of [[tax]] breaks for big corporations and wealthy CEOs - tr ...
   ... ists who rig the rules of the road and riddle our [[tax]] code with special interest favors and corporate l ...
   ... oblem spending hundreds of billions of dollars on [[tax]] breaks for big corporations and a permanent occup ...
   ... rovide struggling homeowners relief by offering a [[tax]] credit to low- and middle-income Americans that w ...
   ... our health care system, we also have to reform a [[tax]] code that rewards wealth over work - a 10,000-pag ...
   ... page after page of special interest loopholes and [[tax]] shelters; a tax code that continues George Bush's ...
   ... of special interest loopholes and tax shelters; a [[tax]] code that continues George Bush's billion-dollar ...
   ... giveaways to big corporations and wealthy CEOs; a [[tax]] code that has plunged this country deeper and dee ...
   ... Cain once said that he couldn't vote for the Bush [[tax]] breaks in good conscience because they were too s ...
   ... hanged about John McCain, because these same Bush [[tax]] cuts are now his central economic policy. Not onl ...
   ... ly that, but he is now calling for a new round of [[tax]] giveaways that are twice as expensive as the orig ...
   ... sive. His policy will spend nearly $2 trillion on [[tax]] breaks for corporations, including $1.2 billion f ...
   ... ernment spending wants to spend $1.2 billion on a [[tax]] break for Exxon Mobil. That isn't just irresponsi ...
   ... I'll take a different approach. I will reform our [[tax]] code so that it's simple, fair, and advances oppo ...
   ... mpany. I'll shut down the corporate loopholes and [[tax]] havens, and I'll use the money to help pay for a ...
   ... I'll use the money to help pay for a middle-class [[tax]] cut that will provide $1,000 of relief to 95% of  ...
   ... amilies. I'll make oil companies like Exxon pay a [[tax]] on their windfall profits, and we'll use the mone ...
   ... mplementing will somehow make up for his enormous [[tax]] giveaway indicates that John McCain was right whe ...
   ... e a continuation of Bush economic policies - more [[tax]] cuts to the wealthy, more corporate tax breaks, m ...
   ... es - more tax cuts to the wealthy, more corporate [[tax]] breaks, more mountains of debt, and little to no  ...
   ... , and self-reliance. They don't like seeing their [[tax]] dollars wasted. But we also believe in an Americ  ...
```

Figure 6.5 *KWIC* concordance listings with an augmented context up to fifty characters.

N	Concordance
1	They don't like seeing their tax dollars wasted. But we also believe
2	tax cuts to the wealthy, more corporate tax breaks, more mountains of debt, and
3	of Bush economic policies – more tax cuts to the wealthy, more corporate
4	somehow make up for his enormous tax giveaway indicates that John McCain
5	make oil companies like Exxon pay a tax on their windfall profits, and we'll use
6	money to help pay for a middle-class tax cut that will provide $1,000 of relief to
7	shut down the corporate loopholes and tax havens, and I'll use the money to
8	a different approach. I will reform our tax code so that it's simple, fair, and
9	wants to spend $1.2 billion on a tax break for Exxon Mobil. That isn't just
10	policy will spend nearly $2 trillion on tax breaks for corporations, including
11	but he is now calling for a new round of tax giveaways that are twice as
12	McCain, because these same Bush tax cuts are now his central economic
13	said that he couldn't vote for the Bush tax breaks in good conscience because
14	will try to define me with the same old tax-and-spend label that his side has
15	big corporations and wealthy CEOs; a tax code that has plunged this country
16	interest loopholes and tax shelters; a tax code that continues George Bush's
17	page of special interest loopholes and tax shelters; a tax code that continues
18	care system, we also have to reform a tax code that rewards wealth over work –
19	homeowners relief by offering a tax credit to low- and middle-income
20	hundreds of billions of dollars on tax breaks for big corporations and a
21	rig the rules of the road and riddle our tax code with special interest favors and
22	and infrastructure on the altar of tax breaks for big corporations and

Figure 6.6 *KWIC* concordance listings with sentence context.

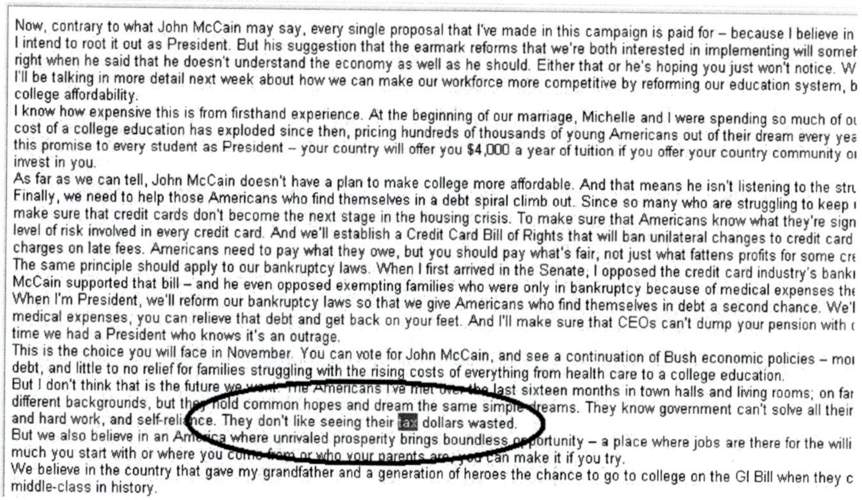

Now, contrary to what John McCain may say, every single proposal that I've made in this campaign is paid for – because I believe in I intend to root it out as President. But his suggestion that the earmark reforms that we're both interested in implementing will somel right when he said that he doesn't understand the economy as well as he should. Either that or he's hoping you just won't notice. W I'll be talking in more detail next week about how we can make our workforce more competitive by reforming our education system, b college affordability.

I know how expensive this is from firsthand experience. At the beginning of our marriage, Michelle and I were spending so much of o cost of a college education has exploded since then, pricing hundreds of thousands of young Americans out of their dream every ye this promise to every student as President – your country will offer you $4,000 a year of tuition if you offer your country community or invest in you.

As far as we can tell, John McCain doesn't have a plan to make college more affordable. And that means he isn't listening to the stru Finally, we need to help those Americans who find themselves in a debt spiral climb out. Since so many who are struggling to keep t make sure that credit cards don't become the next stage in the housing crisis. To make sure that Americans know what they're sign level of risk involved in every credit card. And we'll establish a Credit Card Bill of Rights that will ban unilateral changes to credit card charges on late fees. Americans need to pay what they owe, but you should pay what's fair, not just what fattens profits for some cre The same principle should apply to our bankruptcy laws. When I first arrived in the Senate, I opposed the credit card industry's bankr McCain supported that bill – and he even opposed exempting families who were only in bankruptcy because of medical expenses the When I'm President, we'll reform our bankruptcy laws so that we give Americans who find themselves in debt a second chance. We'l medical expenses, you can relieve that debt and get back on your feet. And I'll make sure that CEOs can't dump your pension with c time we had a President who knows it's an outrage.

This is the choice you will face in November. You can vote for John McCain, and see a continuation of Bush economic policies – mor debt, and little to no relief for families struggling with the rising costs of everything from health care to a college education. But I don't think that is the future we want. The Americans I've met over the last sixteen months in town halls and living rooms; on far different backgrounds, but they hold common hopes and dream the same simple dreams. They know government can't solve all their and hard work, and self-reliance. They don't like seeing their ⬛ dollars wasted.

But we also believe in an America where unrivaled prosperity brings boundless opportunity – a place where jobs are there for the willi much you start with or where you come from or who your parents are, you can make it if you try.

We believe in the country that gave my grandfather and a generation of heroes the chance to go to college on the GI Bill when they c middle-class in history.

Figure 6.7 Showing text with sentence containing concordance and keyword.

This facility of browsing the text forwards and backwards from the point of occurrence of the keyword allows access to as much context as the researcher may need to explore specific patterns, usage and so on in detail. In spite of this, the basic strategy that is most widely used is simply to specify *n* words on either side.

6.1.2 Sorting concordance outputs

Keywords with a large number of occurrences are particularly difficult to cope with as it is not straightforward to detect patterns of usage. Some concordance packages allow the user to specify the order in which the occurrences of a keyword might be listed in the concordance. The most usual order is that in which they occur in the text (see all examples above). However, other possibilities, such as alphabetical ordering of what comes to the right or left of the keyword are particularly interesting and revealing, as instances of the particular pattern can be brought together. Consider the concordances for *make* in Figure 6.8, extracted from our sample text back in Chapter 5 (Barack Obama's speech on the economy[3]). Note that the concordances have been sorted alphabetically according to the keyword's first word on the right.

Examining the data reveals that: (1) *make sure* is a possible collocation, as it occurs four out of seventeen times; (2) *make* is transitive verb, as it is followed normally by an object noun phrase (i.e. *make an enormous difference*) and in one instance we find that the object noun phrase precedes the verb and its subject (*the decisions we make*); and (3) *make up for* is a possible prepositional phrasal verb.

---

3. www.nytimes.com/2008/06/09/us/politics/09transcript-obama.html

```
           ... and a long-term agenda to [[make]] America competitive in a global  ...
    ... place where that investment would [[make]] an enormous difference is in  ...
                ... doesn't have a plan to [[make]] college more affordable. And that  ...
       ... our planet, the decisions we [[make]] in November and over the  ...
             ... a plan that will actually [[make]] it easier - easier -  ...
              ... your parents are, you can [[make]] it if you try. We  ...
     ... workers and their families. I'll [[make]] oil companies like Exxon pay  ...
         ... kind of transparency won't just [[make]] our homeowners more secure, it  ...
       ... homeowners more secure, it will [[make]] our markets more stable, and  ...
              ... week about how we can [[make]] our workforce more competitive by  ...
        ... whether they'll be able to [[make]] payments. This kind of transparency  ...
           ... in the housing crisis. To [[make]] sure that Americans know what  ...
           ... credit cards, we have to [[make]] sure that credit cards don't  ...
          ... debt a second chance. We'll [[make]] sure that if you can  ...
               ... on your feet. And I'll [[make]] sure that CEOs can't dump  ...
              ... also find a way to [[make]] trade work for American workers. ...
    ... interested in implementing will somehow [[make]] up for his enormous tax  ...
```

Figure 6.8 Concordance lines sorted by first word to the right of the keyword *make*.

```
                ... 1.2 billion on a [[tax]] break for Exxon Mobil. That  ...
         ... couldn't vote for the Bush [[tax]] breaks in good conscience because  ...
       ... to the wealthy, more corporate [[tax]] breaks, more mountains of debt, ...
            ... spend nearly $2 trillion on [[tax]] breaks for corporations, including $1. ...
             ... of billions of dollars on [[tax]] breaks for big corporations and  ...
       ... infrastructure on the altar of [[tax]] breaks for big corporations and  ...
             ... the road and riddle our [[tax]] code with special interest favors  ...
              ... also have to reform a [[tax]] code that rewards wealth over  ...
            ... approach. I will reform our [[tax]] code so that it's simple,  ...
     ... corporations and wealthy CEOs; a [[tax]] code that has plunged this  ...
          ... loopholes and tax shelters; a [[tax]] code that continues George Bush's  ...
       ... homeowners relief by offering a [[tax]] credit to low- and middle-income  ...
             ... help pay for a middle-class [[tax]] cut that will provide $1,  ...
            ... Bush economic policies - more [[tax]] cuts to the wealthy, more  ...
       ... McCain, because these same Bush [[tax]] cuts are now his central  ...
           ... They don't like seeing their [[tax]] dollars wasted. But we also  ...
            ... make up for his enormous [[tax]] giveaway indicates that John McCain  ...
                ... for a new round of [[tax]] giveaways that are twice as  ...
     ... down the corporate loopholes and [[tax]] havens, and I'll use the  ...
           ... companies like Exxon pay a [[tax]] on their windfall profits, and  ...
     ... of special interest loopholes and [[tax]] shelters; a tax code that  ...
```

Figure 6.9 Concordance lines sorted by first word to the right of the keyword *tax*.

Similarly, sorting the concordances for *tax* to the first word on the right (Figure 6.9) reveals interesting word clusters: *tax break(s), tax code, tax credit, tax cut(s), tax dollars, tax giveaway(s), tax havens* and *tax shelters*.

The concordance lines can not only be sorted by the first word to the right of the keyword; most packages allow more sophisticated combined sorting criteria, for example sorting primarily according to the alphabetical order of the word following the keyword (first right) and secondarily according to the alphabetical order of the word preceding the keyword, also known as *zig-zag* sorting. Figure 6.10 displays such an example. The positive contribution of this sorting is that possible lexical clusters and/or different word classes are highlighted. We realize that *sudden* can be an adjective: *...so sudden and violent..., ...so sudden and peremptory*; a noun: *...on a sudden..., of a sudden...*; or an adverb: *...come sudden...* Additionally, we also observe that *sudden* as an adjective can be functionally both predicative (*...was so sudden...*) and attributive (*...a sudden bounce..., ...a sudden gasp*, etc.).

For very frequent keywords many concordance lines are produced and the examination of the occurrences can be very time-consuming and difficult. Some

```
... death. And, indeed, the shock was so [[sudden]] and violent, that we took it for grant...
... s issued from the cabin with orders so [[sudden]] and peremptory, that after all it was...
... the season in those Icy Seas, and the [[sudden]] and violent storms to which they are e...
... ly,there is no telling now; but, on a [[sudden]], as the eightieth or ninetieth bucket...
... mises; but I tore from her, and with a [[sudden]] bodily rush dashed myself full against...
... d strain at the bows, the boats gave a [[sudden]] bounce upwards, as a small icefield wil...
... substance, said, that the cause of his [[sudden]] convalescence was this;-at a critical...
... ifficulties and worrying, prospects of [[sudden]] disaster, peril of life and limb; all...
... ship. But at this critical instant a [[sudden]] exclamation was heard that took every...
... Immsman could handle the spokes. The [[sudden]] exclamations of the crew must have alar...
... anging round him in the pantry, by his [[sudden]] fits of the palsy. Nor did the whetst...
... need should be. In a countryman, this [[sudden]] flame of friendship would have seemed...
... s we thus lay entranced, the occasional [[sudden]] frantic spectacles in the distance evi...
... arders, seemed amazingly tickled at the [[sudden]] friendship which had sprung up between...
... onster's run was a brief one. Giving a [[sudden]] gasp, he tumultuously sounded. With a...
... I could not help it now; and giving a [[sudden]] grunt of astonishment he began feeling...
... t may be-a larger and nobler foe; of a [[sudden]], he bore down upon its advancing prow,...
... wise. And once Daggoo, seized with a [[sudden]] humor, assisted Dough-Boy's memory by...
... That was sudden, now; but squalls come [[sudden]] in hot latitudes. I've heard that the...
... tretched out like a wand, and at brief [[sudden]] intervals he continued his cries. To b ...
... Dick. But the whale rushed round in a [[sudden]] maelstrom; seized the swimmer between h...
... t of sight. ""He goes aft. That was [[sudden]], now; but squalls come sudden in hot l...
... aback; though, indeed, at times by the [[sudden]] onset of a large rolling wave, the boea...
... roared the Guernseyman, flying into a [[sudden]] passion. "Oh! Keep cool-cool? Yes, ...
... fe in hand, he had but given loose to a [[sudden]], passionate, corporal animosity; and w...
... eemed threatening to cut it in two; the [[sudden]] profound dip into the watery glens and...
... as to choking Stubb, when a rat made a [[sudden]] racket in the hold below. And poor lit...
```

Figure 6.10 Concordance lines sorted by first word right and first left of the keyword.

packages allow not just sorting according to the criteria seen above, but also to limit the number of occurrences, for example, by extracting just a specified number of concordances arranged in their original sequence or a randomly selected sample of concordances.

So far we have limited our text/corpus search examples to a unique keyword form: *crisis, bank, tax, make* and *sudden*. However, researchers are mostly interested not in single word forms or types, but in the lemma with all its variants: inflections and/or derivations. In English, most regular nouns, verbs, adjectives and adverbs are made up of a word stem/base which does, generally, not alter and to which various endings are added in a regular system of morphology. For example, the inflected forms of the lemma verb form *look*: *look, looks, looked* and *looking*. Many concordance packages allow the use of *wildcard characters*. These *wildcard characters* may be used to make a search more flexible. The standard wildcard characters are:

- "*", matching 0 or more characters
- "%", matching 0 or 1 character; and
- "?", matching exactly 1 character.

If we perform a search for *look**, where "*" stands for 0 or any number of characters, we get the result shown in Figure 6.11.

The occurrences are displayed in their order of occurrence within the original text. To get a neater presentation, we can sort them alphabetically by their keywords. This would group all instances into: *look, looked, looking* and *looks* (Figure 6.12).

Altogether we have 336 matches for *look** found in *Moby Dick*. However, if we examine the matches in Figure 6.11 carefully, we notice some "intruders" such as *lookest* and *looker*. A more exhaustive check of the full concordance list reveals

```
... s previous were out of sight of land. [[Look]] at the crowds of water-gazers there. ...
... some seated upon the pier-heads; some [[looking]] over the bulwarks of ships from China; ...
... sign of "The Crossed Harpoons"-but it [[looked]] too expensive and jolly there. Further...
... ood invitingly open. It had a careless [[look]], as if it were meant for the uses of t...
... eard a forlorn creaking in the air; and [[looking]] up, saw a swinging sign over the door...
... an emigrant from there. AS the light [[looked]] so dim, and the place, for the time, lo...
... ed so dim, and the place, for the time, [[looked]] quiet enough, and the dilapidated litt...
... dilapidated little wooden house itself [[looked]] as if it might have been carted here f...
... a marvellous difference, whether thou [[lookest]] out at it from a glass window where th...
... arpooneer is it?""Oh. no," said he, [[looking]] a sort of diabolically funny, "the har...
... to spend the rest of the evening as a [[looker]] on. Presently a rioting nooise was he...
... all ready to knock me down! Still, [[looking]] round me again, and seeing no possible...
... pping in before long. I'll have a good [[look]] at him then, and perhaps we may become...
... the way. But I stood irresolute; when [[looking]] at a clock in the corner, the Lord ...
... stranger entered the room, and without [[looking]] towards the bed, placed his candle a go...
... nd there stuck over with large blackish [[looking]] squares. Yes, it's just as I thought, ...
... forehead. His bald purplish head now [[looked]] for all the world like a mildewed skull...
... e might take a fancy to mine-heavens! [[Look]] at that tomahawk! But there was no t...
... lukes again and go to sleep. Queequeg, [[look]] here-you sabbee me, I sabbee-you thi...
... eally kind and charitable way. I stood [[looking]] at him a moment. For all his tatooin...
... gs he was on the whole a clean, comely [[looking]] cannibal. What's all this fuss I have...
... us times-this same arm of his, I say, [[looked]] for all the world like a strip of that...
... sat up in bed, stiff as a pike-staff, [[looking]] at me, and rubbing his eyes as if he di...
...s, and whom I had not as yet had a good [[look]] at. They were nearly all whalemen; chi...
... m his Indian voyage. That man next him [[looks]] a few shades lighter; you might say a ...
... silence. And not only that, but they [[looked]] embarrassed. Yes, here were a set of s...
... frequently offer to view the queerest [[looking]] nondescripts from foreign parts. Even...
```

Figure 6.11 Fragment of a concordance listing for *look**.

```
... e. '"What do you think? What does it [[look]] like?' '"Like a lanyard for your bag...
... dspikes, my hearties. Captain, by God, [[look]] to yourself; say the word; don't be a f...
... ves down in the forecastle there, men? [[Look]] to those handspikes, my hearties. Capt...
... with both hands on Perth's shoulders; "[[Look]] ye here-HERE-can ye smoothe out a se...
... play; no more gaffs and pikes to-day, [[Look]] ye here!" jingling the leathern bag, a ...
... ,"flinging the pouch upon the anvil. "[[Look]] ye, blacksmith, these are the gathered...

... an emigrant from there. AS the light [[looked]] so dim, and the place, for the time, lo...
... the whale? Gone down again?" But he [[looked]] too nigh the boat; for as if bent upon...
... . I told him yes; whereat I thought he [[looked]] pleased, perhaps a little complimented...
... ed so dim, and the place, for the time, [[looked]] quite enough, and the dilapidated litt...
... silence. And not only that, but they [[looked]] embarrassed. Yes, here were a set of s...
... sign of "The Crossed Harpoons"-but it [[looked]] too expensive and jolly there. Further...

... vessels parted; the crew of the Pequod [[looking]] with grave, lingering glances towards...
... ging about there for?" muttered Stubb, [[looking]] on from the forecastle. "That Parsee s...
... ck! It is a mild, mild wind, and a mild [[looking]] sky. On such a day-very much such a ...
... pocket a small vial of sand, and then [[looking]] from the ship to the vial, seemed ther...
... ut it is a mild, mild wind, and a mild [[looking]] sky; and the air smells now, as if it...
... ry was heard-a cry and a rushing-and [[looking]] up, they saw a falling phantom in the a..
... slowly, stealthily, and half sideways [[looking]], he placed the loaded musket's end agai..
... r the Line-fiery hot, I tell ye! He's [[looking]] this way-come, oakum; quick. Here we...

... e saddest sights you can see. The head [[looks]] a sort of reproachfully at him, with a ...
... 'em up again. What a leg this is! It [[looks]] like a real live leg, filled down to not...
... ped on the American line-tub, the boat [[looks]] as if it were pulling off with a prodi...
... ing out precisely what the whale really [[looks]] like. And the only mode in which you,...
... ys now-hist!" "I look, you look, he [[looks]]; we look, ye look, they look." "Why,...
...edy enterprise. But now it's done, it [[looks]] much like Pompey's Pillar. There are,...
... -hist! again." "I look, you look, he [[looks]]; we look, ye look, they look." "Well...
... tail, is only two inches in width, and [[looks]] something like a white billiard-ball. ...
```

Figure 6.12 Fragments of a keyword-ordered concordance listing for *look**.

additionally *look-e, lookee, look-out(s)* and *looks-pale*. Another interesting feature is an inconsistency found in Melville's spelling: we find *look-outs* as well as *lookouts*. These non-relevant concordances account for twenty-five lines out of 336 matches, or roughly 7.5 per cent of mismatches.

Some concordance packages allow the use of lemma lists. These lists are mere text files containing a plain text list of lemmas with items like this:

```
... "Moby Dick?" shouted Ahab. "Do ye know [[the white whale]] then, Tash?" "Does he fan-tail a lit...
... the excited old man: "A sharp eye for [[the white whale]]; a sharp lance for Moby Dick!" "God...
... by thrusting through the wall? To me, [[the white whale]] is that wall, shoved near to me. Somet...
... e thing is chiefly what I hate; and be [[the white whale]] agent, or be the white whale principal, ...
...e; and be the white whale agent, or be [[the white whale]] principal, I will wreak that hate upon...
... ; and to cries and maledictions against [[the white whale]], the spirits were simultaneously quaffe...
... Whelped somewhere by the sharkish sea. [[The white whale]] is their demigorgon. Hark! The inferna...
... as for those who, previously hearing of [[the white whale]], by chance caught sight of him; in the...
... ny brave hunters, to whom the story of [[the white whale]] had eventually come. Nor did wild ru...
... t watery spaces, the outblown rumors of [[the White Whale]] did in the end incorporate with themse...
... y those rumors, at least, had heard of [[the White Whale]], few of those hunters were willing to...
... o, as at last coming to be linked with [[the White Whale]] in the minds of the superstitiously in ...
... that after repeated, intrepid assaults, [[the White Whale]] had escaped alive; it cannot be much m...
... gained his distinctive appellation of [[the White Whale]]; a name, indeed, literally justified b...
... llecutal and spiritual exasperations. [[The White Whale]] swam before him as the monomaniac inca...
... at times his hate seemed almost theirs; [[the White Whale]] as much their insufferable foe as his; ...
... e as his; how all this came to be-what [[the White Whale]] was to them, or how to their unconscious...
       ... The Whiteness of The Whale. What [[the white whale]] was to Ahab, has been hinted; what, at...
... hat most of the deadly encounters with [[the white whale]] had taken place; there the waves were...
... in a miscellaneous hunt; if by chance [[the White Whale]], spending his vacation in seas far rem...
... ming, unappeasedly steadfast hunter of [[the white whale]]; this Ahab that had gone to his hammock...
```

Figure 6.13 Fragment of the multiple keyword search: *the white whale*.

LOOK → LOOKS, LOOKED, LOOKING
BE → AM, ARE, WAS, WERE, IS
GO → GOES, GOING, GONE, WENT

A simple lemma file containing only those word forms we want to be extracted gets rid of this problem, and we are just given those linguistic items we want to examine.

A keyword search can also be performed not just for single items but also for multiple word forms. Consider Figure 6.13, where we have a search for the multiple keyword cluster *the white whale* in *Moby Dick*.

An extension to this facility is the use of additional search criteria, for example, using the criteria of range of words; that is, searching for word *a* followed by word *b* within a certain range of words, using the wildcard character "@". The range of words covered by @ is set within the search criteria. Figure 6.14 displays a concordance listing for the word *either* followed by *or* within a range of two to nine words. We discover that the most frequent range is just two words between *either* and *or.*

More sophisticated concordance software allows us not just to list occurrences of two words with a specific range of words in between, but to produce lists of occurrences with two or more specific words occurring simultaneously in the same concordance sentence, irrespective of the distance between the words. Figure 6.15 displays concordances for *love* and *heart** within the same concordance context (i.e. sentence).

Figure 6.16 displays concordances for occurrences of *love, heart*, god* and *lord* within the same concordance context (i.e. sentence).

Clearly, concordances are a very valuable source of linguistic evidence as they show the context in which a keyword occurs. Although the use of concordance lists is essentially a qualitative and not a quantitative technique, concordances are an immensely useful source of information that allow researchers to assess the behaviour of individual words. Only after observing this behaviour and taking decisions on it can we proceed with a quantitative assessment. The numerous options present in many concordance packages (some of which are illustrated here) facilitate enormously the process of observing and distinguishing linguistic patterns and linguistic

```
...    act from him, dramatically regarded, if [[either by birth or]] other circumstances, he have what seem...
... he was every day visible to the crew; [[either standing in his pivot-hole, or]] seated upon an ivory stool he had; or...
...    ication of the Leviathan, founded upon [[either his baleen, or]] hump, or fin, or teeth; notwithstandin...
... suddenly, and, bearing down upon them, [[either stave their boats to splinters, or]] drive them back in consternation to th...
...    asing such over this round globe, they [[either lead us on in barren mazes or]] midway leave us whelmed. CHAPTE...
... I know not. But my life for it he was [[either practically conversant with his subject, or]] else marvelously tutored by some expe...
... e. Here is a vital point; for you must [[either satisfactorily settle this matter with yourself, or]] for ever remain an infidel as to one o...
...    moment followed moment, and no sign of [[either the sinker, or]] the diver could be seen. Some hands n...
...    k to tinker a parcel of old hoops?"" [[Either do that, sir, or]] waste in one day more oil than we may m...
... the deck, unless Ahab was before them;[[either standing in his pivot-hole, or]] exactly pacing the planks between two u...
```

Figure 6.14 Concordances for *either...or* within a range of two to nine words.

29 Jesus answered: "The first is, 'Heare, O Israel, Jehovah our God is one Jehovah, 30 and you must [[love]] Jehovah your God with your whole [[heart]] and with your whole soul and with your whole mind and with your whole strength.

```
...Hear, O Israel, Jehovah our God is one Jehovah, 30 and you must  [[love]]  Jehovah your God with your whole heart and with your whole...
...have faith in "mighty ones," and the greatest commandment is to "  [[love]]  the Lord your God with all your heart, soul, mind and strength...
...ealism_tinged poetry that distinguishes Grace Pool from ordinary  [[love]]  song/broken heart pop fluff.
                          Only time keeps us apart forever in my heart,  [[love]]  you always Joy.
                          Only time keeps us apart forever in my heart,  [[love]]  you always Joy.
        ... surveillance, but in Christ_like, open_hearted, non-judgemental  [[love]].
   As my son loped on ahead, the strains of Neil Young wailing Only  [[Love]]  Can Break Your Heart wafted from behind a half-opened...
... exercises in stylistic refinement and intensification, In the Mood for  [[Love]]  is a departure; a heartaching, eye-bewitching masterwork...
      ... Three of Hearts Sherilyn Fenn is cured of her lesbianism by the  [[Love]]  of a Baldwin (Billy, to add insult to injury).
                                                                  (I  [[love]]  you Pop) Forever in our hearts, by dauther Michelle...
                                  It's hard to lose someone you  [[love]].  The one that's been part of all that's been important in you...
     ... Mom are in Heaven, Surrounded by God's loving care, Parents  [[love]]  remains in our hearts, strong, God, guide our footsteps, As...
                                                           Your  [[love]]  is always with me, Locked in my heart to stay.
        ... our precious Mom up above, from her children And give her our  [[love]].
                                                To have, to  [[love]],  and then to part, Is the greatest sorrow of one's heart.
                    In life we loved you dearly. In death we  [[love]]  you still. In our hearts we hold a memory. That no one else...
             ... up above, Tell her we miss her terribly, And give her all our  [[love]]  To Our Precious Sister: When evening shades are falling...
         ... never close, We miss you more than anyone knows, With tender  [[love]]  and deep regret, We who loved you will never forget.
          ... and you're not there, With a broken heart we whisper low, We  [[love]]  you both and miss you so.
```

Figure 6.15 Fragment of concordances for *love* and *heart** within the same context.

One does not have faith in "mighty ones," and the greatest commandment is to "[[love]] the [[Lord]] your God with all your heart, soul, mind and strength" (Mark 12:30).

```
...h in "mighty ones," and the greatest commandment is to "love the  [[Lord]]  your God with all your heart, soul, mind and strength" (Mark...
   ..Jesus answered. The fist [commandment]; is, Hear, O Israel; The  [[Lord]]  our God, the Lord is one; and you shall love the Lord your...
       The fist [commandment]: is, Hear, O Israel: The Lord our God, the  [[Lord]]  is one; and you shall love the Lord your God with all your...
O Israel: The Lord our God, the Lord is one; and you shall love the  [[Lord]]  your God with all your heart, and with all your soul, and with...
   ... originated on Sinai with Moses and is recited daily: O Israel, the  [[Lord]]  our God is One— to this, as he matured, more was added...
              ..part of his deepest consciousness. And thou shat love the  [[Lord]]  thy God with all the heart, and with all thy soul, and with all...
```

Figure 6.16 Fragment of concordances for *love, heart**, *god* and *lord* within the same context.

behaviours, and can, additionally, be the basis for further analysis such as collocation analysis.

6.2 Collocations

There has been a lot of theoretical and applied research on collocations. Still, the definition of collocation may be rather different depending on the researchers' interests and standpoints.

The importance of collocations has been stressed in extensive literature and can be summarized as follows:

- Collocational information indicates which words co-occur frequently with other words and how they combine to form bigger constituents within a sentence.
- Human beings mostly determine word senses from context. Co-occurrence information tells us which word forms appear close together with other word forms. Words that are commonly found in the same context as a given word can be thought of as making up a neighbourhood of that word.
- From a cognitive point of view, human language acquisition is governed by the law of maximum efficiency. In other words, data compression and word association are performed to minimize storage demands in the brain. These chunks and associations are considered to be patterns or structures that repeatedly appear in a variety of contexts.

  In its broadest sense, *collocation* is more or less equivalent to "recurrent word combination". In the Firthian tradition, however, it is generally used in a stricter sense: a collocation consists of two or more words which have a strong tendency to be used together. According to Firth, "collocations of a given word are statements of the habitual or customary places of that word".[4] For example, in English you say *rancid butter*, not *sour butter*, or *burning ambition* instead of *firing ambition*.
- Methodologically, collocation analysis is viewed as essentially a probabilistic phenomenon consisting of identifying statistically significant collocations and excluding chance combinations. In collocation analysis, interest normally centres on the extent to which the actual pattern of these occurrences differs from the pattern that would have been expected, assuming a random distribution of forms. Any significant difference can be taken as, at least, preliminary evidence that the presence of one word in the text affects the occurrence of another in some way.

6.3 Measuring collocation strength

The simplest form of collocation analysis can be performed by using simple concordances and producing a wordlist out of them. Let us illustrate this with an example.

---

4. Firth (1968: 181).

```
     ... finds means to kill your joys with [[love]]; And I, for winking at your discords...
  ... good the friar's words, Their course of [[love]], the tidings of her death: And here...
     ... and there's my master, One that you [[love]]. Who is it?
     ... thy sea-sick weary bark! Here's to my [[love]]! O true apothecary! Thy drugs are...
     ... how may I Call this a lightning? O my [[love]]! My wife! Death, that hath suck'd the...
     ... me to fury: O! be gone: By heaven, I [[love]] thee better than myself. For I come...
     ... was an emperor. Ah me! How sweet is [[love]] itself possess'd. When but love's...
     ... as heaven itself? O! in this love, you [[love]] your child so ill, That you run mad.
     ... as high as heaven itself? O! in this [[love]], you love your child so ill, That  you ...
  ... overthrown! O love! O life! Not life, but [[love]] in death! Despis'd, distressed, ...
     By cruel cruel thee quite overthrown! O [[love]]! O life! Not life, but love in death!
     ... why, lady! File, you slug-a-bed! Why, [[love]], I say! Madam! Sweet-heart! why.
          ... cell; And gave him what becomed [[love]] I might. Not stepping o'er the...
     To Mantua, with my letters to thy lord. [[Love]], give me strength! And strength...
       To live an unstain'd wife to my sweet [[love]]. Hold, then; go home, be merry.
     ... him. So will ye. I am sure, that you [[love]] me. If I do so, it will be of more…
  ... you love me. I will confess to you that I [[love]] him. So will ye, I am sure, that you...
     ... to you. Do not deny to him that you [[love]] me. I will confess to you that I love...
     ... I may be a wife. That may be must be, [[love]], on Thursday next. What must be...
       And therefore have I little talk'd of [[love]]; For Venus smiles not in a hose of...
  ... tender, To answer 'I'll not wed. "I cannot [[love]]." 'I am too young, 'I pray you, pardon...
     ... thankful even for hate, that is meant [[love]]. How now! How now, chop-logic!...
     ... and cannot come to him, To wreak the [[love]] I bore my cousin Tybalt Upon his...
     ... have done: some grief shows much of [[love]]; But much of grief shows still some...
     ... or thou look'st pale. And trust me, [[love]], in my eye so do you: Dry sorrow...
```

Figure 6.17 Fragment of the concordance list for *love*.

```
       Their course of love, the tidings of her [[death]]: And here he writes that he did...
     ... give his father, And threaten'd me with [[death]], going in the vault, If I departed not...
       ... I brought my master news of Juliet's [[death]]; And then in post he came from...
                ... for it wrought on her The form of [[death]]: meantime I writ to Romeo That he...
        ... Tybalt's doomsday, whose untimely [[death]] Banish'd the new-made...
     ... of your woes, And lead you even to [[death]]: meantime forbear, And let...
     ... daughter's bosom. O me! This sight of [[death]] is as a bell, That warms my old...
     ... noise. Lady, come form that nest Of [[death]], contagion, and unnatural sleep: A...
          ... And fearfully did menace me with [[death]], If I did stay to look on his intents.
       ... Kiss A dateless bargain to engrossing [[death]]! Come, bitter conduct, come,...
     ... fair? Shall I believe That unsubstantial [[death]] is amorous, And that the lean...
     ... this a lightning? O my love! my wife! [[Death]], that hath suck'd the honey of thy...
     ... their keepers call A lightning before [[death]]: O! how may I Call this a lightning?...
       How oft when men are at the point of [[death]] Have they been merry! Which their...
  ... vault a feasting presence full or light. [[Death]], lie thou there, by a dead man...
         Can vengeance be pursu'd further than [[death]]? Condemned villain, I do...
         Thou detestable maw, thou womb of [[death]], Gorg'd with the dearest morsel of...
     ... course. Why I descend into this bed of [[death]], Is partly, to behold my lady's...
     ... mortal drugs I have; but Mantua's law Is [[death]] to any he that utters them. Art...
          ... a poison now, Whose sale is present [[death]] in Mantua, Here lives a caitiff...
     ... part in her you could not keep from [[death]], But heaven keeps his part in...
        O love! O life! not life, but love in [[death]]! Despis'd, distressed, hated, ...
     ... wronged, spited, slain! Most detestable [[death]], by thee beguil'd, By cruel cruel...
  ... thing to rejoice and solace in, And cruel [[death]] hath catch'd it from my sight! O...
            ... by him. Death is my son-in law, [[Death]] is my heir; My daughter he hath....
```

Figure 6.18 Fragment of the concordance list for *death*.

Imagine we are interested in extracting those words that most often occur together with the words *love* and *death* in Shakespeare's *Romeo and Juliet*. The first thing to do is to extract concordance lines for *love* and *death* (Figures 6.17 and 6.18).

Recall that collocations are understood as "the occurrence of two or more words within a short space of each other in a text".[5] Consequently, concordance lines can be taken to be such a "short space" limit, as their context is limited to a certain range on each side. Therefore, if we compute a frequency wordlist out of the concordance lines for *love* and *death* in *Romeo and Juliet*, then we are likely to find most of the collocates for *love* and *death*. Furthermore, in order to refine the analysis, we shall

---

5. Sinclair (1991: 170).

extract only content words. Table 6.1 shows the twenty most frequently occurring words on either side of *love* and *death* respectively.

Table 6.1 Co-occurring words with *love* and *death* in *Romeo and Juliet.*

Love		Death	
Word	Frequency	Word	Frequency
NIGHT	15	BANISHED	12
LIKE	12	LOVE	8
COME	11	LIFE	8
HATE	11	COME	7
ROUGH	11	EXILE	7
DEATH	10	LIKE	7
DEAR	9	CALL	5
SWEET	9	CRUEL	5
FAIR	8	LAW	5
SAYS	8	PART	5
GIVE	7	POISON	5
TAKE	7	SAY	5
TENDER	7	FLOWER	4
TRUE	7	LET	4
YOUNG	7	LIES	4
GRACE	6	LIGHTNING	4
HEAVEN	6	LOOK	4
LADY	6	WIFE	4
LIFE	6	WOE	4
LIGHT	6	WORD	4

The data obtained by means of this meta-analysis of the concordance lists for *love* and *death* in *Romeo and Juliet* show which words most frequently co-occur with them. Regarding *love* we find *night, like, come, hate, rough, death* and so on, and among *death* we get *love, banished, life, come, exile, like, call, cruel* and so on. We could go further and say that when Shakespeare was writing on *love* in his *Romeo and Juliet,* he associated it with concepts or meanings related to *night, hate, death, dear, sweet* and so on. Similarly, the idea he wanted to convey when dealing with *death* in *Romeo and Juliet* has to do with *love, banished, life, exile, cruel, law* and so on. A further interesting feature is the fact that although both concepts, *love* and *death,* are situated diametrically apart for most of us, they are very much interrelated in *Romeo and Juliet: death* is a highly occurring word in the context of *love,* and vice versa. Furthermore, it is also likely that other high frequency words would be rejected as collocates if we were to use a more sophisticated and accurate analytical method. In addition, we could also investigate how the words occurring with *love* and *death* are distributed in relation to the keywords: for example, in which positions with respect to *love* the word *dear* occurs, and how often. Tables 6.2 and 6.3 display the distributions of the co-occurring words with *love* and *death*; note that the context has been reduced to just five words on both sides.

Table 6.2 Distribution of word occurring with *love*.

	Total	Total left	Total right	L5	L4	L3	L2	L1	R1	R2	R3	R4	R5
DEATH	5	2	3	1	0	0	1	0	0	2	0	0	1
DEAR	5	4	1	0	0	0	0	4	0	1	0	0	0
BLIND	4	2	2	0	0	1	0	1	0	2	0	0	0
SAYS	3	1	2	0	0	0	1	0	2	0	0	0	0
SHAPE	3	3	0	0	0	0	3	0	0	0	0	0	0
GRACE	3	3	0	0	2	0	1	0	0	0	0	0	0
SWEET	3	3	0	0	0	0	1	2	0	0	0	0	0
GENTLEMAN	3	0	3	0	0	0	0	0	0	1	0	0	2
HATE	3	2	1	0	2	0	0	0	0	0	0	0	1
PRICKING	2	1	1	0	1	0	0	0	0	1	0	0	0

Table 6.3 Distribution of word occurring with *death*.

	Total	Total left	Total right	L5	L4	L3	L2	L1	R1	R2	R3	R4	R5
LOVE	5	3	2	1	0	0	2	0	0	1	0	0	1
LAW	4	3	1	0	0	1	1	1	0	0	0	0	1
BANISHMENT	3	0	3	0	0	0	0	0	0	1	1	1	0
UNTIMELY	2	2	0	0	0	0	0	2	0	0	0	0	0
COLD	2	2	0	0	0	1	0	1	0	0	0	0	0
COUSIN'S	2	2	0	0	0	0	0	2	0	0	0	0	0
PRINCE	2	1	1	0	1	0	0	0	0	0	0	1	0
EXILE	2	2	0	0	0	1	1	0	0	0	0	0	0
SON	2	1	1	0	0	1	0	0	0	0	1	0	0
THREATEN'D	2	2	0	0	0	1	0	1	0	0	0	0	0

The distributional data adds more information on where the co-occurring words normally appear with respect to the keyword they go with. Of course, reducing the context to just five words on each side of the keyword has eliminated many co-occurring words as they fall outside this context. Some revealing hints of this are that, for instance, in the case of *love*, its co-occurrences *dear, shape, grace* and *sweet* normally occur in front or before *love*. Do they function as pre-nominal modifiers of *love*? *Gentleman* occurs generally after *love*. Other co-occurrences are distributed more evenly and are found either left or right of *love*: *death, blind, says, hate* and *pricking*. Similarly, *death* has one co-occurrence that normally appears to its right: *banishment*, whereas *law, untimely, cold, cousin's, exile* and *threaten'd* normally preface it. *Love, prince* and *son* exhibit a less "biased" distribution.

This data are undoubtedly revealing about the lexical configuration and lexical selection of Shakespeare's *Romeo and Juliet*. However, this is not enough to reach any conclusion about what Shakespeare actually wanted to convey with the concepts of *love* and *death* in *Romeo and Juliet*. It is just a very crude basis for analysing collocations, but it may be useful as a starting point. There are many interesting hints in the data that might be worth looking into in a more systematic and analytical way.

Let us analyse in a little more depth some of the co-occurrences for *love* in *Romeo and Juliet*: *death, dear, blind, shape, grace* and *sweet*. We shall start by gathering some basic data on *Romeo and Juliet* and the word *love* and its context:

- The whole play of *Romeo and Juliet* accounts for: 24,104 words or tokens.
- In *Romeo and Juliet*
  - *loves* occurs 138 times
  - *death* 72 times
  - *dear* 26 times
  - *blind* 5 times
  - *shape* 5 times
  - *grace* 5 times
  - *sweet* 36 times.

Our aim is to compare the behaviour of the words *death, dear, blind, shape, grace* and *sweet* in the whole play to their behaviour in the context of *love*. In other words, do *death, dear, blind, shape, grace* and *sweet* behave the same way in *Romeo and Juliet* as a whole as they do in proximity to *love*? To perform this comparison we need to know the extension of both contexts: the whole play and the *love*-context. We know the size of *Romeo and Juliet* in words: 24,104 words, but we do not know the total number of tokens in the *love*-context. To find this, we need to count the total concordance lines for *love* (138) and multiply them by the span or words on both sides. Remember that we truncated the concordance lines for *love* to five words on each side (see Tables 6.2 and 6.3). Consequently, as each concordance line has ten words (five words on each side of the keyword *love*), the overall context for *love* is:

138 × 10 = 1,380 words

We can now tabulate the data for the words *death, dear, blind, shape, grace* and *sweet* in the whole play and in the context of the word *love* (Table 6.4).

Table 6.4 Occurrences for *death, dear, blind, shape, grace* in the whole play and in the context of the word *love*.

	Romeo and Juliet	Love
Death	72	5
Dear	26	5
Blind	5	4
Shape	5	3
Grace	5	3
Sweet	36	3

To compare the occurrences in both contexts, we need to consider the different text lengths they occur in (total play: 24,104 tokens; *love*-context: 1,380 tokens) and calculate their percentage rates within the two contexts. For example, for death in the whole play and in the *love*-context we get:

$$death(RJ) = \left(\frac{72}{24,104}\right) \times 100 = 0.2987$$

$$death(love) = \left(\frac{6}{1,380}\right) \times 100 = 0.4348$$

This means that *death* is relatively more frequent in the context of *love* than in the whole of the play. Table 6.5 gives all the percentage rates for *death, dear, blind, shape, grace* and *sweet*.

Table 6.5 Percentage rates for *death, dear, blind, shape, grace* in both contexts.

	Romeo and Juliet	Love
Death	0.2987	0.3623
Dear	0.1079	0.3623
Blind	0.0207	0.2899
Shape	0.0207	0.2174
Grace	0.0207	0.2174
Sweet	0.1494	0.2174

If a word *w* is more frequent in context *a* than in context *b*, we might intuitively interpret it as that *w* is somehow more attracted by the words of *a* than those of *b*. In our example above, the difference between the contexts is that one context is the whole play and the other a particular context consisting of 138 concordance lines in each of which the word *love* is present. Therefore, the behaviour in the whole-play context would be generic or representative of how a specific word behaves with all the words that conform that context. In contrast, the behaviour in the *love*-context is specific. So if a word has the same relative occurrence in both contexts, we can consider this word to be non-context-specific. If the word is more frequent in the specific context, then we could say that this word is somehow "attracted" by the word(s) present in that context. Therefore, we might think that this word is context-specific. Finally, if the word is relatively more frequent in the generic context than in the specific one, we can conclude that this word is somehow "rejected" by the words in the specific context.

A brief look at the data reveals that *death* and *sweet* are more or less equally frequent in both contexts. So, we might consider them as words with a similar behaviour within the contexts of *love* and within the generic context (whole play). However, if we have a glace at the remaining words: *dear, blind, shape* and *grace*, we detect much greater differences. To get a more accurate view of the different behaviours, we can calculate how many times the relative frequency in one context is greater than in the other one (Table 6.6).

Table 6.6 Difference rates for *death, dear, blind, shape, grace* in both contexts.

	Romeo and Juliet	Love	Diff = Love/RJ
Death	0.2987	0.3623	1.21
Dear	0.1079	0.3623	3.36
Blind	0.0207	0.2899	14.00
Shape	0.0207	0.2174	10.50
Grace	0.0207	0.2174	10.50
Sweet	0.1494	0.2174	1.46

Table 6.6 shows now that *dear, blind, shape* and *grace* in the two contexts exhibit great differences: *dear* is three times more frequent in the *love*-context than in the whole play, while *blind* is fourteen times, and *shape* and *grace* are ten times more frequent. These figures are particularly revealing as these words (*dear, blind, shape* and *grace*) are clearly much more prominent in the proximity of *love* and this might lead us to think that there may be some lexical-semantic attraction between them and the word *love*.

However, these differences cannot be properly assessed without applying an appropriate measure of significance to the results. In statistical terms, a collocation is significant if the probability of a word co-occurring with another lexical item (the node) within a specific context or span (i.e. concordance line, sentence, etc.) is greater than might be expected by pure chance. In what follows, we shall consider some of these measures and explain how this probability is calculated and how it reflects statistical significance.

6.3.1 *z*-score

Perhaps the most common statistical measure used is the *z*-score. First introduced by Berry-Rogghe,[6] the *z*-score, to put it succinctly, compares the observed frequency between a lexical node and its collocate to the expected frequency and evaluates the difference between these values. In order to calculate the *z*-score we need the following data:

- the total number of words (tokens) of the whole text or corpus = T_c
- the total occurrences of the specific collocation within the whole text or corpus = F_c
- the total occurrences of the specific collocation within the specific context (span); this is the observed frequency = O
- the total number of words (tokens) of the specific context (span) = T_s.

---

6. Berry-Rogghe (1973).

Let us apply this to an example. Recall our example above where we found a number of words in *Romeo and Juliet* that co-occurred very frequently within the span of the node word *love: death, dear, blind, shape, grace* and *sweet.* The data for these co-occurrences are given in Table 6.7.

Table 6.7 Data needed for *z*-score calculation.

	T_c	F_c	O	T_s
Death	24.104	72	5	1.380
Dear	24.104	26	5	1.380
Blind	24.104	5	4	1.380
Shape	24.104	5	3	1.380
Grace	24.104	5	3	1.380
Sweet	24.104	36	3	1.380

To calculate the expected frequency *E* of a given word, we first need to obtain its probability within the whole text or corpus. This is expressed as:

$$p = \frac{F_c}{T_c}$$

That is, we divide the total occurrences of that word in the text/corpus by the total number of tokens of the text/corpus. Thus, for example, the probability of *death* in *Romeo and Juliet* is:

$$p(death) = \frac{72}{24,104} = 0.00298$$

If *death* is randomly distributed throughout the text, then its expected frequency in the context of *love* (totalling 1,380 tokens) should be:

$$E = p \times T_s$$
$$E(death) = 0.00298 \times 1,380 = 4.122$$

We now have all the data to calculate the *z*-score. This is done using the following formula:

$$z = \frac{(O - E)}{\sqrt{E(1 - p)}}$$

The *z*-score for *death* within the context of *love* is:

$$z = \frac{(5 - 4.122)}{\sqrt{4.122(1 - 0.00298)}} = \frac{0.8779}{\sqrt{4.1097}} = 0.433$$

For a collocation to be statistically significant, a useful cut-off measure is around 3; more precisely, for a collocation to be statistically significant at 0.01 (1% level), the z-score should be at least 2.576. The figure obtained for *death* within the context of *love* is very low (0.433) and does not show any significant variation between the occurrence of *death* within the context of *love* and its occurrences throughout the whole play. Therefore, we conclude that *love* does not exert any lexical influence on *death*; that is, they are lexically unrelated and its behaviour within the proximity of *love* is similar to the way it behaves with all the other words that make up *Romeo and Juliet.*

Table 6.8 gives the z-score for all the words (*death, dear, blind, shape, grace* and *sweet*).

Table 6.8 z-scores for *death, dear, blind, shape, grace* and *sweet.*

	T_c	F_c	O	T_s	p	E	z-score
Death	24.104	72	5	1,380	0.0029	4.1221	0.4330
Dear	24.104	26	5	1,380	0.0011	1.4885	2.8796
Blind	24.104	5	4	1,380	0.0002	0.2863	6.9419
Shape	24.104	5	3	1,380	0.0002	0.2863	5.0726
Grace	24.104	5	3	1,380	0.0002	0.2863	5.0726
Sweet	24.104	36	3	1,380	0.0015	2.0611	0.6545

A detailed comparison of the z-scores reveals that *dear, blind, shape* and *grace* are four significant collocations of *love* in *Romeo and Juliet* at the 0.01 level. In contrast, neither *death* nor *sweet* reach the threshold level of 2.576 and we conclude that they are not statistically significant. This might be a starting point for further investigation and for looking into the way in which Shakespeare lexically and semantically related his concept of *love* in *Romeo and Juliet.* There is objective evidence that words such as *dear, blind, shape* and *grace* are conceptually interrelated with *love.*

The more strongly connected two items are, the higher the z-score will be. A z-score close to 0 indicates that the co-occurrence of the two items is largely due to chance. Finally, a z-score can also be negative, indicating that the two words are more frequent in isolation than in co-occurrence. This is an interesting feature, as it may be an indication of the words repelling each other.

6.3.2 Mutual information

Another statistical measure is *mutual information*[7] (*MI*). MI is a formula borrowed from the area of theoretical computer science known as information theory.

The *MI* score helps us to find the words most closely associated with a given node and measures the strength of their association. Unlike the z-score, it does not evaluate

---

7. See Church and Hanks (1990) and Church *et al.* (1991).

the difference between observed and expected frequencies, but compares the joint versus isolated occurrences. Hence, it aims to measure the amount of information that the observation of one word gives about the likely occurrence of the other.

MI compares the probability of observing word w_1 and word w_2 together (which is the joint probability) with the probabilities of observing w_1 and w_2 independently (by chance). This is expressed by the formula:

$$MI = \log_2 \frac{P(w_1, w_2)}{P(w_1) \times P(w_2)}$$

If there is a genuine association between w_1 and w_2, then the joint probability $p(w_1, w_2)$ will be much larger than chance: $p(w_1) \times p(w_2)$; consequently the *MI* score will be greater than 0. If there is no relationship between w_1 and w_2, then $p(w_1, w_2)$ and $p(w_1) \times p(w_2)$ will be equal or very similar, and *MI* will be around 0. And finally, if w_1 and w_2 repel each other, that is, w_1 and w_2 are in complementary distribution, the *MI* score will be negative.

The probabilities are calculated as follows: $p(w_1)$ and $p(w_2)$ are estimated by counting the individual occurrences of w_1 and w_2 in the whole text/corpus and normalizing the result by the total number of words (tokens) of the whole text or corpus; the joint probability $p(w_1, w_2)$ is calculated by counting the number of co-occurrences[8] of w_1 and w_2 and normalizing the result by the total number of words (tokens) of the whole text or corpus.

Let us apply this collocation formula to the same example above, *Romeo and Juliet*, where we found a number of words that co-occurred very frequently within the span of the node word *love*: *death, dear, blind, shape, grace* and *sweet*. The data needed to calculate the *MI* score are given in Table 6.9. Note that observed values are not given for *love*, as they refer to the co-occurrence with *love* and we are not interested in whether it co-occurs with itself or not. What we want to examine is the co-occurrence of *love* with other lexical items, namely *death, dear, blind, shape, grace* and *sweet*.

Table 6.9 Data on *death, dear, blind, shape, grace* and *sweet* with *love*.

w_1	w_2	Freq. w_1	Freq. w_2	Freq. (w_1, w_2)
Love	Death	138	72	5
Love	Dear	138	26	5
Love	Blind	138	5	4
Love	Shape	138	5	3
Love	Grace	138	5	3
Love	Sweet	138	36	3

---

8. This is the same as the *observed frequency*.

To illustrate the application of the formula, we shall calculate the *MI* score for the co-occurrence *death*. Note that we need to multiply the coefficient by the total number of words (tokens) of the whole text or corpus; in our case *Romeo and Juliet*, totalling 24,104 tokens.

$$MI = \log_2\left(\frac{5}{138 \times 72}\right) \times 24,104 = \log_2 12.1296 = 3.6004$$

A strict statistical significance ratio for *MI* scores is not given and some researchers[9] suggest a score of 1.58 as a cut-off point, which is the same as taking the cut-off for cases where the numerator is three or more times greater than the denominator. Note that 1.58 is roughly the logarithm of 3 to the base of 2. Therefore a ratio of 3:1 can be used as a cut-off point. Back to our example, we discover that the *MI* score for *death* (3.6004) is significant, and we can conclude that *death* is a collocation of *love*. However, this contradicts the finding above where it turned out not to be a collocation of *love*, according to the *z*-score estimated.

Table 6.10 gives the *MI* score for all the words (*death, dear, blind, shape, grace* and *sweet*).

Table 6.10 *MI* scores for *death, dear, blind, shape, grace* and *sweet*.

w_1	w_2	Freq. w_1	Freq. w_2	Freq. (w_1,w_2)	*MI*
Love	Death	138	72	5	3.6004
Love	Dear	138	26	5	5.0699
Love	Blind	138	5	4	7.1265
Love	Shape	138	5	3	6.7114
Love	Grace	138	5	3	6.7114
Love	Sweet	138	36	3	3.8634

It is interesting that not only *death*, but all the co-occurrences, are given as statistically significant collocations for *love*. This contrasts sharply with the statistically significant *z*-scores given above.

It seems as if *MI* gives too much weight to low frequency events. For example, suppose that in *Romeo and Juliet*, we had word *x* that occurs once and word *a* that also occurs once, and suppose *x* and *a* co-occur. Now consider a different word *y* that occurs twice and word *b* that occurs twice, too, and imagine *y* and *b* co-occur twice, and so on. Table 6.11 gives the *MI* scores for five fictitious words showing this behaviour and an additional sixth word that occurs 1,000 times.

---

9. See Barnbrook (1996).

Table 6.11 *MI* scores for six fictitious words.

w_1	w_2	Freq. w_1	Freq. w_2	Freq. (w_1, w_2)	*MI*
X	A	1	1	1	14.5569
Y	B	2	2	2	13.5569
Z	C	3	3	3	12.9720
U	D	4	4	4	12.5569
V	E	5	5	5	12.2350
W	F	1,000	1,000	1,000	4.5912

Surprisingly, the more a word co-occurs with a node word, the smaller its *MI* score is. In order to correct this and to give more weight to frequent events, the numerator of the *MI* formula is taken to the power of three.[10] The cube of the numerator produces a more effective coefficient for collocation extraction. Thus, we get:

$$MI3 = \log_2 \frac{(p(w_1, w_2))^3}{p(w_1) \times p(w_2)}$$

This improves the scores significantly and in a more realistic way: more frequent co-occurrences get higher *MI* scores. Table 6.12 gives the new estimations of our fictitious words using *MI3*, the correct *MI* formula.

Table 6.12 *MI3* scores for six fictitious words.

w_1	w_2	Freq. w_1	Freq. w_2	Freq. (w_1, w_2)	MI
X	A	1	1	1	14.5569
Y	B	2	2	2	15.5569
Z	C	3	3	3	16.1419
U	D	4	4	4	16.5569
V	E	5	5	5	16.8789
W	F	1,000	1,000	1,000	24.5227

If we apply *MI3* to our example in *Romeo and Juliet* we get the results shown in Table 6.13.

Before we interpret these *MI3* scores, let us go back for a moment to the ratio 3:1 as a cut-off point for *MI*, that is, the idea that the numerator should roughly be at least three times greater than the denominator. If we applied the same ratio to *MI3* scores, we would need to raise the numerator to the cube. This would give a ratio of 3^3:1, that is, 27:1, which is not very straightforward to interpret. Instead, if we can calculate the logarithm of 27 to the base of 2, we get 4.75, which is the cut-off point to use for *MI3*.

---

10. See Gaussier and Langé (1994).

Table 6.13 *MI3* scores for *death, dear, blind, shape, grace* and *sweet.*

w_1	w_2	Freq. w_1	Freq. w_2	Freq. (w_1,w_2)	*MI3*
Love	Death	138	72	5	8.2443
Love	Dear	138	26	5	9.7138
Love	Blind	138	5	4	11.1265
Love	Shape	138	5	3	9.8814
Love	Grace	138	5	3	9.8814
Love	Sweet	138	36	3	7.0334

A brief look at Table 6.13 reveals that all co-occurrences are significant according to *MI3*, which is exactly the same as happened above with *MI*, except that *MI3*, additionally, gives more weight to frequent events, which is a major handicap for *MI*.

If we rank the data according to their scores using the three measures (Table 6.14), we notice a high correlation between all three scores, which is a clear sign of their validity for collocation extraction, not necessarily related to their accuracy. This is a different issue we shall tackle in section 6.3.4.

Table 6.14 Comparing *z*-score, *MI* and *MI3* scores for *death, dear, blind, shape, grace* and *sweet.*

	z-score		*MI*		*MI3*	
	Score	Rank	Score	Rank	Score	Rank
Death	0.4330	6	3.6004	6	8.2443	5
Dear	2.8796	4	5.0699	4	9.7138	4
Blind	6.9419	1	7.1265	1	11.1265	1
Shape	5.0726	2	6.7114	2	9.8814	2
Grace	5.0726	2	6.7114	2	9.8814	2
Sweet	0.6545	5	3.8634	5	7.0334	6

6.3.3 Log-likelihood or G^2

The statistic *log-likelihood* (LL)[11] or G^2 can also be used to indicate the collocational strength holding between two words.

Typically, the *LL* determines whether word w_1 is a collocation of another word w_2 by taking the ratio between how often it occurs in a text/corpus compared to how often it would be expected to occur based on the model of chance (independence). An *LL* score of 0 implies that the data fits the hypothesized model perfectly, meaning that w_1 exhibits complete independence with respect to w_2. It is very similar to the chi-square as the hypothesized model is calculated according to the data on a contingency table. The difference is in the formula used to calculate the collocation value.

---

11. See Dunning (1993). Note that we have already used *LL* in Chapter 5 (section 5.2) when dealing with keyword extraction.

For the *LL* calculation we need to consider the contingency table shown in Table 6.15, where *a* = the frequency of the co-occurrence; *b* = the number of instances where the node does not co-occur with the collocate; *c* = the number of instances where the collocate does not co-occur with the node; and *d* = the number of words in the corpus minus the number of occurrences of the node and the collocate.

Table 6.15 Contingency table for *LL* calculation.

	W_2	Not-W_2	
W_1	a	b	a+b
Not-W_1	c	d	c+d
	a+c	b+d	a+b+c+d

Let us complete the contingency table with our data on the co-occurrence of *death* with the node word *love* (Table 6.16). Recall that the total number of words (tokens) of the whole text or corpus, in our case *Romeo and Juliet*, is 24,104.

Table 6.16 Contingency table for *LL* calculation: *death*.

	W_2	Not-W_2	
W_1	5	133	138
Not-W_1	67	23,894	23,961
	72	24,027	24,099

Next, we need to insert the values in to the *LL* formula:

$$LL = 2 \times [a \times \log(a) + b \times \log(b) + c \times \log(c) + d \times \log(d) - (a + b) \times \log(a + b) \\ - (a + c) \times \log(a + c) - (b + d) \times \log(b + d) - (c + d) \times \log(c + d) \\ + (a + b + c + d) \times \log(a + b + c + d)]$$

giving:

$$LL = 2 \times [5 \times \log(5) + 133 \times \log(133) + 67 \times \log(67) + 23{,}894 \times \log(23{,}894) \\ - (138) \times \log(138) - (72) \times \log(72) - (24{,}027) \times \log(24{,}027) - (23{,}961) \\ \times \log(23{,}961) + (24{,}099) \times \log(24{,}099)] \\ = 7.05081$$

The higher the *LL*-value, the more significant is the difference between two frequency scores. An *LL*-value of 3.8 or higher is significant at the level of $p < 0.05$ and an *LL*-value of 6.6 or higher is significant at $p < 0.01$. Considering the *LL*-value for *death* with respect to its co-occurrence with *love*, we can conclude that it is a statistically significant collocation at $p < 0.05$, as its *LL*-value, 7.05, is greater than 3.8.

Table 6.17 gives all the *LL*-values for *death, dear, blind, shape, grace* and *sweet* within the proximity of the node word *love* in *Romeo and Juliet.*

Table 6.17 *LL*-values for *death, dear, blind, shape, grace* and *sweet.*

	LL-value	Significance level: $p < 0.05$
Death	7.05	Sig.
Dear	11.54	Sig.
Blind	15.82	Sig.
Shape	10.56	Sig.
Grace	10.56	Sig.
Sweet	4.74	Sig.

LL, as *MI* and *MI3* did, demonstrates that all collocations are statistically significant. The ranked collocation strengths show a perfect correlation between *z*-score and *MI*, and minor differences between *z*-score/*MI* and *MI3*; however, major divergences can be noted between *z*-score/*MI*/*MI3* and *LL* (Table 6.18).

Table 6.18 Comparing ranked scores: *z*-score, *MI*, *MI3* and *LL*.

	z-score	*MI*	*MI3*	*LL*-value
Death	6	6	5	5
Dear	4	4	4	2
Blind	1	1	1	1
Shape	2	2	2	3
Grace	2	2	2	3
Sweet	5	5	6	6

For a neater quantitative comparison, let us standardize the scores of all four collocation measures by means of this formula:[12]

$$z = \frac{score - mean}{SD}$$

This will enable us to make a full comparison of all four scores. The ordered standardized measures are given in Table 6.19 and Figure 6.19.

Almost no discrepancies are found between *z*-score and *MI*; there are minor differences between *z*-score/*MI* and *MI3* (*dear* and *death*), and *MI3* and *LL* (*shape, grace* and *dear*), while important divergences appear between *z*-score/*MI* and *LL* (*shape, grace, dear, sweet* and *death*).

---

12. This was introduced earlier in Chapter 1 (section 1.6). Do not confuse *z*-score with standardized *z*-values, although there are important similarities (see Barnbrook 1996).

Table 6.19 Comparing standardized scores: *z*-score, *MI, MI3* and *LL*.

	z-score	*MI*	*MI3*	*LL*-value
Blind	1.3049	1.0429	1.2615	1.5065
Shape	0.5941	0.7751	0.3968	0.1332
Grace	0.5941	0.7751	0.3968	0.1332
Dear	−0.2397	−0.2839	0.2804	0.3890
Sweet	−1.0857	−1.0623	−1.5810	−1.3864
Death	−1.1700	−1.2320	−0.7401	−0.7833

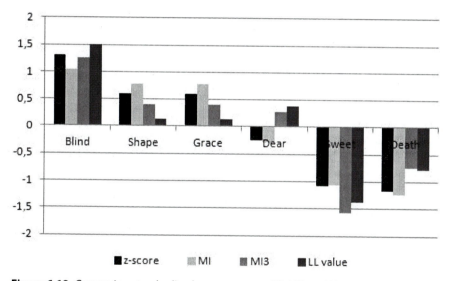

Figure 6.19 Comparing standardized scores: *z*-score, *MI, MI3* and *LL*.

A quantitative comparison among the different collocation scores (Table 6.20) reveals that in the collocation *blind* the greatest divergence is found between *MI* and *LL* (0.4636); in *shape* between *MI* and *LL* (0.6419); in *grace* between *MI* and *LL* (0.6419); in *dear* between *MI* and *LL* (0.6729); in *sweet* between *MI* and *MI3* (0.5187); and in *death* between *MI* and *MI3* (0.4919).

It seems that these discrepancies are most prominent between *MI* and *LL*, and between *MI* and *MI3*. Divergences among the collocation strength scores between *MI* and *LL* emerge with low frequency words: *blind* (5), *shape* (5), *grace* (5) and *dear* (26), whereas with more frequent words (*death*: 72 and *sweet*: 36) the greatest score differences are obtained between *MI* and *MI3*.

Table 6.20 Divergences among *z*-score, *MI*, *MI3* and *LL*.

Blind	*z*-score	*MI*	*MI3*
MI	0.262		
MI3	0.0434	0.2186	
LL	0.2016	0.4636	0.245

Shape	*z*-score	*MI*	*MI3*
MI	0.181		
MI3	0.1973	0.3783	
LL	0.4609	0.6419	0.2636

Grace	*z*-score	*MI*	*MI3*
MI	0.181		
MI3	0.1973	0.3783	
LL	0.4609	0.6419	0.2636

Dear	*z*-score	*MI*	*MI3*
MI	0.0442		
MI3	0.5201	0.5643	
LL	0.6287	0.6729	0.1086

Sweet	*z*-score	*MI*	*MI3*
MI	0.0234		
MI3	0.4953	0.5187	
LL	0.3007	0.3241	0.1946

Death	*z*-score	*MI*	*MI3*
MI	0.062		
MI3	0.4299	0.4919	
LL	0.3867	0.4487	0.0432

The sum of all divergences (Table 6.21) ratifies the fact that the most outstanding differences are found between *MI* and *LL* (3.1931), and between *MI* and *MI3* (2.5501), whereas the smallest divergences are between *z*-score and *MI*.

Table 6.21 Sum of divergences.

	z-score	*MI*	*MI3*
MI	0.7536		
MI3	1.8833	2.5501	
LL	2.4395	3.1931	1.1186

To explore these divergences more, we shall examine all four measures in a more exhaustive way in the next section.

6.3.4 Comparing collocational measures

Let us start by applying all four formulae above (*z*-score, *MI*, *MI3* and *LL*) to the co-occurrences of the word form *whale* in Melville's novel *Moby Dick*. In order to compare the measures, we shall first calculate the statistically significant collocations (Table 6.22) by means of the four measures, leaving just the twenty-five most prominent content word collocations.

At first glance we can see coincidences among the various measures regarding the words most strongly correlated with the node: *sperm, white, Greenland,* and so on, particularly among *z*-score, *MI3* and *LL*, but not *MI*.

Table 6.22 Significant collocations ranked by scores.

z-score	MI	MI3	LL
SPERM	COPPERED	SPERM	SPERM
WHITE	QUOG	WHITE	WHITE
GREENLAND	SCRAGG	GREENLAND	STEAD
SCRAGG	HORNED	FISHERY	GREENLAND
QUOG	TRUMPA	SHIP	DAD
COPPERED	DAD	BOAT	SHIP
HORNED	HUMPBACKED	GREAT	FISHERY
HUMPBACKED	DEPOSED	ALONGSIDE	BOAT
FISHERY	STEAD	QUOG	GREAT
ALONGSIDE	SIGHTING	COPPERED	PHYSETER
PHYSETER	TITLES	SCRAGG	QUOG
SIGHTING	PHYSETER	ENGLISH	ALONGSIDE
STEAD	SPECTRALLY	HUMPBACKED	ENGLISH
DEPOSED	BASIN	HEADED	HORNED
TRUMPA	CONFINE	SPOUT	SPOUT
DAD	CIRCUMSPECTLY	HORNED	BODY
TITLES	VACATION	BODY	SHIPS
PUDDING	GIBBERING	HUNTERS	DEAD
ICEBERG	USURPER	SHIPS	SIGHTING
HYENA	ALIMENT	DEAD	TITLES
SPOUTING	FOIBLE	AMERICAN	HEADED
HEADED	BREECHING	LINE	LINE
STRICKEN	COLNETT'S	STRICKEN	HUNTERS
ELEPHANT	TOPMAUL	ELEPHANT	AMERICAN
RAISES	COLLATED	SPOUTING	ELEPHANT

For a better comparison we shall sort the list alphabetically, so that the differences in their contents are easier to spot (Table 6.23). Additionally, the rank order is given with each collocation.

This sorting highlights two things:

- Some words are not found to be statistically significant collocations by some measures.
- Some words are ranked differently based on the collocational strength obtained by the various measures.

As already mentioned, there are some parallels between three of the measures (z-score, MI3 and LL) regarding the most prominent collocations. This suggests that *sperm*, *white* and *Greenland* strongly collocate with *whale*. *Elephant* is also ranked similarly by z-score, MI3 and LL. Other important rank similarities are found between MI3 and LL: *American*, *boat*, *body*, *dead*, *great*, *horned*, *line*, *Quog*, *ship*, *ships* and *spout*. We also find rank similarities between z-score and MI: *horned*, *humpbacked*, *Physetter*, *Quog*, *Scragg*, *sighting* and *stead*. These coincidences

Table 6.23 Collocates ordered alphabetically with rank order.

z-score	MI	MI3	LL
	20. ALIMENT		
10. ALONGSIDE		8. ALONGSIDE	12. ALONGSIDE
		21. AMERICAN	24. AMERICAN
	14. BASIN		
		6. BOAT	8. BOAT
		17. BODY	16. BODY
	22. BREECHING		
	16. CIRCUMSPECTLY		
	23. COLLATED		
	25. COLNETT'S		
	15. CONFINE		
6. COPPERED	1. COPPERED	10. COPPERED	
16. DAD	6. DAD		5. DAD
		20. DEAD	18. DEAD
14. DEPOSED	8. DEPOSED		
24. ELEPHANT		24. ELEPHANT	25. ELEPHANT
		12. ENGLISH	13. ENGLISH
9. FISHERY		4. FISHERY	7. FISHERY
	21. FOIBLE		
	18. GIBBERING		
		7. GREAT	9. GREAT
3. GREENLAND		3. GREENLAND	4. GREENLAND
22. HEADED		14. HEADED	21. HEADED
7. HORNED	4. HORNED	16. HORNED	14. HORNED
8. HUMPBACKED	7. HUMPBACKED	13. HUMPBACKED	
		18. HUNTERS	23. HUNTERS
20. HYENA			
19. ICEBERG			
		22. LINE	22. LINE
11. PHYSETER	12. PHYSETER		10. PHYSETER
18. PUDDING			
5. QUOG	2. QUOG	9. QUOG	11. QUOG
25. RAISES			
4. SCRAGG	3. SCRAGG	11. SCRAGG	
		5. SHIP	6. SHIP
		19. SHIPS	17. SHIPS
12. SIGHTING	10. SIGHTING		19. SIGHTING
	13. SPECTRALLY		
1. SPERM		1. SPERM	1. SPERM
		15. SPOUT	15. SPOUT
21. SPOUTING		25. SPOUTING	
13. STEAD	9. STEAD		3. STEAD
23. STRICKEN		23. STRICKEN	
17. TITLES	11. TITLES		20. TITLES
	24. TOPMAUL		
15. TRUMPA	5. TRUMPA		
	19. USURPER		
	17. VACATION		
2. WHITE		2. WHITE	2. WHITE

might suggest that these co-occurrences can be considered strong collocations. However, *MI* highlights different collocations as prominent.

Let us now analyse which measures extract which collocations. We shall use the technique proposed in section 5.4 for wordlist comparisons. As we are going to compare four different collocation lists, each one corresponding to four different collocation measures (*z*-score, *MI*, *MI3* and *LL*), we would need to take list 1 once, list 2 twice, list 3 four times and list 4 eight times. The frequencies of the meta-frequency list would range from 1 to 15, indicating the memberships shown in Table 6.24:

Table 6.24 Collocation membership according to measure used.

Frequency	Collocation measure(s)	Collocation
1	*z*-score	HYENA, ICEBERG, PUDDING
2	*MI*	ALIMENT, BASIN, CIRCUMSPECTLY, CONFINE, GIBBERING, SPECTRALLY, USURPER, VACATION
3	*z*-score – *MI*	DEPOSED, TRUMPA
4	*MI3*	HEADED, HUNTERS
5	*z*-score – *MI3*	
6	*MI* – *MI3*	
7	*z*-score – *MI* – *MI3*	COPPERED, HUMPBACKED, SCRAGG
8	*LL*	
9	*z*-score – *LL*	
10	*MI* – *LL*	
11	*z*-score – *MI* – *LL*	DAD, PHYSETER, SIGHTING, STEAD, TITLES
12	*MI3* – *LL*	BOAT, BODY, DEAD, ENGLISH, GREAT, SHIP, SHIPS, SPOUT
13	*z*-score – *MI3* – *LL*	ALONGSIDE, FISHERY, GREENLAND, SPERM, WHITE
14	*MI* – *MI3* – *LL*	
15	*z*-score – *MI* – *MI3* – *LL*	HORNED, QUOG

Examining the collocations that have been highlighted by just the *z*-score (*hyena*, *iceberg* and *pudding*), we can see that they occur in the text relatively few times: three, five and five times respectively. This is even more noticeable in those collocations only present in the *MI* list – *aliment, basin, circumspectly, confine, gibbering, spectrally*, *usurper* and *vacation* – and also those collocations in both the *z*-score list and the *MI* one – *deposed* and *Trumpa*. All these only occur once in *Moby Dick*. It seems as if *z*-score and *MI* artificially inflate the significance of low frequency co-occurring words. This point is reinforced by the fact that other more frequent words in *Moby Dick* do not occur within *z*-score and *MI*. For example, *headed* and *hunters*. These two words have relatively high frequencies in the novel, twenty-five (*headed*) and twenty-eight (*hunters*), and are downgraded by the *z*-score and the *MI*, and what is more, not even noticed as collocations. These findings are also supported by the rank of the words in the lists of *z*-score and *MI* compared with *MI3*: *coppered* is ranked sixth by the *z*-score, first by the *MI*, but tenth by the *MI3*. Similar ranking is found in the case of *humpbacked* and *Scragg*, which, again, are ranked much higher in the the *z*-score and *MI* lists than in the *MI3* one, or *horned* and *Quog*, which again are ranked much higher in *z*-score and *MI* than in *MI3* and *LL*.

It is interesting that there is no collocation exclusively highlighted by *LL*. It seems as if *MI3* and *LL* do not inflate the significance of low frequency words and behave in similar ways.

A Spearman correlation analysis on the collocation ranks based on the collocational strength obtained by the various measures gives the results shown in Table 6.25.

Table 6.25 Correlations among *z*-score, *MI*, *MI3* and *LL*.

			z-score	*MI*	*MI3*	*LL*
Spearman rho	*z*-score	Correlation coefficient	1.000	0.615	0.725	0.622
		Sig. (2-tailed)	.	0.033	0.005	0.031
		N	24	12	13	12
	MI	Correlation coefficient	0.615	1.000	0.800	−0.086
		Sig. (2-tailed)	0.033	.	0.104	0.872
		N	12	25	5	6
	MI3	Correlation coefficient	0.725	0.800	1.000	0.958
		Sig. (2-tailed)	0.005	0.104	.	0.000
		N	13	5	25	20
	LL	Correlation coefficient	0.622	−0.0086	0.958	1.000
		Sig. (2-tailed)	0.031	0.872	0.000	.
		N	12	6	20	25

The data reveal that the collocation ranks of the *z*-score correlate significantly with all other measures. However, *MI* only shows significant correlation with

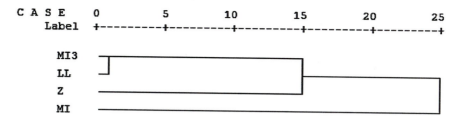

Figure 6.20 Hierarchical cluster analysis on collocations.

z-score. The *z*-score, *MI3* and *LL* all correlate significantly with one another; the rank correlation between *MI3* and *LL* is particularly high.

As already mentioned, some collocations are not found to be statistically significant by some measures and do not appear in some lists. Hierarchical cluster analysis (Figure 6.20) shows that in this respect the two most similar measures are *MI3* and *LL*. The *z*-scores reveal important differences with *MI3* and *LL*, whereas the most significant difference is produced by *MI*. *MI* behaves in a very peculiar way as it includes and highlights some completely different collocations from those produced by *z*-score, *MI3* and *LL*. This outsider-behaviour of the *z*-score and, in particular, the *MI* is mainly due to the way they artificially inflate the significance of low frequency co-occurring words and downgrade more frequent words.

It is very difficult to conclude which measure is the more accurate or precise for collocation extraction. However, the strong similarities between *MI3* and *LL* indicate their validity and effectiveness for extracting collocation. However, it is probably better not to discard *a priori* the other two measures, *z*-score and *MI*, but to retain them in order to use and contrast as many sources of information as possible when exploring and analysing collocations by taking advantage of more than one measure.

6.3.5 Lexical constellation: a hierarchical model of collocations

As mentioned above, a significant collocation can be defined in statistical terms as the probability of one lexical item co-occurring with another word or phrase within a specified linear distance or span being greater than might be expected from pure chance.

In this section, we shall re-examine some basic notions regarding collocations with reference to real data. This, we are confident, will give us a more comprehensive view of the complex interrelationships (semantic, lexical, syntactic, etc.) between co-occurring linguistic items.

Three starting positions are taken:

- We understand collocates in the stricter sense, as already discussed in section 6.2 above: that is, words that have a strong tendency to co-occur around a node word (the word that is being studied) in a concordance (co-text around the node).

- In order to avoid bias in favour of any data, we shall concentrate on the occurrences of one lemma within a single semantic domain: the Spanish noun *mano* (hand).[13]
- No optimal span is taken for granted.[14] We shall use the full sentence as the concordance (although important collocates can be missed due to anaphoric reference).

To make sure that we are actually focusing on the same semantic context, we shall first extract all instances (full sentences) containing *mano*, both in singular and plural form, and next, classify all occurrences semantically by means of the various definitions for *mano*.

This preliminary distributional analysis will allow us to isolate the various meanings and to concentrate on individual meanings or identical semantic contexts. In the analysis that follows, we shall concentrate on one specific meaning of *mano* ("layer of paint, varnish or other substance put on a surface at one time"; see Figure 6.21).

As already noted, no preliminary assumptions are made regarding relevant or optimal window size or span. We shall simply start by taking the whole sentence in the belief that full sentences are more likely to contain complete ideas, meanings and so on. A complete meaning as represented in a full sentence is, we believe, the best guarantee for keeping the meaning of the node word. It is true that each word (node) exerts a significant influence on its neighbouring words, and even perhaps on some words outside the sentence range. Consequently, fixing a span beforehand might often distort the *unity of meaning* or *complete meaning* in a sentence. We tend to think that words outside the range of a sentence are not likely to affect the *meaning unity* of other sentences, nor are they strongly associated with node words within other sentences, but this does not generally seem to be the case.

Figure 6.22 shows the co-occurrence distribution relative to the distance from the node word. The *x*-axis illustrates the position relative to the node word: positive values indicate the co-occurring items following the node word, whereas negative ones precede it. The *y*-axis displays the total number of co-occurring items. Clearly, the closer we get to the node, the more co-occurrences we find (six tokens at positions −3, −2, −1, +1, and five tokens at +2), which is indeed nothing new. The skewed negative distribution of the data is however interesting. This clearly indicates that items co-occurring with the node are not necessarily distributed normally (note the superimposed trendline).

Next, we shall calculate the *z*-scores of all co-occurrences in order to elucidate which co-occurring items are actually most relevant or statistically significant. The distribution of significant collocates (*z*-scores) produces the graph shown in Figure 6.23, where the *x*-axis displays the position relative to the node word and the *y*-axis the number of statistically significant collocates.

---

13. Extracted from the *CUMBRE* Corpus.
14. Note that most concordance software (e.g. WordSmith) takes a span of five words on each side for collocation analysis.

(1) ... porque han cambiado una ventana, porque ha cambiado eso, se ha hecho un piquete el albañil del pueblo, que ha puesto ahí la ventana y le ha dado yeso y ha pintado encima, o ha hecho una roza para el enchufe y se ha pasado por la nariz de un angelote, o por la mano de una virgen, pues, tranquilamente, luego le ha dado una {MANO} de yeso y a correr.

(2) Si algún tono no tiene la intensidad deseada, aplique otra {MANO} de pintura.

(3) - ¿Te quedó bien la {MANO}?

(4) Después se les da a las cuentas una {MANO} de esmalte especial para protegerlas.

(5) Profesora de la Universidad Autónoma de Madrid, fundadora y directora del Museo de Artes y Tradiciones Populares, especialista en etnografía y autora de varios libros sobre estos temas, Guadalupe González-Hontoria estudia, en la primera parte de su obra, todo lo relacionado con los "ritos" del nacimiento: exvotos y velas de cera, la rosa de Jericó, cintas de Santa Casilda, báculo de Santo Domingo de Silos, colcha y velas de San Ramón, cruz de Caravaca para el parto, amuletos infantiles -lunares, crómicos -, objetos para proteger a los niños, cunas y cuévanas, silletas y taburetes para el parto, protectores, mantillas de cristianar, jarros y tortas de bautizo, indumentarias del neófito, "cuentas de leche" para la crianza, pilas bautismales, "almorratxas" o botijos, {MANOS} de sal, "figas" de azabache, parideras, trajes de "tamarco" y un largo etcétera de utensilios y voces que subyugarían al maestro Azorín.

(6) Con unas vigas de cemento, unas {MANOS} de cal, y tejas nuevas, no hay viento que la tumbe.

Figure 6.21 Concordance sentences for *MANO (layer of paint, etc.).*

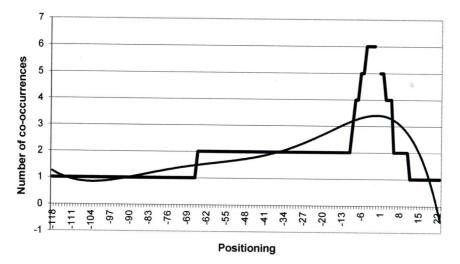

Figure 6.22 Distribution of co-occurrences versus trendline.

In order to get a more accurate and neater visual representation of the distribution of the significant collocates than the zigzag curve in Figure 6.23, we shall normalize the data of the y-axis (number of significant collocates), by dividing the number of significant collocates found at each position by their positioning with respect to the

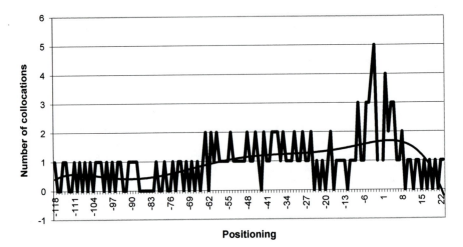

Figure 6.23 Distribution of collocates versus trendline.

node word (Figure 6.24). The *y*-axis represents the relative number of significant collocates.

Figure 6.24 visually represents the extent of the node's influence on its immediate environment: its *lexical gravity*.[15] The graph stresses the attraction of *MANO(layer of paint, etc.)*, which is greatest in the immediate environment and wears off with distance. This is indeed a fact we have already established (see a zoom display from −10 to +10; Figure 6.25).

If we compare the actual gravity with the trendline, we realize that there is a kind of correlation between the relative number of significant collocates and the node distance, particularly close to the node word. By looking at Figure 6.25, we can with some confidence state that the most relevant collocational context for *MANO(layer of paint, etc.)* is between −8 and +6. It is also interesting that data around the node tends to have a more normal distribution than overall. However, evidence shows that fixing an optimal span could be misleading as the appearance of significant collocates is likely to exceed these pre-established limits.

Against the background of this data, it becomes clear that the distribution of significant collocates is not necessarily normal and this has important consequences.

One important finding from our empirical data is that there are many statistically significant collocations quite far away from the node word. If this is true, then we are likely to miss many collocations if we reduce the analytical span to just −5 to +5. On the other hand, it also seems unlikely and/or dubious that co-occurrences very far away from the node are actually statistically significant collocations, irrespective of the significance value obtained. Why and how do these co-occurrences produce

---

15. See Sinclair *et al.* (1998) and Mason (1997).

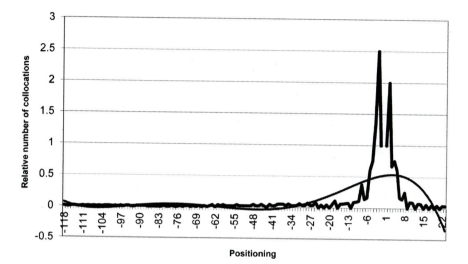

Figure 6.24 Gravity versus trendline.

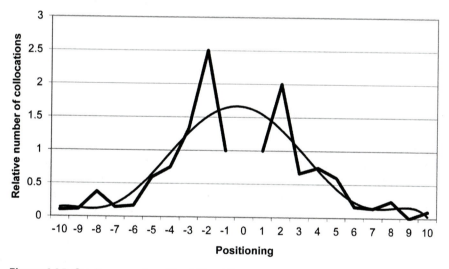

Figure 6.25 Gravity versus trendline (-10, +10).

statistically significant value? One possible reason might be that not all significant collocates are actually attracted by the node; only some are. Others are likely to be attracted by other significant collocates. What matters here is not just the span or extent of the influence of the node on its immediate environment but the fact that statistically significant collocates within the same environment are not necessarily attracted by the same node. This introduces a striking difference in standard collocation analysis; we understand that collocates within the same environment build ordered and structured frames: not flat lexical frames (the traditional view of collocates), but complex interrelated hierarchies similar to *constellations* consisting of a nucleus (e.g. the sun) which attracts various planets, with each planet attracting various other moons. Collocates form lexico-conceptual multi-dimensional frames: lexical constellations. Constellations themselves can be substructures (subsets) of others (e.g. the Solar System as part of the Milky Way) or superstructures (supersets) subsuming other structures (e.g. the Solar System containing Jupiter and its moons).

Evidence shows that words exert some influence on others, forming units (semantic units, tone units, syntactic structures such as phrases, etc.). Furthermore, these units are to some extent cognitively, spatially and temporally limited, although not necessarily universally fixed or equally limited. Several principles speak in favour of this: minimal attachment, right association and lexical preferences. This means that the attraction domain of the node needs to be not just limited but also constrained, although not necessarily fixed or universally predetermined: the extent of influence is likely to vary depending on grammatical category, semantic range, and so on. This assumption significantly reduces the range of variability of the various possible attraction domains (optimal spans) of node words. In addition, this also fits in with the unification-based assumption of the *constellation* principle: ordered hierarchical elements forming autonomous structures, substructures or superstructures.

This explains the appearance of significant collocates for *MANO(layer of paint, etc.)* found at positions −99, −89, −38, −28, −19 and +20, among others. If they are not attracted by the node word, then which items exert their influence on them and attract them? We might explain these facts as follows: the high *z*-scores categorize them as significant collocates within the sentence context *MANO(layer of paint, etc.)*; however, they are likely to be attracted by other words, not necessarily by *mano*. That is, these collocates are part of another unit, not the immediate unit or vicinity of the node word.

From the data, it becomes apparent that, for instance, *profesora* (−118) – a significant collocate within the concordance sentence of *MANO(layer of paint, etc.)* – might not be semantically attracted by *mano*, but by other lexical items within the same context, for example by *Universidad* (position −115). And *Autónoma* (−114) is probably attracted by *Universidad* (position −115), too. The reason for these significant collocates, within the context sentences of *MANO(layer of paint, etc.)*, is not related to the influence *mano* exerts on them, but to the fact that they are attracted by other items. Indeed, they seem to be part of a different unit (i.e. part of a different phrase). This means that the direct influence of some words on others is not just limited but also somehow structured.

To illustrate this, let us take one concordance sentence for *MANO(layer of paint, etc.)*: "Si algún tono no tiene la intensidad deseada, aplique otra {MANO} de pintura" ("If the shade hasn't got the desired intensity, apply another layer of paint"). The *mano* sentence contains six statistically significant collocates: *algún, tono, intensidad, deseada, aplique* and *pintura*, distributed from −9 to +2 (a positively skewed influence distribution). The collocational distribution for *mano* is displayed in Table 6.26.

Table 6.26 Collocation distribution for *mano*.

		Positioning					
		−10	−9	−8	−7	−6	−5
Freq.	1	Si	algún	tono	No	tiene	la

		Positioning					
		−4	−3	−2	−1	+1	+2
Freq.	1	intensidad	deseada	aplique	Otra	de	pintura

A simple flat collocational analysis would just reveal that there are six collocates likely to be statistically significant for *mano*. Furthermore, if we had fixed the optimum span to −5 to +5 or −4 to +4, we would have missed at least two: *algún* and *tono*.

To know more about the possible lexical hierarchy, we start by calculating the expected co-occurrence probability of all possible significant collocate tuples (combinations) within the same sentence, that is, the probability that event *x* will occur, given that event *y* has already occurred. For example, the co-occurrence probabilities for the two collocates *tono* and *intensidad* found within the context of *MANO(layer of paint, etc.)* are shown in Table 6.27.

Table 6.27 Co-occurrence probabilities.

	Tono		*Intensidad*
Intensidad	11	*Tono*	11
Without *intensidad*	640	Without *tono*	1,037
	651		1,048

Intensidad occurs 1048 times in the corpus and *tono* 651 times. Both items co-occur eleven times in the same sentence. This co-occurrence data could help us to determine the direction of attraction. Thus, the co-occurrence probability of finding *intensidad*, given *tono*, would be:

$$p(i|t) = \frac{11}{1,048} = 0.0105$$

Whereas the probability of finding *tono* given *intensidad* would be:

$$p(t|i) = \frac{11}{651} = 0.0169$$

This information reveals that *tono* is lexically less tied to *intensidad* and more likely to appear without it, whereas *intensidad* is much more dependent on *tono* and less likely to occur without it. The probability figures indicate that the lexical attraction is mutual and bi-directional, but not equidistant: *tono* exerts a greater influence and attraction on *intensidad* than vice versa.

Once the attraction direction procedure has been established, we shall determine all possible tuples of *mano* by means of the statistically significant collocates produced (namely, *tono, intensidad, deseada, aplique* and *pintura*). We shall discard *algún* as it is not a content word or an open-class lexical item. Potentially, the possible tuples or combinations within the same context sentence for *mano* range from single-word ones up to six-word clusters (the total number of statistically significant collocates plus the node word *mano*) – the sum of all combinations of *r* objects (number of co-occurring items) from *n* (set of statistically significant collocates). Thus, the combination of *r* objects from *n* is calculated as follows:

$$C(n,r) = \frac{n!}{(n-r)!\, r!}$$

This gives:

One-word tuples: $C(6, 1) = 6$
Two-word tuples: $C(6, 2) = 15$
Three-word tuples: $C(6, 3) = 20$
Four-word tuples: $C(6, 4) = 15$
Five-word tuples: $C(6, 5) = 6$
Six-word tuples: $C(6, 6) = 1$

This gives an overall total of sixty-three possible order-independent combinations for *mano* (6 + 15 + 20 + 15 + 6 + 1). However, the singletons (single-word combinations) are practically irrelevant as they just indicate their own probability of occurrence in the corpus, irrespective of co-occurrence with other items.

According to the data and probability calculations for *tono* and *intensidad* above, the attraction direction is somehow inherently determined by the observed frequency. This means that, between two items, the one that occurs more often in a language model (i.e. corpus) is likely to exert a greater influence on the less occurring one(s). This explains why we do not care about the actual order of the combinations as this is to some extent predetermined by the observed frequencies of their constituents.

In order to concentrate on the really significant combinations, we shall take a number of preliminary decisions. First, all singletons will be discarded as they do not give any information as to which other items they combine with. Next, we shall discard all combinations with an occurrence frequency equal to 1. The reason is that all significant collocates occur at least once, that is, whenever they co-occur in the concordance sentence itself under investigation. Consequently, combinations with a frequency lower than 2 are irrelevant, as they do not contribute anything to their association power with other items. So, among all potential combinations, we shall discard the hapax tuples (combinations with an occurrence frequency of 1) and the singletons (one-word combinations). The significant combinations are displayed in Table 6.28.

Table 6.28 Significant combinations for *mano*.

Token(s)	Frequency (corpus)	Probability (corpus)
mano, pintura	17	6.19820×10^{-14}
tono, intensidad	11	4.01060×10^{-14}
pintura, tono	8	2.91680×10^{-14}
mano, tono	7	2.55220×10^{-14}
mano, intensidad	6	2.18760×10^{-14}
intensidad, deseada	3	1.09380×10^{-14}
mano, aplique	2	7.29200×10^{-15}
tono, deseada	2	7.29200×10^{-15}
tono, intensidad, deseada	2	4.40306×10^{-22}

It is important to point out here that the probability calculations for tuples with more than one constituent differ significantly from the one for singletons. The probability of occurrence of a single-word combination in a corpus is straightforward as we simply need to divide its total number of occurrences in the corpus by the total number of tokens this corpus has. For instance, the occurrence probability of *mano* would be:

$$p(mano) = freq(mano) / token(corpus)$$
$$p(mano) = 5{,}902 / 16{,}561{,}199$$
$$p(mano) = 3.56 \times 10^{-4}$$

However, to calculate the probability of a multiple-word combination, we cannot divide the total number of occurrences of this tuple by the corpus tokens. This would be wrong. In order to find the probability of occurrence of a tuple with r constituents, we need to divide its frequency of occurrence by the number of potential r-word tuples in the corpus, that is, all possible combinations with r objects taken from n, or $C(n, r)$, where n stands for the number of tokens the corpus is made of and r for the number of items each combination or tuple consists of. $C(16{,}561{,}199, 2)$ indicates all possible combinations of two objects within a corpus of 16,561,199 tokens. Thus, the probability of the two-word combination *mano-pintura* co-occurring within the same sentence (in the CUMBRE Corpus) is calculated by:

$$p(mano,pintura) = freq(corpus) / C(16{,}561{,}199, 2)$$
$$p(mano,pintura) = 17 / (16{,}561{,}199 \times 16{,}561{,}198)$$
$$p(mano,pintura) = 6.19 \times 10^{-14}$$

Going back to the above tables of the most likely combinations, we find that the most likely tuple for *mano* is *mano–pintura*. This means that, in fact, *mano* is responsible for its co-occurrence with *pintura*, but not necessarily the other way round, as *mano* is more likely to be found than *pintura*. This also applies to the tuple *tono–intensidad*, producing these two ordered pairs:

```
mano      (pintura
          )

tono      (intensidad
          )
```

This means that the collocate *intensidad*, although significant within the context of *MANO(layer of paint, etc.)*, is not directly attracted by *mano* but by another significant collocate (*tono*) within the same context. The third most likely combination is *pintura–tono*. Here we now have the missing link between *mano–pintura* and *tono–intensidad*. The two previous combinations can be merged and reduced into a single structure, giving:

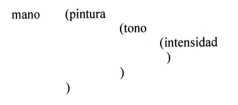

```
mano      (pintura
                (tono
                     (intensidad
                      )
                )
          )
```

The next tuple *mano–tono* is already included in the structure above, and indicates that *mano* does indeed attract *tono*. However, the evidence shows that it is actually *pintura* that exerts a greater influence on *tono*, or, in other words, *mano* attracts *tono* by means of *pintura*. If it were not for *pintura*, it is unlikely that *tono* would be a collocate of *mano* or, at least, directly attracted by it. A similar case is that of *mano–intensidad*. The next combination, *intensidad–deseada*, enlarges the structure into:

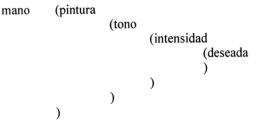

```
mano      (pintura
                (tono
                     (intensidad
                          (deseada
                           )
                      )
                )
          )
```

Mano–aplique brings along a new directly attracted collocate of *mano*:

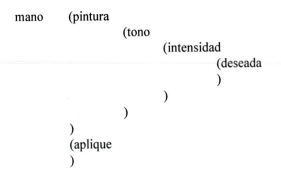

```
mano      (pintura
                (tono
                     (intensidad
                          (deseada
                           )
                      )
                )
          )
          (aplique
           )
```

and finally, *tono–deseada* and *tono–intensidad–deseada* which are already included in the structure above.

We conclude that, in this sample sentence, within the context of *MANO(layer of paint, etc.)*, *mano* is the dominant collocate or node as it directly attracts *pintura* and *aplique* and indirectly attracts most of the collocates (*tono, intensidad* and *aplique*), except for *deseada*. The resulting collocational hierarchy is:

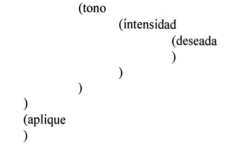

In a more visual mode, this is similar to a three-dimensional star constellation (Figure 6.26), where the dominant element is *mano* attracting *pintura* and *aplique*; *pintura* attracts *tono*; *tono* attracts *intensidad*; and *intensidad* attracts *deseada*.

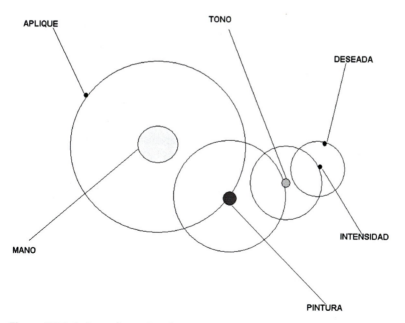

Figure 6.26 A three-dimensional star constellation for *mano*.

This does not mean that *mano* does not attract *tono*; it does, in fact. However, there is evidence that this attraction is not direct, but by means of an intermediate item or lexical structure formed by *pintura*.

As discussed, the notion of constellation goes far beyond that of collocation. So far, most of the research and work centred on collocational analysis has merely been aiming at finding the best quantitative method to automatically extract the most relevant or significant collocates of a given node word or keyword (defined by *z-score*, *MI*, *MI3*, *log-likelihood*, etc.). The data that researchers get by means of these statistical techniques are simply a list of items likely to be attracted by the node word or keyword under investigation. Divergences and even discrepancies among the results, depending on the statistical method used, have led some researchers to refine these mathematical models, either by considering new variables (e.g. word distance) or establishing cut-offs or constraints, such as discarding low frequency items or determining optimum spans. The discrepancies and differences among the various significance measures still remain and debate continues: there seems to be no ideal method yet. The wisest method is to use as much information as possible in exploring collocation and to take advantage of the different perspectives provided by the use of more than one measure. Similarly, cut-offs are problematic. Where should the borderline between low and high frequency items be established? Or, what is the best span for collocational analysis? Recent trends are to find or calculate the optimal span for each word, in the belief that each word exerts a different influence on its environment.

6.4 Qualitative and quantitative data analysis: an example

An important advantage of collocation analysis is that it allows us to focus our attention on specific aspects of the contexts of words already selected for investigation through concordance lines. Collocations can help organize the context into major patterns, and we can use our knowledge of those patterns to assess the general behaviour patterns of the language or the uses being made of particular words within the text. This can make it much easier to identify phrases and idioms, to differentiate among different meanings of a single word form or to determine the range of syntactic features.

Imagine we are interested in examining the lemma *keep* in order to know about its grammatical patterning, collocations, syntagmatic relations, and so on. The first thing we do is extract the occurrences of the lemma *keep* (*keep, keep'em, keeping, keeps, kept*) in a corpus,[16] by means of the standard concordance package, using a fixed span of six words on either side of the keyword (Figure 6.27).

For the following analysis, we include closed-class items, focusing particularly on prepositions, since they are likely to be relevant when dealing with verbs (think

---

16. Arts sub-corpus of *Corpus Collection B*, totalling 178,143 tokens (Scott and Jones 1994).

```
...eraser to use for what purpose, how to  [[keep]] a sheet clean by masking or tacking dow...
...cle Knacker's to see the new horses. To  [[keep]] a pony in the middle of a town, and ke...
...answering their questions and trying to  [[keep]] a conversation going while cooking a c...
...views about the company her son should  [[keep]] and used to embarrass him by vetting hi...
             ...o tears. `Not Bones!" `To  [[keep]] Bones, would you rather go on with the ...
     ...ive. `Might be a bit of trouble.  [[Keep]] clear. Bit nervous, this one. Bin in ba...
...a stringy-looking tie that would never  [[keep]] closed up to the collar itself. His ve...
...been doing throughout the action. They  [[keep]] coming, like immigrants, or refugees, 1...
...r other writers he published. I did not  [[keep]] copies of my letters to him _ or to an...
...they had to stay put if they wanted to  [[keep]] designing. There were almost no ...
...neck, pushing him down. `Bloody hell!  [[Keep]] down! It's the fuzz!" Keeping be...
...my girl. You owe it to your parents to  [[keep]] him off the premises." `Is he th...
           ...ed an old brown photograph. `You  [[keep]] him here, and say your prayers, and all...
...nd she babysat nearly every evening to  [[keep]] him in good oats (not Uncle Knacker's) ...
...ep a pony in the middle of a town, and  [[keep]] him fit, was hard work, as he had to be...
...e willed him to, because she slaved to  [[keep]] him up to it. When she looked at poor l...
...to deteriorate, although nothing could  [[keep]] him from his garden and the prize bird...
...t the subject of his letters, he cannot  [[keep]] his mind off poetry for more than a fe...
...guessed that some instinct told Sam to  [[keep]] his mouth shut about the knacker-yard ...
...here the author's genitals were wont to  [[keep]] house. Gregory Woods...
...he home, the more labour is required to  [[keep]] it fit== ; the more labour required, t...
...treasure for this purpose, if one could  [[keep]] it. Otherwise a spoon sufficed. The pe...
        ... ambition in life?" `You joking?  [[keep]] lot of the old man's hair mostly." ...
...the kind of parson I go to. Some would  [[keep]] me trotting round the parish all day: ...
...nto the bed; his chattering teeth would  [[keep]] me awake after he himself had fallen in...
...e rather narrow gate and was trying to  [[keep]] Midnight from eating a lavender bush by...
...ncouraged by our drawing instructors to  [[keep]] notebooks and to draw whenever we coul...
...rd pencil, but one had to be careful to  [[keep]] one's hands off the sheet to avoid spo...
      ... much better." `You'd be able to  [[keep]] order, sir. I mean, it's not enough to ...
...cks his head, to hold it up. But if you  [[keep]] pulling on the reins he'll get cross."...
...ur nags then?" Sebastian asked. `Better  [[keep]] that one away from the others" _ he no...
...er, were not such that he could hope to  [[keep]] the beautiful daughter of the former m...
```

Figure 6.27 Fragment of the concordance list for the lemma *keep*.

of prepositional or phrasal verbs, idioms, and the like). Co-occurrence frequency data distribution can be very useful in this respect. Table 6.29 shows the data for the verb lemma *keep* (with a frequency threshold of 3).

Given this data, a first approach could be to group the words in column *1-Right* (words that immediately follow *keep*) according to their parts-of-speech; we get:

- determiners: *the*, *a* and *his* (there is no instance where *his* is a possessive pronoun)
- prepositions: *up*, *in* and *to*
- pronouns: *him*.

Table 6.29 Co-occurrence data for the lemma *keep*.

2-Left		1-Left		1-Right		2-Right	
6	he	23	to	16	the	6	with
3	that	5	he	7	a	3	a
3	and	4	and	7	up	3	of
		3	I	6	his	3	to
		3	would	6	him	3	hands
		3	could	3	in		
		3	of	3	to		

The right hand side association power of *keep* can now be typified as:

- KEEP + *preposition (up, in, to)*
- KEEP + *pronoun (him)*
- KEEP + *determiner (the, a, his).*

Next we shall obtain all the co-occurrences for *keep*, calculate the statistical significance and focus on those which are statistically significant (see Table 6.30).

Table 6.30 Statistically significant collations for *keep*.

Types	z-scores	Types	z-scores	Types	z-scores
pony	43.9385	out	11.7460	you	8.1570
hands	40.5193	would	11.5532	one	8.1073
themselves	35.3342	me	11.5533	to	7.5132
feet	34.6111	their	9.8399	by	7.9934
going	28.7131	my	9.6589	that	7.7026
your	22.2411	from	9.4379	not	7.6211
off	21.1105	he	9.2571	an	7.4307
up	20.2812	his	9.2347	which	7.2160
always	19.0351	they	9.2025	for	7.0078
house	17.5473	are	9.1621	It	6.8140
because	16.8926	but	9.1038	was	6.4644
down	15.9125	we	8.8348	is	6.1069
could	15.5327	were	8.7933	in	5.3022
him	15.0464	with	8.7079	a	4.6564
well	14.6175	she	8.7819	and	4.3028
our	14.1252	all	8.3567	I	4.5055
if	14.0867	her	8.2738	of	3.6182
some	12.6192	on	8.1045	the	2.0622

A quick glance at the z-scores for *keep* in Table 6.30 reveals that the probability of *in* co-occurring with *keep* is quite low, compared with *to* and *up*. The latter two combinations are statistically very significant, particularly *up* (20.2812). It is difficult to make assumptions here, due to the small sample analysed, but the z-scores point to one hypothesis: KEEP + *up* and KEEP + *to* may form lexical units (prepositional verbs or phrasal verbs), such as in:

*The jargon they **kept** up was delicious for me to hear.*

*Commentary on form is **kept** to a minimum and is almost entirely superficial.*

However, it seems very unlikely that *in* is part of the verb and it is probably part of the prepositional phrase (PP) that follows the verb (see its low *z*-score: 5.3022), as in:

> *Hoomey knew it was a suggestion for sugarlumps, which he **kept** in his pocket.*

Regarding determiners, these do not occur alone; they precede or *determine* a noun or noun head. We can go further and say that *keep* is able to associate on its right hand side noun phrases (NPs) of the type:

- NP 6 Pr; (*You **keep** him here, and say your prayers, and all will be well*)
- NP 6 Det (Adj) N; (*My uncle will go on **keeping** the horses if we want them.- He **keeps** a sleeping bag up there, stuffed behind the old ventilator pipes, and he sleeps in with her.- He was **keeping** his feet well out of the way, following where his horse ate*).

The above is true, as *keep* is a transitive verb. Consequently, we could with some degree of certainty say that the high co-occurrence frequency of pronouns and determiners with the verb *keep* is not due to the configuration of any particular phrase but due to the transitivity of *keep*.

Regarding its association with prepositions, we have three prepositions which are directly attached to the verb (*up, in, to*), and three others which occur within a word distance of two (*2-Right: with, of, to*). A first hypothesis could be that the co-occurrence of KEEP + *preposition* (*up, in* or *to*) attracts other prepositions. If we look at the concordance list, this is only true for *up*, which attracts *with* in four out of six occasions, as in:

> *To **keep** up with this pace, that is, just to carry out the work that...*

This produces the following syntactic frames for KEEP + *preposition*:

- KEEP + *up*
- KEEP + *up* + *with*
- KEEP + *to*
- KEEP + *in*.

The first three are very likely to form phrasal verbs or prepositional verbs, as already discussed, but not *in*, which is part of what follows, a PP in this case. In addition, KEEP + *up* + *with* might be a phrasal prepositional verb.

The three non-directly attached prepositions (*with, of, to*) have different syntactic patterns with respect to those directly attached ones (*up, to, in*). *With, of* and *to* allow another constituent to be placed in between the verb KEEP and the preposition itself; see for instance:

*... but where one **keeps** <u>faith with</u> it by negation and suffering...*

*One Jew with a pencil stuck behind his ear **kept** <u>gesticulating with</u> his hands and...*

*... that for so long helped to **keep** <u>the Jews of</u> Eastern Europe in medieval ghettoes*

The allowed "intruder" is either a present participle or an NP:

- KEEP + *NP / present participle* + *with*
- KEEP + *NP* + *of*
- KEEP + *NP* + *to.*

An interesting syntactic difference among these non-directly attached prepositions is that in the first two instances (KEEP + *NP/present participle* + *with* and KEEP + *NP* + *of*) the prepositions are part of a PP, that is, the PP that complements the preceding NP or present participle, whereas in KEEP + *NP* + *to*, the verb seems to form a kind of discontinuous phrase, and the preposition might, therefore, be thought to be part of the verb:

*...it was insisted that they **keep** <u>themselves to themselves</u>...*

We also find the determiner *a* in position *2-Right*, which indicates that whenever *keep* has the pattern:

KEEP + ... + a...

the determiner introduces an NP, and this might be some hint of transitivity. The transitive instances with this pattern we have detected are the two phrasal or prepositional verbs:

KEEP + *up* + *a*: ...***keeping** <u>up a</u> house*

KEEP + *to* + *a*: *Commentary on form is **kept** <u>to a</u> minimum...*

However, in the case of KEEP + *in*, the NP that follows is not a direct object but part of an adverbial PP headed by the preposition *in*:

*... which he **kept** <u>in his pocket</u>*

Finally, the exploration of the right hand side association of *keep* takes us to *hand*. Its high *z*-score (40.5193) provides evidence of some kind of idiomatic expression:

KEEP + *Det(Poss)* + *hands*: *...and **keeping** his hands away from the ever questing...*

Let us now analyse the left hand side association. This side can be interpreted straightforwardly and indicates clearly that *keep* can only be a verb. The word forms heading *keep* are:

- the infinitive particle *to*: *You'd be able to **keep** order, sir*
- the pronouns *I* and *he* (subjects of the verb): *I **kept** the past alive out of a desire for revenge*
- the modal verbs *would* and *could*: both require a non-finite verb form to their right: *Some would **keep** me trotting round the parish all day*
- the preposition *of*, which requires a non-finite verb form, in instances such as: ... *the habit of **keeping** themselves to themselves was not easily lost.*

Note that this has by no means been an exhaustive analysis of *keep* collocation patterns and phrases, but is just an illustration of the potential of using quantitative data in combination with qualitative linguistic data. In addition, for the sake of simplicity and clarity, we have deliberately reduced the collocation data (*freq ≥ 3*) and the concordance sets.

As already noted, the identification of phrases goes far beyond simple syntactic frame identification and it may lead us to important syntactic, lexical and semantic discoveries about the behaviour of words, collocates and phrases: *the sociology of words*.

Appendix 1
Standard normal distribution

z	p	z	p	z	p	z	p
−4.0	0.00003	−1.9	0.02872	0.1	0.53983	2.1	0.98214
−3.9	0.00005	−1.8	0.03593	0.2	0.57926	2.2	0.98610
−3.8	0.00007	−1.7	0.04456	0.3	0.61791	2.3	0.98928
−3.7	0.00011	−1.6	0.05480	0.4	0.65542	2.4	0.99180
−3.6	0.00016	−1.5	0.06681	0.5	0.69146	2.5	0.99379
−3.5	0.00023	−1.4	0.08076	0.6	0.72575	2.6	0.99534
−3.4	0.00034	−1.3	0.09680	0.7	0.75804	2.7	0.99653
−3.3	0.00048	−1.2	0.11507	0.8	0.78814	2.8	0.99744
−3.2	0.00069	−1.1	0.13566	0.9	0.81594	2.9	0.99813
−3.1	0.00097	−1.0	0.15865	1.0	0.84134	3.0	0.99865
−3.0	0.00135	−0.9	0.18406	1.1	0.86433	3.1	0.99903
−2.9	0.00187	−0.8	0.21185	1.2	0.88493	3.2	0.99931
−2.8	0.00256	−0.7	0.24196	1.3	0.90320	3.3	0.99952
−2.7	0.00347	−0.6	0.27425	1.4	0.91924	3.4	0.99966
−2.6	0.00466	−0.5	0.30853	1.5	0.93319	3.5	0.99977
−2.5	0.00621	−0.4	0.34457	1.6	0.94520	3.6	0.99984
−2.4	0.00820	−0.3	0.38209	1.7	0.95543	3.7	0.99989
−2.3	0.01072	−0.2	0.42074	1.8	0.96407	3.8	0.99993
−2.2	0.01390	−0.1	0.46017	1.9	0.97128	3.9	0.99995
−2.1	0.01786	0.0	0.50000	2.0	0.97725	4.0	0.99997
−2.0	0.02275						

Appendix 2
Examples of appropriate statistics

Nominal scale	Ordinal scale	Interval scale	Ratio scale
Chi-square	Median	Mean	Coefficient of
Phi coefficient	Interquartile range	Standard deviation	variation
Cramér's V	Spearman's correlation	Pearson correlation	Sign test
Contingency	coefficient	coefficient	Median test
coefficient	Kendall's tau	t-test	
Uncertainty	Kolmogorov Smirnov test	Analysis of variance	
coefficient	Kendall coefficient of	Multivariate analysis of	
Kappa	concordance	variance	
Likelihood ratio	Friedman two-way anova	Factor analysis	
Goodman &	Mann–Whitney U-test	Regression	
Kruskal tau	Wald–Wolfowitz	Multiple correlation	
McNemar	Kruskal–Wallis	Sign test	
Cochran Q	Sign test	Median test	
	Median test		

Appendix 3
t-distribution

df	0.5	0.2	0.1	0.05	0.02	0.01	0.002	0.001
				p				
1	1.000	3.078	6.314	12.71	31.82	63.66	318.3	636.6
2	0.816	1.886	2.920	4.303	6.965	9.925	22.33	31.60
3	0.765	1.638	2.353	3.182	4.541	5.841	10.21	12.92
4	0.741	1.533	2.132	2.776	3.747	4.604	7.173	8.610
5	0.727	1.476	2.015	2.571	3.365	4.032	5.893	6.869
6	0.718	1.440	1.943	2.447	3.143	3.707	5.208	5.959
7	0.711	1.415	1.895	2.365	2.998	3.499	4.785	5.408
8	0.706	1.397	1.860	2.306	2.896	3.355	4.501	5.041
9	0.703	1.383	1.833	2.262	2.821	3.250	4.297	4.781
10	0.700	1.372	1.812	2.228	2.764	3.169	4.144	4.587
11	0.697	1.363	1.796	2.201	2.718	3.106	4.025	4.437
12	0.695	1.356	1.782	2.179	2.681	3.055	3.930	4.318
13	0.694	1.350	1.771	2.160	2.650	3.012	3.852	4.221
14	0.692	1.345	1.761	2.145	2.624	2.977	3.787	4.140
15	0.691	1.341	1.753	2.131	2.602	2.947	3.733	4.073
16	0.690	1.337	1.746	2.120	2.583	2.921	3.686	4.015
17	0.689	1.333	1.740	2.110	2.567	2.898	3.646	3.965
18	0.688	1.330	1.734	2.101	2.552	2.878	3.610	3.922
19	0.688	1.328	1.729	2.093	2.539	2.861	3.579	3.883
20	0.687	1.325	1.725	2.086	2.528	2.845	3.552	3.850
21	0.686	1.323	1.721	2.080	2.518	2.831	3.527	3.819
22	0.686	1.321	1.717	2.074	2.508	2.819	3.505	3.792
23	0.685	1.319	1.714	2.069	2.500	2.807	3.485	3.767
24	0.685	1.318	1.711	2.064	2.492	2.797	3.467	3.745
25	0.684	1.316	1.708	2.060	2.485	2.787	3.450	3.725
26	0.684	1.315	1.706	2.056	2.479	2.779	3.435	3.707
27	0.684	1.314	1.703	2.052	2.473	2.771	3.421	3.690
28	0.683	1.313	1.701	2.048	2.467	2.763	3.408	3.674
29	0.683	1.311	1.699	2.045	2.462	2.756	3.396	3.659
30	0.683	1.310	1.697	2.042	2.457	2.750	3.385	3.646

Appendix 4
F-distribution

*df*2	*df*1 = 1	2	3	4	5	6	7	8	9	10	12	24
2	18.51	19.00	19.16	19.25	19.30	19.33	19.35	19.37	19.38	19.40	19.41	19.45
3	10.13	9.55	9.28	9.12	9.01	8.94	8.89	8.85	8.81	8.79	8.74	8.64
4	7.71	6.94	6.59	6.39	6.26	6.16	6.09	6.04	6.00	5.96	5.91	5.77
5	6.61	5.79	5.41	5.19	5.05	4.95	4.88	4.82	4.77	4.74	4.68	4.53
6	5.99	5.14	4.76	4.53	4.39	4.28	4.21	4.15	4.10	4.06	4.00	3.84
7	5.59	4.74	4.35	4.12	3.97	3.87	3.79	3.73	3.68	3.64	3.57	3.41
8	5.32	4.46	4.07	3.84	3.69	3.58	3.50	3.44	3.39	3.35	3.28	3.12
9	5.12	4.26	3.86	3.63	3.48	3.37	3.29	3.23	3.18	3.14	3.07	2.90
10	4.96	4.10	3.71	3.48	3.33	3.22	3.14	3.07	3.02	2.98	2.91	2.74
11	4.84	3.98	3.59	3.36	3.20	3.09	3.01	2.95	2.90	2.85	2.79	2.61
12	4.75	3.89	3.49	3.26	3.11	3.00	2.91	2.85	2.80	2.75	2.69	2.51
13	4.67	3.81	3.41	3.18	3.03	2.92	2.83	2.77	2.71	2.67	2.60	2.42
14	4.60	3.74	3.34	3.11	2.96	2.85	2.76	2.70	2.65	2.60	2.53	2.35
15	4.54	3.68	3.29	3.06	2.90	2.79	2.71	2.64	2.59	2.54	2.48	2.29
16	4.49	3.63	3.24	3.01	2.85	2.74	2.66	2.59	2.54	2.49	2.42	2.24
17	4.45	3.59	3.20	2.96	2.81	2.70	2.61	2.55	2.49	2.45	2.38	2.19
18	4.41	3.55	3.16	2.93	2.77	2.66	2.58	2.51	2.46	2.41	2.34	2.15
19	4.38	3.52	3.13	2.90	2.74	2.63	2.54	2.48	2.42	2.38	2.31	2.11
20	4.35	3.49	3.10	2.87	2.71	2.60	2.51	2.45	2.39	2.35	2.28	2.08
21	4.32	3.47	3.07	2.84	2.68	2.57	2.49	2.42	2.37	2.32	2.25	2.05
22	4.30	3.44	3.05	2.82	2.66	2.55	2.46	2.40	2.34	2.30	2.23	2.03
23	4.28	3.42	3.03	2.80	2.64	2.53	2.44	2.37	2.32	2.27	2.20	2.01
24	4.26	3.40	3.01	2.78	2.62	2.51	2.42	2.36	2.30	2.25	2.18	1.98
25	4.24	3.39	2.99	2.76	2.60	2.49	2.40	2.34	2.28	2.24	2.16	1.96
26	4.23	3.37	2.98	2.74	2.59	2.47	2.39	2.32	2.27	2.22	2.15	1.95
27	4.21	3.35	2.96	2.73	2.57	2.46	2.37	2.31	2.25	2.20	2.13	1.93
28	4.20	3.34	2.95	2.71	2.56	2.45	2.36	2.29	2.24	2.19	2.12	1.91
29	4.18	3.33	2.93	2.70	2.55	2.43	2.35	2.28	2.22	2.18	2.10	1.90
30	4.17	3.32	2.92	2.69	2.53	2.42	2.33	2.27	2.21	2.16	2.09	1.89
40	4.08	3.23	2.84	2.61	2.45	2.34	2.25	2.18	2.12	2.08	2.00	1.79
60	4.00	3.15	2.76	2.53	2.37	2.25	2.17	2.10	2.04	1.99	1.92	1.70
120	3.92	3.07	2.68	2.45	2.29	2.18	2.09	2.02	1.96	1.91	1.83	1.61

Appendix 5
Pearson product-moment correlation coefficient

N (number of pairs)	p			
	0.1	0.05	0.02	0.01
1	0.988	0.997	0.9995	0.9999
2	0.9	0.95	0.98	0.99
3	0.805	0.878	0.934	0.959
4	0.729	0.811	0.882	0.917
5	0.669	0.754	0.833	0.874
6	0.622	0.707	0.789	0.834
7	0.582	0.666	0.75	0.798
8	0.549	0.632	0.716	0.765
9	0.521	0.602	0.685	0.735
10	0.497	0.576	0.658	0.708
11	0.476	0.553	0.634	0.684
12	0.458	0.532	0.612	0.661
13	0.441	0.514	0.592	0.641
14	0.426	0.497	0.574	0.628
15	0.412	0.482	0.558	0.606
16	0.4	0.468	0.542	0.59
17	0.389	0.456	0.528	0.575
18	0.378	0.444	0.516	0.561
19	0.369	0.433	0.503	0.549
20	0.36	0.423	0.492	0.537
21	0.352	0.413	0.482	0.526
22	0.344	0.404	0.472	0.515
23	0.337	0.396	0.462	0.505
24	0.33	0.388	0.453	0.495
25	0.323	0.381	0.445	0.487
26	0.317	0.374	0.437	0.479

N (number of pairs)	p			
	0.1	0.05	0.02	0.01
27	0.311	0.367	0.43	0.471
28	0.306	0.361	0.423	0.463
29	0.301	0.355	0.416	0.456
30	0.296	0.349	0.409	0.449
35	0.275	0.325	0.381	0.418
40	0.257	0.304	0.358	0.393
45	0.243	0.288	0.338	0.372
50	0.231	0.273	0.322	0.354
60	0.211	0.25	0.295	0.325
70	0.195	0.232	0.274	0.302
80	0.183	0.217	0.256	0.284
90	0.173	0.205	0.242	0.267
100	0.164	0.195	0.23	0.254

Appendix 6
U-distribution for the Mann–Whitney test

	4	5	6	7	8	9	10	11	12	13	14	15	16	17	18	19	20
1	–	–	–	–	–	–	–	–	–	–	–	–	–	–	–	–	–
2	–	–	–	–	0	0	0	0	1	1	1	1	1	2	2	2	2
3	–	0	0	0	2	2	3	3	4	4	5	5	6	6	7	7	8
4	0	1	2	3	4	4	5	6	7	8	9	10	11	11	12	13	13
5		2	3	5	6	7	8	9	11	12	13	14	15	17	18	19	20
6			5	6	8	10	11	13	14	16	17	19	21	22	24	25	27
7				8	10	12	14	16	18	20	22	24	26	28	30	32	34
8					13	15	17	19	22	24	26	29	31	34	36	38	41
9						17	20	23	26	28	31	34	37	39	42	45	48
10							23	26	29	33	36	39	42	45	48	52	55
11								30	33	37	40	44	47	51	55	58	62
12									37	41	45	49	53	57	61	65	69
13										45	50	54	59	63	67	72	76
14											55	59	64	67	74	78	83
15												64	70	75	80	85	90
16													75	81	86	92	98
17														87	93	99	105
18															99	106	112
19																113	119
20																	127

Appendix 7
Sign test

N	X	Y	p	N	X	Y	p	N	X	Y	p
1	.	.	.	41	14	28	0.02753	81	32	50	0.04483
2	.	.	.	42	15	28	0.04356	82	32	51	0.03524
3	.	.	.	43	15	29	0.03154	83	33	51	0.04752
4	.	.	.	44	16	29	0.04877	84	33	52	0.03753
5	.	.	.	45	16	30	0.03570	85	33	53	0.02946
6	1	6	0.03125	46	16	31	0.02590	86	34	53	0.03985
7	1	7	0.01563	47	17	31	0.03999	87	34	54	0.03142
8	1	8	0.00781	48	17	32	0.02930	88	35	54	0.04221
9	2	8	0.03906	49	18	32	0.04438	89	35	55	0.03342
10	2	9	0.02148	50	18	33	0.03284	90	36	55	0.04460
11	2	10	0.01172	51	19	33	0.04887	91	36	56	0.03545
12	3	10	0.03857	52	19	34	0.03648	92	37	56	0.04701
13	3	11	0.02246	53	19	35	0.02701	93	37	57	0.03751
14	3	12	0.01294	54	20	35	0.04022	94	38	57	0.04945
15	4	12	0.03516	55	20	36	0.03003	95	38	58	0.03961
16	4	13	0.02127	56	21	36	0.04405	96	38	59	0.03155
17	5	13	0.04904	57	21	37	0.03314	97	39	59	0.04173
18	5	14	0.03088	58	22	37	0.04794	98	39	60	0.03336
19	5	15	0.01921	59	22	38	0.03634	99	40	60	0.04388
20	6	15	0.04139	60	22	39	0.02734	100	40	61	0.03520
21	6	16	0.02660	61	23	39	0.03962	101	41	61	0.04604
22	6	17	0.01690	62	23	40	0.03002	102	41	62	0.03707
23	7	17	0.03469	63	24	40	0.04296	103	42	62	0.04823
24	7	18	0.02266	64	24	41	0.03277	104	42	63	0.03896
25	8	18	0.04329	65	25	41	0.04635	105	42	64	0.03130
26	8	19	0.02896	66	25	42	0.03558	106	43	64	0.04087
27	8	20	0.01916	67	26	42	0.04980	107	43	65	0.03295
28	9	20	0.03570	68	26	43	0.03846	108	44	65	0.04281
29	9	21	0.02412	69	26	44	0.02949	109	44	66	0.03462
30	10	21	0.04277	70	27	44	0.04139	110	45	66	0.04476
31	10	22	0.02945	71	27	45	0.03193	111	45	67	0.03631
32	10	23	0.02006	72	28	45	0.04437	112	46	67	0.04674
33	11	23	0.03508	73	28	46	0.03442	113	46	68	0.03802
34	11	24	0.02431	74	29	46	0.04739	114	47	68	0.04872
35	12	24	0.04096	75	29	47	0.03695	115	47	69	0.03975
36	12	25	0.02882	76	29	48	0.02863	116	47	70	0.03227
37	13	25	0.04703	77	30	48	0.03954	117	48	70	0.04150
38	13	26	0.03355	78	30	49	0.03079	118	48	71	0.03379
39	13	27	0.02370	79	31	49	0.04217	119	49	71	0.04327
40	14	27	0.03848	80	31	50	0.03299	120	49	72	0.03532

Appendix 8
Chi-square distribution

df	p		
	0.05	0.01	0.001
1	3.84	6.64	10.83
2	5.99	9.21	13.82
3	7.82	11.35	16.27
4	9.49	13.28	18.47
5	11.07	15.09	20.52
6	12.59	16.81	22.46
7	14.07	18.48	24.32
8	15.51	20.09	26.13
9	16.92	21.67	27.88
10	18.31	23.21	29.59
12	21.03	26.22	32.91
15	25	30.58	37.7
20	31.41	37.57	45.32
24	36.42	42.98	51.18
30	43.77	50.89	59.7
40	55.76	63.69	73.41
50	67.51	76.15	86.66
60	79.08	88.38	99.62
70	90.53	100.42	112.31
80	101.88	112.33	124.84
90	113.15	124.12	137.19
100	124.34	135.81	149.48

Appendix 9
Spearman rank correlation coefficient

			p			
n	0.10	0.05	0.025	0.01	0.005	0.001
4	0.8000	0.8000				
5	0.7000	0.8000	0.9000	0.9000		
6	0.6000	0.7714	0.8286	0.8857	0.9429	
7	0.5357	0.6786	0.7450	0.8571	0.8929	0.9643
8	0.5000	0.6190	0.7143	0.8095	0.8571	0.9286
9	0.4667	0.5833	0.6833	0.7667	0.8167	0.9000
10	0.4424	0.5515	0.6364	0.7333	0.8167	0.8667
11	0.4182	0.5273	0.6091	0.7000	0.7818	0.8364
12	0.3986	0.4965	0.5804	0.6713	0.7455	0.8182
13	0.3791	0.4760	0.5549	0.6429	0.7273	0.7912
14	0.3626	0.4593	0.5341	0.6220	0.6978	0.7670
15	0.3500	0.4429	0.5179	0.6000	0.6747	0.7464
16	0.3382	0.4265	0.5000	0.5824	0.6536	0.7265
17	0.3260	0.4118	0.4853	0.5637	0.6324	0.7083
18	0.3148	0.3994	0.4716	0.5480	0.6152	0.6904
19	0.3070	0.3895	0.4579	0.5333	0.5975	0.6737
20	0.2977	0.3789	0.4451	0.5203	0.5684	0.6586
21	0.2909	0.3688	0.4351	0.5078	0.5545	0.6455
22	0.2829	0.3597	0.4241	0.4963	0.5426	0.6318
23	0.2767	0.3518	0.4150	0.4852	0.5306	0.6186
24	0.2704	0.3435	0.4061	0.4748	0.5200	0.6070
25	0.2646	0.3362	0.3977	0.4654	0.5100	0.5962
26	0.2588	0.3299	0.3894	0.4564	0.5002	0.5856
27	0.2540	0.3236	0.3822	0.4481	0.4915	0.5757
28	0.2490	0.3175	0.3749	0.4401	0.4828	0.5660
29	0.2443	0.3113	0.3685	0.4320	0.4744	0.5567
30	0.2400	0.3059	0.3620	0.4251	0.4665	0.5479

Bibliography

Agresti, A. (1990) *Categorical Data Analysis*. Bognor Regis: Wiley.

Allen, J. (1995) *Natural Language Understanding*. Redwood, CA: Benjamin/Cummings Publishing Company.

Allwood, J., Andersson, L. G. & Dahl, Ö. (1977) *Logic in Linguistics*. Cambridge: Cambridge University Press.

Alt, M. (1990) *Exploring Hyperspace*. Maidenhead: McGraw-Hill.

Anderberg, M. R. (1973) *Cluster Analysis for Applications*. New York: Academic Press.

Anshen, F. (1978) *Statistics for Linguists*. Rowley, MA: Newbury House.

Atwell, E. (1987) "Constituent-Likelihood Grammar". In R. Garside, G. Leech & G. Sampson (eds) *The Computational Analysis of English: A Corpus-Based Approach*. London and New York: Longman, 34–67.

Baayen, R. H. (1993) "Statistical Models for Word Frequency Distributions: A Linguistic Evaluation". *Computers and Humanities* 26: 347–63.

Baayen, R. H. (1994) "Derivational productivity and text typology". *Journal of Quantitative Linguistics* 1: 16–34.

Baayen, R. H. (2001) *Word Frequency Distribution*. Dordrecht: Kluwer Academic Publishers.

Baayen, R. H. & Lieber, R. (1997) "Word Frequency Distributions and Lexical Semantics". *Computers and the Humanities* 30: 281–91.

Bar-Hillel, Y. (1964) *Language and Information*. Reading, MA: Addison Wesley Publishing Company.

Barnbrook, G. (1996) *Language and Computers*. Edinburgh: Edinburgh University Press.

Bennett, S. & Bowers, D. (1976) *Multivariate Techniques for Social and Behavioural Sciences*. London: Macmillan.

Berber Sardinha, A. P. (1997) "Lexical Co-occurrence: A Preliminary Investigation into Business English Phraseology". *Letras & Letras* 13(1): 15–23.

Berry-Rogghe, G. L. M. (1973) "The Computation of Collocations and their Relevance in Lexical Studies". In A. J. Aitken, R. Bailey & N. Hamilton-Smith (eds) *The Computer and Literary Studies*. Edinburgh: Edinburgh University Press, 103–12.

Berry-Rogghe, G. L. M. (1974) "Automatic Identification of Phrasal Verbs". In J. L. Mitchell (ed.) *Computers in the Humanities*. Edinburgh: Edinburgh University Press, 16–26.

Biber, D. (1988) *Variation Across Speech and Writing*. Cambridge: Cambridge University Press.

Biber, D. (1993) "Co-occurrence Patterns among Collocations: A Tool for Corpus-Based Lexical Knowledge Acquisition". *Computational Linguistics* 19(3): 531–8.

Biber, D. (1995) *Dimensions of Register Variation*. Cambridge: Cambridge University Press.

Brainerd, B. (1974) *Weighing Evidence in Language and Literature: A Statistical Approach*. Toronto and Buffalo: University of Toronto Press.

Brown, D. J. (1988) *Understanding Research in Second Language Learning. A Teacher's Guide to Statistics and Research Design*. Cambridge: Cambridge University Press.

Butler, C. (1985a) *Statistics in Linguistics*. Oxford: Basil Blackwell.

Butler, C. (1985b) *Computers in Linguistics*. Oxford: Basil Blackwell.

Cantos, P. (1995) "Tratamiento informático y obtención de resultados". In A. Sánchez, R. Sarmiento, P. Cantos & J. Simón, J. (eds) *CUMBRE. Corpus lingüístico del español contemporáneo: fundamentos, metodología y análisis.* Madrid: SGEL, 39–70.

Cantos, P. (1996) *Lexical Ambiguity, Dictionaries and Corpora.* Murcia: Servicio de Publicaciones de la Universidad de Murcia.

Cantos, P. (2000) "Investigating Type-Token Regression and its Potential for Automated Text Discrimination". In P. Cantos & A. Sánchez (eds) *Corpus-based Research in English Language and Linguistics* (Monográfico. Cuadernos de Filología Inglesa). Murcia: Servicio de Publicaciones de la Universidad de Murcia, 71–92.

Cantos, P. (2001) "An Attempt to Improve Current Collocation Analysis". In P. Rayson, A. Wilson, T. McEnery, A. Hardie & S. Khoja (eds) *Technical Papers Volume 13: Proceedings of the Corpus Linguistics 2001 Conference.* Lancaster: Lancaster University Press, 100–108.

Cantos, P. (2003) "Do We Need Statistics When We Have Linguistics?" *DELTA* 18(2): 233–71.

Cantos, P. & Sánchez, A. (2001) "Lexical Constellations: What Collocates Fail to tell". *International Journal of Corpus Linguistics* 6(2): 199–228.

Carroll, J. D. (1970) "An Alternative to Juilland's Usage Coefficient for Lexical Frequencies and a Proposal for a Standard Frequency Index (SFI)". *Computer Studies in the Humanities and Verbal Behaviour* 3(2): 61–5.

Chen, Y. & Leimkuhler, F. (1989) "A Type-Token Identity in the Simon-Yule Model of Text". *Journal of the American Society for Information Science* 40: 45–53.

Chipere, N., Malvern, D., Richards, B. & Duran, P. (2001) "Using a Corpus of School Children's Writing to Investigate the Development of Vocabulary Diversity". In P. Rayson, A. Wilson, T. McEnery, A. Hardie & S. Khoja (eds) *Technical Papers Volume 13. Special Issue. Proceedings of the Corpus Linguistics 2001 Conference.* Lancaster: Lancaster University Press, 126–33.

Church, K. W. & Hanks, P. (1990) "Word Association Norms, Mutual Information and Lexicography". *Computational Linguistics* 16(1): 22–9.

Church, K. W., Gale, W., Hanks, P. & Hindle, D. (1991) "Using Statistics in Lexical Analysis". In U. Zernik (ed.) *Lexical Acquisition: Exploiting On-line Resources to Build a Lexicon.* Hillsdale, NJ: Lawrence Erlbaum Associates, 115–64.

Clear, J. (1993) "From Firth Principles: Computational Tools for the Study of Collocation". In M. Baker, G. Francis & E. Tognini-Bonelli (eds) *Text and Technology.* Amsterdam: Benjamins: 271–92.

Clogg, C. C. & Shihadeh, E. S. (1994) *Statistical Models for Ordinal Variables.* London: Sage.

Coulmas, F. (1981) "Introduction: Conversational Routine". In F. Coulmas (ed.) *Conversational Routine: Explorations in Standardized Communication Situations and Pre-patterned Speech.* The Hague: Mouton, 1–17.

Cowie, A. P. (1981) "The Treatment of Collocations and Idioms in Learners' Dictionaries". *Applied Linguistics* 2: 223–35.

Coxon, A. P. M. (1982) *The User's Guide to Multidimensional Scaling.* London: Heinemann.

Cruse, D. A. (1986) *Lexical Semantics.* Cambridge: Cambridge University Press.

Cureton, E. E. & D'Agostino, R. B. (1983) *Factor Analysis: An Applied Approach.* London: Lawrence Erlbaum Associates.

Daille, B. (1994) "Extraction Automatique de Norms Composés Terminologiques". Ph.D. thesis, University of Paris 7.

Daille, B. (1995) "Combined Approach for Terminology Extraction: Lexical Statistics and Linguistic Filtering". *UCREL Technical Papers Volume 5. Combined Approach for Terminology Extraction: Lexical Statistics and Linguistic Filtering.* Lancaster: University of Lancaster Press.

Damerau, F. J. (1975) "The Use of Function Word Frequencies as Indicators of Style". *Computing in the Humanities* 9: 271–80.

De Hann, P. & van Hout, R. (1986) "A Loglinear Analysis of Syntactic Constraints on Postmodifying Clauses". In J. Aarts & W. Meijs (eds) *Corpus Linguistics II: New Studies in the Analysis and Exploration of Computer Corpora.* Amsterdam: Rodopi, 79–98.

Dunning, T. (1993) "Accurate Methods for the Statistics of Surprise and Coincidence". *Computational Linguistics* **19**(1): 61–74.

Edmundson, H. P. (1963) "A Statistician's View of Linguistic Models and Language Data Processing". In P. L. Garvin (ed.) *Natural Language and the Computer*. New York: McGraw Hill, 151–79.

Ellegård, A. (1959) "Statistical Measurement of Linguistic Relationship". *Language* **35**(2): 131–56.

Ellegård, A. (1962) *A Statistical Method for Determining Authorship*. Gothenburg: Acta Universitas Gothoburgensis.

Embleton, S. M. (1986) *Statistics in Historical Linguistics*. Bochum: Brockmeyer Verlag.

Firth, J. (1968) "A Synopsis of Linguistic Theory 1930–1955". In F. R. Palmer (ed.) *Selected Papers of J. R. Firth 1952–59*. Bloomington, IN: Indiana University Press, 168–205.

Fleiss, J. L. (1981) *Statistical Methods for Rates and Proportions*. New York: Wiley.

Gale, W. A. & Church, K. W. (1993) "A Program for Aligning Sentences in Bilingual Corpora". *Computational Linguistics* **19**(1): 75–102.

Gale, W. A., Church, K. W. & Yarowsky, D. (1992) "A Method for Disambiguating Word Senses in a Large Corpus". *Computers and the Humanities* **26**(5–6): 415–39.

Gale, W. A. & Sampson, G. (1995) "Good-Turing Frequency Estimation without Tears". *Journal of Quantitative Linguistics* **2**: 217–37.

Garside, R. (1987) "The CLAWS Word Tagging System". In R. Garside, G. Leech & G. Sampson (eds) *The Computational Analysis of English*. London and New York: Longman, 30–41.

Garside, R., Leech, G. & McEnery, A. (eds) (1997) *Corpus Annotation*. London: Addison-Wesley-Longman.

Gaussier, E. & Langé, J.-M. (1994) "Some Methods for the Extraction of Bilingual Terminology". In D. Jones & H. Somers (eds) *New Methods in Language Processing*. London: UCL Press, 145–53.

Geffroy, A., Lafon, P., Seidel, G. & Tournier, M. (1973) "Lexicometric Analysis of Co-occurrences". In A. J. Aitkien, R. Bailey & N. Hamilton-Smith (eds) *The Computer and Literary Studies*. Edinburgh: Edinburgh University Press, 113–33.

Geffroy, A., Guilhaumou, J., Hartley, A. & Salem, A. (1976) "Factor Analysis and Lexicometrics: Shifters in Some Texts of the French Revolution (1793–1794)". In A. Jones & R. F. Churchhouse (eds) *The Computer in Literary and Linguistic Studies*. Cardiff: University of Wales Press, 177–93.

Ghiselli, E. E., Campbell, J. P. & Zedeck, S. (1981) *Measurement Theory for the Behavioural Sciences*. Oxford: W. H. Freeman.

Gilbert, G. N. (1984) *Modelling Society: An Introduction to Loglinear Analysis for Social Researchers*. London: George Allen & Unwin.

Gilbert, N. (1993) *Analysing Tabular Data*. London: UCL Press.

Goldstein, H. (1995) *Multilevel Statistical Methods* (2nd edn). London: Edward Arnold.

Greenbaum, S. (1974) "Some Verb-Intensifier Collocations in American and British English". *American Speech* **49**: 79–89.

Gries, T. (2008) "Dispersions and Adjusted Frequencies in Corpora". *International Journal of Corpus Linguistics* **13**(4): 403–37.

Guthrie, J. (1993) "A Note on Lexical Disambiguation". In C. Souter & E. Atwell (eds) *Corpus-Based Computational Linguistics*. Amsterdam: Rodopi, 225–37.

Halliday, M. A. K. (1991) "Corpus Studies and Probabilistic Grammar". In K. Aijmer & B. Altenberg (eds) *English Corpus Linguistics*. London and New York: Longman, 30–43.

Hann, M. N. (1973) "The Statistical Force of Random Distribution". *ITL* **20**: 31–44.

Haskel, P. I. (1971) "Collocations as a Measure of Stylistic Variety". In R. A. Wisbey (ed.) *The Computer in Literary and Linguistic Research*. Cambridge: Cambridge University Press, 159–69.

Hatch, E. M. & Lazaraton, A. (1991) *The Research Manual: Design and Statistics for Applied Linguistics*. New York: Newbury House Publishers.

Haztivassiloglou, V. (1994) "Do We Need Linguistics When We Have Statistics? A Comparative Analysis of the Contributions of Linguistic Cues to Statistical Word Grouping System". In J. L. Klavans & P. Resnik (eds) *The Balancing Act. Combining Symbolic and Statistical Approaches to Language*. Cambridge, MA: MIT Press, 67–94.

Herdan, G. (1962) *The Calculus of Linguistic Observations*. The Hague: Mouton and Co.

Herdan, G. (1964) *Quantitative Linguistics*. London: Butterworths.

Hockey, S. (1980) *A Guide to Computer Applications in the Humanities*. London: Duckworth.

Hofland, K. (1991) "Concordance Programs for Personal Computers". In S. Johansson & A.-B. Stenström (eds) *English Computer Corpora*. Berlin and New York: Mouton de Gruyter, 283–306.

Holmes, D. I. (1994) "Authorship Attribution". *Computers and the Humanities* 28: 87–106.

Hood-Roberts, A. H. (1965) *A Statistical Linguistic Analysis of American English*. The Hague: Mouton and Co.

Hoyle, R. H. (ed.) (1995) *Structural Equation Modelling: Concepts, Issues and Applications*. London: Sage.

Hughes, A. & Woods, A. J. (1983) "Interpreting the Performance on the Cambridge Proficiency Examination of Students of Different Language Backgrounds". In A. Hughes & D. Porter (eds) *Current Developments in Language Testing*. London: Academic Press, 123–44.

Hunston, S. & Francis, G. (1999) *Pattern Grammar. A Corpus-driven Approach to the Lexical Grammar of English*. Amsterdam: John Benjamins.

Jones, S. & Sinclair, J. (1973) "English Lexical Collocations. A Study in Computational Linguistics". *Cahiers de Lexicologie* 23(2): 15–61.

Juilland, A., Brodin, D. & Davidovitch, C. (1970) *Frequency Dictionary of French Words*. The Hague: Mouton.

Kilgarriff, A. (1996a) "Which Words Are Particularly Characteristic of Text? A Survey of Statistical Approaches". Technical report. Information Technology Research Institute, University of Brighton, June.

Kilgarriff, A. (1996b) "Using Word Frequency Lists to Measure Corpus Homogeneity and Similarity between Corpora". Technical report. Information Technology Research Institute, University of Brighton, 18 April.

Kilgarriff, A. (1996c) "Corpus Similarity and Homogeneity via Word Frequency". *EURALEX Proceedings*, Gothenburg, Sweden, 121–30.

Kinnear, P. R. & Gray, C. D. (1994) *SPSS for Windows Made Simple*. Hove: Lawrence Erlbaum Associates.

Kita, K., Kato, Y., Omoto, T. & Yano, Y. (1994) "Automatically Extracting Collocations from Corpora for Language Learning". In A. Wilson & T. McEnery (eds) *UCREL Technical Papers Volume 4. Corpora in Language Education and Research. A Selection of Papers from TALC94*. Lancaster: University of Lancaster Press, 53–64.

Krause, P. & Clark, D. (1993) *Representing Uncertain Knowledge*. Dordrecht: Kluwer Academic Publishers.

Krenn, B. & Samuelsson, C. (1997) *The Linguist's Guide to Statistics: Don't Panic*. Saarland University, Saarbrücken. http://nlp.stanford.edu/fsnlp/dontpanic.pdf (accessed June 2012).

Kretzschmar, W. A. & Schneider, E. W. (1996) *Introduction to Quantitative Analysis of Linguistic Survey Data: An Atlas by the Numbers*. Thousand Oaks, CA: Sage Publications.

Krzanowski, W. J. & Woods, A. J. (1984) "Statistical Aspects of Reliability in Language Testing". *Language Testing* 1: 1–20.

Lafon, P. (1984) *Dépouillements et statistiques en lexicométrie*. Geneva: Slatkine-Champion.

Lazarton, A. (2000) "Current trends in research methodology and statistics in applied linguistics". *TESOL Quarterly* 34(1): 175–81.

Lebart, L. & Salem, A. (1994) *Statistique Textuelle*. Paris: Dunod.

Lebart, L., Salem, A. & Barry, L. (1999) "Exploring Textual Data". *Computational Linguistics* 1(1): 165–6.

Leech, G. N. (1995) *Semantics*. Harmondsworth: Penguin.

Leech, G. N., Francis, B. & Xu, X. (1994) "The Use of Computer Corpora in the Textual Demonstrability of Gradience in Linguistic Categories". In C. Fuchs & B. Vitorri (eds) *Continuity in Linguistic Semantics*. Amsterdam and Philadelphia, PA: John Benjamins Publishing Company. 57–76.

Lesk, M. (1986) "Automatic Sense Disambiguation Using Machine Readable Dictionaries: How to Tell a Pine Cone from an Ice Cream Cone". *Proceedings of SIGDOC-86: Fifth International Conference on Systems Documentation*, Toronto, Canada, 24–6

Lewis-Beck, M. S. (ed.) (1993) *Regression Analysis*. London: Sage.

Lovie, A. D. (1981) "On the Early History of ANOVA in the Analysis of Repeated Measure Designs in Psychology". *British Journal of Mathematical and Statistical Psychology* 34: 1–15.

Lyne, A. A. (1985) *The Vocabulary of French Business Correspondence*. Geneva and Paris: Slatkine-Champion.

Mair, C. (2004) "Corpus Linguistics and Grammaticalization Theory: Statistics, Frequencies, and Beyond". In H. Lindqvist & C. Mair (eds) *Corpus Approaches to Grammaticalization*. Amsterdam: John Benjamins, 121–50.

Manly, B. F. J. (1994) *Multivariate Statistical Methods: A Primer* (2nd edn). London: Chapman & Hall.

Marriot, F. H. C. (1974) *The Interpretation of Multiple Observations*. New York and London: Academic Press.

Martin, W., Al, B. & van Sterkenburg, P. (1983) "On the Processing of a Text Corpus: From Textual Data to Lexicographical Information". In R. Hartmann (ed.) *Lexicography: Principles and Practice*. London: Academic Press, 77–87.

Mason, O. (1997) "The Weight of Words: An Investigation of Lexical Gravity". In *Proceedings of PALC'97*. Lodz: Lodz University Press, 361–75.

Maxwell, A. E. (1977) *Multivariate Analysis in Behavioural Research*. London: Chapman & Hall.

McDonald, J., Plate, A. & Schvaneveldt, R. (1990) "Using Pathfinder to Extract Semantic Information from Text". In R. W. Schvaneveldt (ed.) *Pathfinder Associative Networks: Studies in Knowledge Organization*. Norwood, NJ: Ablex, 149–64.

McEnery, T. & Wilson, A. (1996) *Corpus Linguistics*. Edinburgh: Edinburgh University Press.

McEnery, T., Baker, P. & Wilson, A. (1994) "The Role of Corpora in Computer Assisted Language Learning". *Computer Assisted Language Learning* 6(3): 233–48.

McKee, G., Malvern, D. & Richards, B. J. (2000) "Measuring Vocabulary Diversity Using Dedicated Software". *Literary and Linguistic Computing* 15(3): 323–38.

Mitkov, R. (1996) "Anaphor Resolution: A Combination of Linguistic and Statistical Approaches". In S. Botley, J. Glass, A. McEnery & A. Wilson (eds) "Approaches to Discourse Anaphora", *Proceedings of the Discourse Anaphora and Anaphora Resolution Colloquium* (DAARC 96). Lancaster: UCREL, 76–84.

Morrison, D. F. (1976) *Multivariate Statistical Methods* (2nd edn). New York: McGraw-Hill.

Nagao, M. (1984) "A Framework of a Mechanical Translation between Japanese and English by Analogy Principle". In A. Elithorn & R. Banerji (eds) *Artificial and Human Intelligence*. Amsterdam: Elsevier Science Publisher, 173–80.

Nakamura, J. & Sinclair, J. (1995) "The World of Woman in the Bank of English: Internal Criteria for the Classification of Corpora". *Literary and Linguistic Computing* 10(2): 99–110.

Nattinger, J. (1980) "A Lexical Phrase Grammar for ESL". *TESOL Quarterly* 14: 337–44.

Nattinger, J. (1988) "Some Current Trends in Vocabulary Teaching". In C. Carter & M. McCarthy (eds) *Vocabulary and Language Teaching*. London: Longman, 62–82.

Oakes, M. (1998) *Statistics for Corpus Linguistics*. Edinburgh: Edinburgh University Press.

Ooi, V. B. Y. (1998) *Computer Corpus Lexicography*. Edinburgh: Edinburgh University Press.

Overall, J. E. & Klett, C. (1972) *Applied Multivariate Analysis*. New York: McGraw-Hill.

Phillips, M. (1989) *Lexical Structure of Text*. Birmingham: ELR/University of Birmingham.

Quirk, R. & Greenbaum, S. (1985) *A University Grammar of English.* Harlow: Longman.

Renouf, A. & Sinclair, J. (1991) "Collocational Frameworks in English". In K. Aijmer & B. Altenberg (eds) *English Corpus Linguistics.* London and New York: Longman, 128–43.

Rice, J. A. (1988) *Mathematical Statistics and Data Analysis.* Pacific Grove, CA: Wadsworth & Brooks.

Richardson, J. T. E. (1990) "Variants on Chi-square for 2 × 2 Contingency Tables". *British Journal of Mathematical and Statistical Psychology* **43**: 309–27.

Rietveld, T. & van Hout, R. (2005) *Statistics in Language Research: Analysis of Variance.* Berlin: Mouton de Gruyter.

Rosengren, I. (1971) "The Quantitative Concept of Language and its Relation to the Structure of Frequency Dictionaries". *Études de Linguistique Appliquée* (Nlle Sér.) **1**: 103–27.

Sánchez, A. & Cantos, P. (1997) "Predictability of Word Forms (Types) and Lemmas in Linguistic Corpora. A Case Study Based on the Analysis of the CUMBRE Corpus: An 8-Million-Word Corpus of Contemporary Spanish". *International Journal of Corpus Linguistics* **2**(2): 259–80.

Sánchez, A. & Cantos, P. (1998) "El ritmo incremental de palabras nuevas en los repertorios de textos. Estudio experimental comparativo basado en dos corpus lingüísticos equivalentes de cuatro millones de palabras de las lenguas inglesa y española y en cinco autores de ambas lenguas". *Atlantis* **19**(2): 205–23.

Sánchez, A., Sarmiento, R., Cantos, P. & Simón, J. (1995) *CUMBRE. Corpus lingüístico del español contemporáneo: fundamentos, metodología y análisis.* Madrid: SGEL.

Sankoff, D. (2004) "Statistics in Linguistics". *Encyclopedia of the Statistical Sciences,* 5. New York: John Wiley & Sons, 74–81.

Scott, M. (1996) *WordSmith Tools Manual.* Oxford: Oxford University Press.

Scott, M. & Jones, T. (1994) *Corpus Collection B (Academic Texts).* Oxford: Oxford University Press.

Sichel, H. S. (1986) "Word Frequency Distributions and Type-Token Characteristics". *Mathematical Scientist* **11**: 45–72.

Siegel, S. & Castellan, N. J. Jr (1988) *Nonparametric Statistics for the Behavioural Sciences* (2nd edn). London: McGraw-Hill.

Sinclair, J. (1966) "Beginning the Study of Lexis". In C. E. Bazell, J. Catford, M. Halliday and R. Robins (eds) *In Memory of J. R. Firth.* London: Longman, 410–30.

Sinclair, J. (1991) *Corpus, Concordance, Collocation.* Oxford: Oxford University Press.

Sinclair, J. (1995) *Collins Cobuild English Dictionary.* London: HarperCollins Publishers.

Sinclair, J., Mason, O., Ball, J. & Barnbrook, G. (1998) "Language Independent Statistical Software for Corpus Exploration". *Computers and the Humanities* **31**: 229–55.

Smadja, F. A. (1989) "Lexical Co-occurrence: The Missing Link". *Literary and Linguistic Computing* **4**(3): 163–8.

Smadja, F. A. (1991) "Macro-coding the Lexicon with Co-occurrence Knowledge". In U. Zernik (ed.) *Lexical Acquisition: Exploiting On-line Resources to Build a Lexicon.* Hillsdale, NJ: Lawrence Erlbaum Associates, 165–89.

Smadja, F. A. (1992) "XTRACT: An Overview". *Computers and the Humanities* **26**(5–6): 399–414.

Smadja, F. A. & McKeown, K. R. (1990) "Automatically Extracting and Representing Collocations for Language Generation". *Proceedings of the 28th Annual Meeting of the Association for Computational Linguistics.* Pittsburgh, PA: Pittsburgh University Press, 252–9.

Smadja, F. A., McKeown, K. R. & Hatzivassiloglou, V. (1996) "Translating Collocations for Bilingual Lexicons: A Statistical Approach". *Computational Linguistics* **22**(1): 1–38.

Stenström, A.-B. (1984) "Discourse Tags". In J. Aarts & W. Meijs (eds) *Corpus Linguistics.* Amsterdam: Rodopi, 65–81.

Stevens, J. (1992) *Applied Multivariate Statistics for the Social Sciences.* London: Lawrence Erlbaum Associates.

Stewart, I. (1995) "Statistical Sampling". *New Scientist: Inside Science* **82**(6 June).

Stubbs, M. (1995) "Collocations and Semantic Profiles: On the Cause of the Trouble with Quantitative Methods". *Functions of Language* 2(1): 1–33.

Těšitelová, M. & Kohler, R. (1992) *Quantitative Linguistics*. Amsterdam and Philadelphia, PA: John Benjamins Publishing Co.

Thisted, R. & Efron, B. (1987) "Did Shakespeare Write a Newly-Discovered Poem?" *Biometrika* **74**(3): 445–55.

Tognini-Bonelli, E. (2001) *Corpus Linguistics at Work*. Amsterdam: Benjamins.

van de Geer, J. P. (1993a) *Multivariate Analysis of Categorical Data: Applications*. London: Sage.

van de Geer, J. P. (1993b) *Multivariate Analysis of Categorical Data: Theory*. London: Sage.

Wetherill, G. B. (1972) *Elementary Statistical Methods*. London: Chapman & Hall.

Wilcox, R. R. (1995) "ANOVA: A Paradigm for Low Power and Misleading Measures of Effect Size". *Review of Educational Research* **65**: 51–77.

Willett, P. (1980) "Document Clustering Using an Inverted File Approach". *Journal of Information Science* **2**(5), 23–31.

Willett, P. (1988) "Recent Trends in Hierarchic Document Clustering: A Critical Review". *Information Processing and Management* **24**(5): 577–97.

Winer, B. J. (1971) *Statistical Principles in Experimental Design*. New York: McGraw-Hill.

Wolff, J. G. (1991) *Towards a Theory of Cognition and Computing*. Chichester: Ellis Horwood.

Woods, A., Fletcher, P. & Hughes, A. (1986) *Statistics in Language Studies*. Cambridge: Cambridge University Press.

Wright, D. B. (1997) *Understanding Statistics: An Introduction for the Social Sciences*. London: Sage.

Yang, D. H., Cantos, P. & Song, M. (2000) "An Algorithm for Predicting the Relationship between Lemmas and Corpus Size". *International Journal of the Electronics and Telecommunications Research Institute (ETRI)* **22**: 20–31.

Yang, D. H., Song, M., Cantos, P. & Lim, S. J. (2002) "On the Corpus Size Needed for Compiling a Comprehensive Computational Lexicon by Automatic Lexical Acquisition". *Computers in the Humanities* **36**(2), 171–90.

Yardi, M. R. (1946) "A Statistical Approach to the Problem of the Chronology of Shakespeare's Plays". *Sankhya* (Indian Journal of Statistics) **7**(3): 263–8.

Yule, G. U. (1939) "On Sentence Length as a Statistical Characteristic of Style in Prose, with Applications to Two Cases of Disputed Authorship". *Biometrika* **30**: 363–90.

Yule, G. U. (1944) *The Statistical Study of Literary Vocabulary*. Cambridge: Cambridge University Press.

Zernik, U. (1991) "Train 1 vs Train 2: Tagging Word Sense in a Corpus". In U. Zernik (ed.) *Lexical Acquisition: Exploiting On-line Resources to Build a Lexicon*. Hillsdale, NJ: Lawrence Erlbaum Associates, 91–112.

Zipf, G. (1935) *The Psycho-Biology of Language*. Boston, MA: Houghton Mifflin.

Zwick, R. (1993) "Pairwise Comparison Procedures for One-Way Analysis of Variance Designs". In G. Keren & C. Lewis (eds) *A Handbook for Data Analysis in the Behavioural Sciences: Statistical Issues*. Hillsdale, NJ: Lawrence Erlbaum Associates, 43–71.

Index